Y0-DKD-722

WHAT DO YOU KNOW ABOUT ANIMALS?

WHAT DO
YOU KNOW
ABOUT ANIMALS?

WHAT DO YOU KNOW ABOUT ANIMALS?

IAN JACKSON

HAMLYN
London · New York · Sydney · Toronto

for Nicholas

The illustrations in this book have been selected from titles in
the Hamlyn all-colour paperback series.

Published 1973 by the Hamlyn Publishing Group Limited
London   New York   Sydney   Toronto

© Copyright The Hamlyn Publishing Group Limited 1973
ISBN 0 600 39245 7
Printed in Spain by Mateu Cromo, Madrid

CONTENTS

Invertebrates	7
Fishes	67
Amphibians	97
Reptiles	111
Birds	147
Mammals	201

INVERTEBRATES

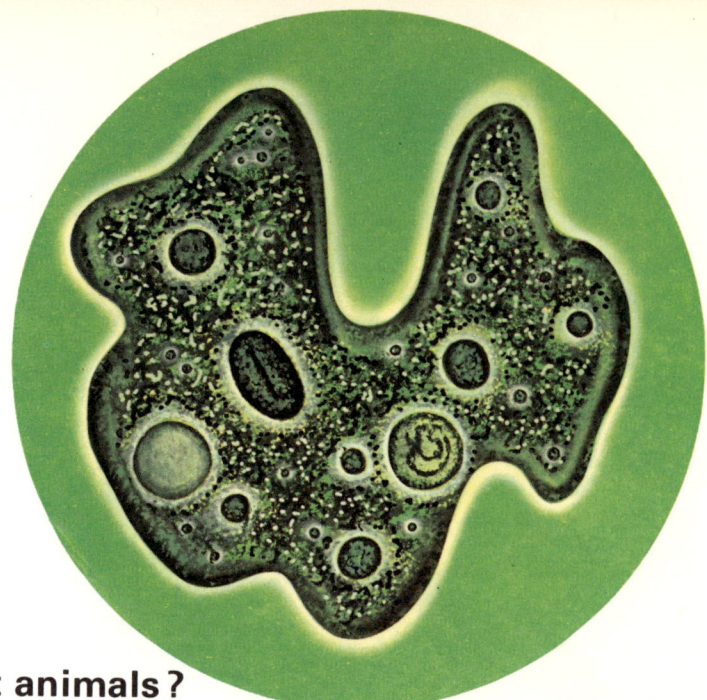

What are the simplest animals?

The protozoans are simple organisms that consist of only one cell. They make up the phylum Protozoa. It is difficult to refer to some of them as either animals or plants because although many are extremely active and catch and eat their food, others, like plants, use the energy of the sun to make their own food. A protozoan is made up of a single microscopic unit of protoplasm (the complex mixture of substances of which all animals and plants are made) enclosed by a membrane and controlled by a central nucleus.

Protozoans live in a remarkable variety of habitats. Although they are essentially aquatic they are found in all bodies of water from small muddy puddles of rainwater to all the oceans of the world. They can even exist in the thin film of moisture which surrounds soil particles and many are parasitic, living within the bodies of other plants and animals. They are very resistant and, if the pond or marsh in which they live dries up, they are able to secrete a protective skin around themselves. In this condition, the cyst, as the protozoan is then called, is able to survive and it returns to life again when favourable conditions occur.

Although extremely small in size and basic in structure, the protozoans are very significant to other members of the animal kingdom. They form the heads of food chains and so provide proteins and vitamins for other more advanced animals. They also play an important role in breaking down plant and animal remains. Parasitic forms cause diseases in man, for example, malaria.

An amoeba creeps slowly along changing its shape all the time.

Chlamydomonas is a protozoan that swims around by lashing the water with two flagellae.

Euglena has a single whip-like flagellum.

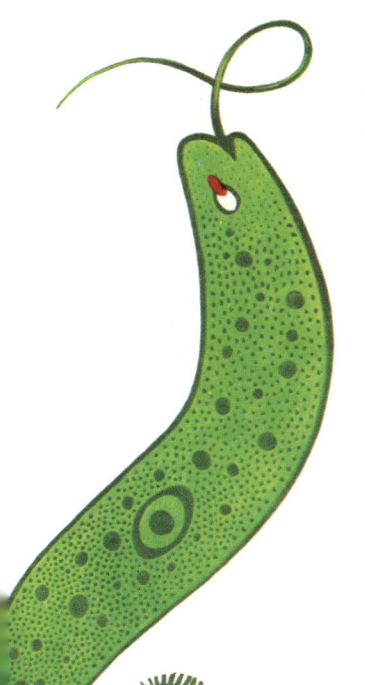

How do these single-celled animals move?

Protozoans move in a variety of ways. The amoeba has no characteristic shape, in contrast to the other protozoans, and moves along the substratum, or surface of objects, in a flowing movement, continually changing its form. The jelly-like protoplasm streams out into thin extensions called *pseudopodia* or 'false-feet' and the rest of the amoeba flows into them. In this way the amoeba slowly creeps about.

The majority of protozoans, however, are more active and lash the water with whip-like flagellae. *Chlamydomonas* and *Euglena* swim jerkily around.

A modification of the same method is seen in *Paramecium* in which the entire surface is covered with rows of short cilia. Their movements are co-ordinated and they beat rythmically in waves, propelling the animal smoothly through the water.

How does *Volvox* differ from other protozoans?

Volvox is a colony of protozoans. It is a group of several thousand individual protozoans arranged to form the wall of a jelly-filled sphere. Some of these individual cells have different functions and in this way *Volvox* and other similar colonies of protozoans are among the first examples of the arrangement of many-celled animals.

Each protozoan of the colony has a pair of flagellae which lash the water in a co-ordinated rythmic sequence. *Volvox* can be seen in pond water as a tiny green ball moving smoothly along in a rolling motion.

Paramecium has a characteristic 'slipper shape' and is covered with rows of short hairs called cilia.

Within this *Volvox* colony can be seen smaller daughter colonies which are released when they have grown large enough.

(*Right*) Some varieties of sponges encrusting a rock on the seashore.

(*Below*) Examples of the different types of spicules produced by sponges. Spicules are secreted by the sponge from salts in the water and form a single skeleton to support the soft body.

What are sponges?

Sponges are very primitive many-celled animals. They live in both fresh and sea water and encrust rocks and underwater objects in strange lumpy masses. Some spread over considerable areas, others hang in finger-like clusters, while others stand erect, branching irregularly up to 5 feet in height. Sponges are interesting because they represent a more advanced stage of development than the colony of protozoans. They belong to the phylum Porifera.

An individual sponge has a definite vase-like shape, and groups of the cells of which it is made are adapted to carry out special tasks. The cells of the wall of the sponge are called 'covering cells', and these protect it and help keep its shape. The inside layer of cells consists of cells bearing a whip-like flagellum to lash the water and make a current, as well as other cells which form pores on the outside of the sponge. Between the two, amoeba-like cells occur and these secrete strengthening rods called 'spicules' which make the sponge rigid.

How do sponges feed if they cannot move?

As the flagellae of the cells inside the sponge beat the water, a current is set up and water is drawn through the tiny pores into the centre of the sponge and then driven out through the hole at the top. Suspended particles of food in the water are caught on the flagellae of the cells and passed back to the amoeba-like cells. Another function of these cells is to absorb the food particles filtered from the water and to transport the digested food to the other parts of the sponge. The cells bearing flagellae can only deal with a certain size of food particle, and so no matter how large the sponge, it must feed on microscopic particles such as bacteria and protozoans suspended in the water.

This cut-away diagram shows the arrangement of the different types of cells within a single individual sponge.

Three examples of commercial sponges in their natural state (before preparation as bathroom sponges). These are from the Mediterranean Sea.

Where do bath sponges come from?

The sponge with which some people regularly soap themselves in the bath is really the skeleton of a particular type of natural sponge. Bath sponges are supported by a framework of a resilient, elastic material called 'spongin', and it is this that makes up the bathroom sponge.

Bath sponges are found in warm shallow seas, and in various parts of the world 'sponge farms' were once established and bath sponges grown from cuttings for eventual sale. Few such farms still exist, but sponges are still grown commercially in the Greek Islands and in the Philippines. The increased use of synthetic sponges – cheaper to produce, although not as hard wearing – has meant that there is now little demand for natural sponges, except for cleaning and polishing in certain industries.

A group of hydras. The illustration below shows a hydra cut away to show the two layers of cells of the body wall and the mouth. A young hydra is growing on the wall.

Are hydras more advanced than sponges?

You might easily overlook a hydra in a pond, lake or stream, because when disturbed, it contracts its body from the normal length of about half-an-inch to a tiny blob of jelly that you can only see if you look very carefully. Most people are more familiar with its marine relatives – the sea anemones, jellyfishes and corals – which are, of course, much larger and more colourful.

This group of animals belongs to the phylum Coelenterata which means simply 'hollow gut'. The hydra is basically a bag with a fringe of tentacles around the mouth at one end, and a disc at the other with which it sticks to a surface.

Instead of a loose arrangement of the cells into groups with different functions (as in the sponges), the body wall of a hydra consists of two definite layers. The cells act together in a much more organized way than those of the sponge. The hydra is also more responsive and active than the sponge and has a network of nerve cells which make up a primitive nervous system. It also has single muscle cells which enable it to bend and contract its body.

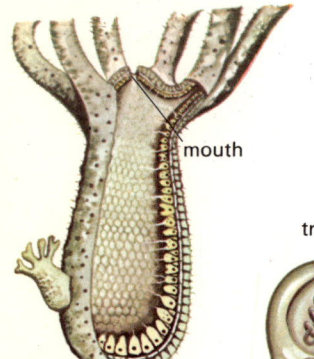

(*Right*) The special stinging and holding cells which arm the tentacles. The cells are stimulated to fire when the trigger is touched by a passing animal.

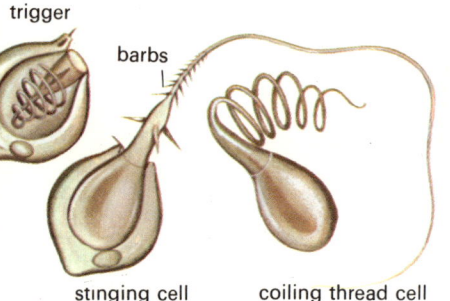

Hydra-like animals live in branching colonies such as *Obelia*. Some polyps of the colony are modified to produce free-swimming stages called medusae which bear the reproductive organs; the underneath view of one is shown.

How do hydras catch their prey?

The tentacles of the hydra, like those of the anemones and jellyfishes, are armed with special stinging cells which fire poisonous barbed threads into any unfortunate creature that happens to brush against them. Other cells of this type release long threads which coil around the prey and help hold it until it can be manoeuvred to the mouth and engulfed. Once inside the bag of the hydra the small water flea or worm is quickly digested and any remains are spat out from the mouth. It is an interesting fact that the hydra can catch and eat much larger animals than the sponge.

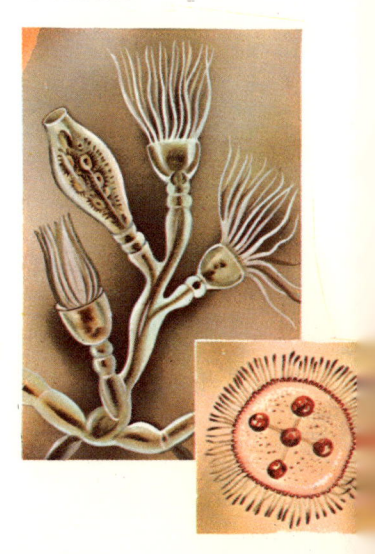

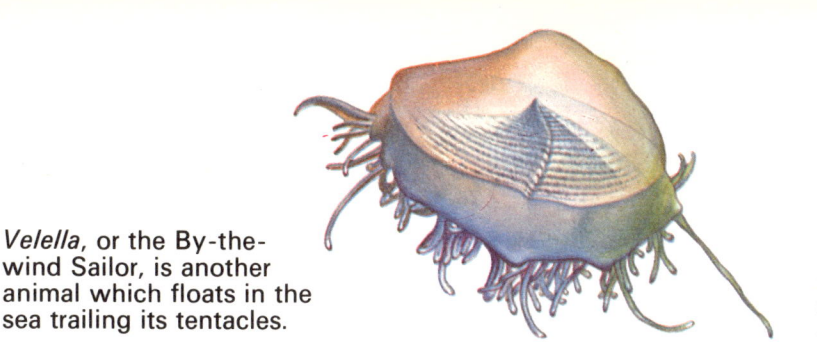

Velella, or the By-the-wind Sailor, is another animal which floats in the sea trailing its tentacles.

What is the Portuguese man-o'-war?

Although it looks very much like a jellyfish, the Portuguese man-o'-war is really a floating colony of hydra-like animals called polyps, clustered together under a gas-filled bladder. The bladder acts as a sail and the Portuguese man-o'-war is driven about the warm seas of the world completely at the mercy of the wind. (A jellyfish, of course, can actively swim.)

The animal itself is about 6 inches long, but the trailing tentacles of the polyps can extend up to 60 feet. The tentacles of some of the polyps bear stinging and holding cells similar to those of the hydra. They can catch and hold fishes as large as mackerel. Once overcome the prey is quickly drawn up within reach of other polyps which eat and digest it.

Sometimes storms drive masses of these animals on to the beaches of seaside towns where they become a serious menace. They are usually left stranded high up the beach and the bladders soon dry and shrivel. The tentacles can still give a nasty sting if touched, however, and bathing is often prevented until the Portuguese men-o'-war are removed.

The Portuguese man-o'-war is common in the warm seas of the world and particularly in the North Atlantic, and areas of the Indian and Pacific Oceans.

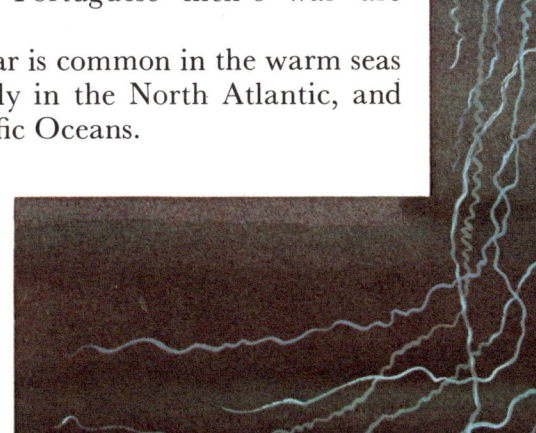

A Portuguese man-o'-war traps fishes in its deadly, trailing tentacles.

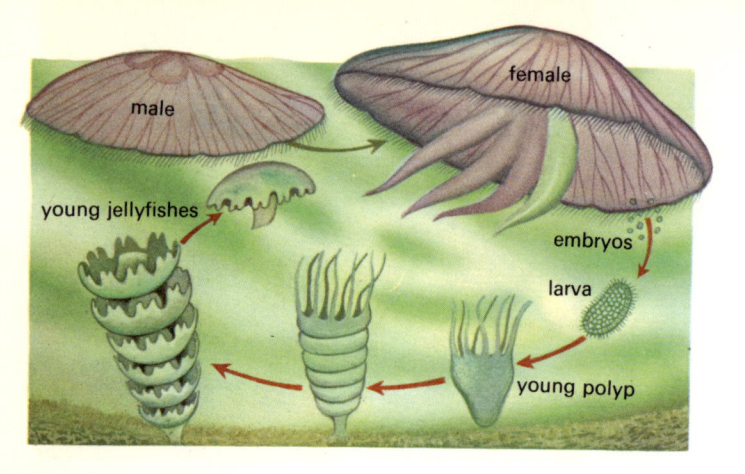

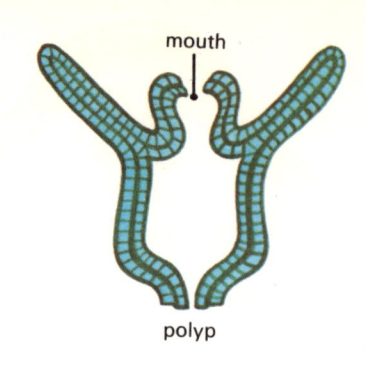

(*Above*) The stages of the life-cycle of a jellyfish. The young larva attaches itself to the sea bed as a polyp. In time young jellyfishes are formed like a stack of saucers and one by one they detach themselves and swim away.

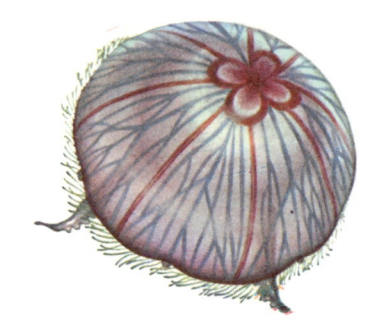

The tentacles of jellyfishes are arranged around the rim of the bell shape. The mouth hangs from the centre on a stalk which is often divided into four 'arms'.

What is a true jellyfish?

True jellyfishes resemble slowly undulating bells which drift majestically through the depths of the oceans, trailing their long tentacles for some distance behind them.

Many of the coelenterates can exist in two forms: either as fixed polyps as typified by the simple hydra, or as free-swimming bell shapes called medusae. *Obelia* (page 12) shows both of these forms but it exists for most of the time in the polyp form and for only a short time, when it is reproducing, in the medusa form. For jellyfishes it is the other way round and they are familiar to us as the free-swimming dome-shaped stage although they do pass through the fixed stage when they are reproducing.

You may have seen a jellyfish stranded on the beach. It is wise not to touch the helpless mass of jelly because the stinging cells of the tentacles can give you a nasty sting, even though the animal may be dead.

How does a jellyfish swim?

If you have ever stared into the water from a boat at sea or even from the end of a pier, you may have been surprised to see a ghostly shape drifting up just near enough to the

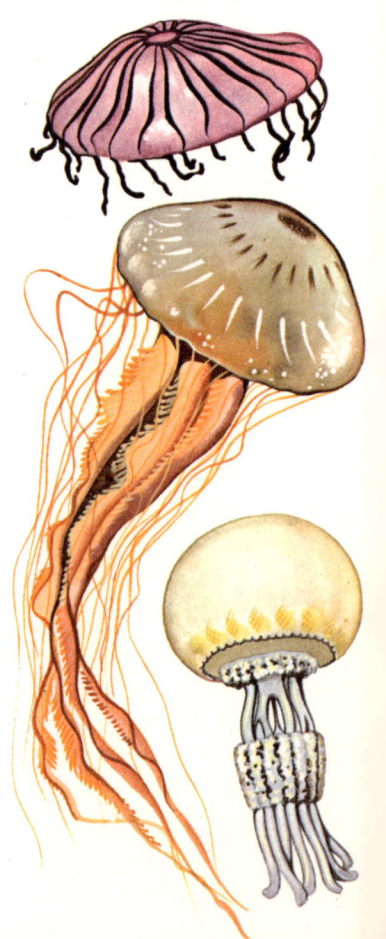

14

mouth

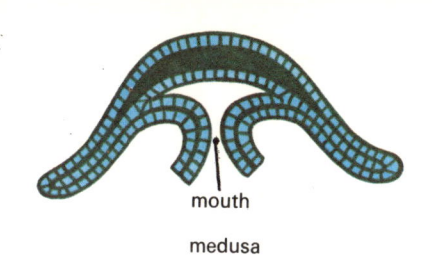

medusa

(*Left and above*) The two forms in which many of the coelenterates live. The free-swimming medusa form, as shown by jellyfishes, is really an upside-down version of the fixed polyp form of the hydras.

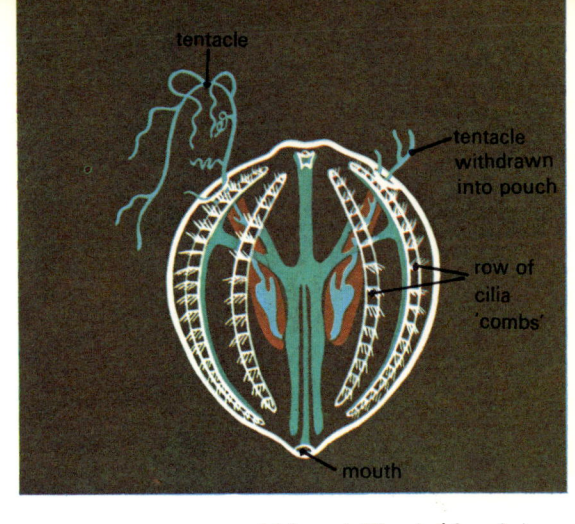

(*Above*) The body plan of a sea gooseberry.

surface for you to make out its milky-white, saucer-shaped outline before sinking from view again. This would have been a swimming jellyfish. If you watch more closely you will see that its pulsating swimming motion is rather like the action of an umbrella slowly opening and closing. The bell contracts forcing out the water it enclosed and driving the jellyfish upwards. The jelly of the jellyfish makes it quite buoyant and so the animal has only to make these regular, lazy contractions to drift along for considerable distances.

What are sea gooseberries?

Sea gooseberries resemble transparent balls of jelly about three-quarters of an inch long. They belong to a curious group of animals (phylum Ctenophora) related to the coelenterates. From the top of the animal radiate eight rows of cilia grouped in little 'combs' which give the group its common name of 'comb jellies'. The rows of cilia beat together to propel the animals through the water. They are not very strong swimmers and masses are often driven together by the wind and currents of the sea.

The comb jellies are closest in body plan to the jellyfishes although there are one or two important differences. The sea gooseberries are usually oval in shape and have only two branched tentacles which they loop through the water in search of prey. The tentacles have special cells which stick to, and entrap, small fishes, shrimps and tiny organisms. Once a creature is caught the tentacle is shortened and the food brushed off into the mouth.

At night, masses of luminous comb jellies provide a shining spectacle flashing and sparkling along the eight lines of combs as they move through the dark water.

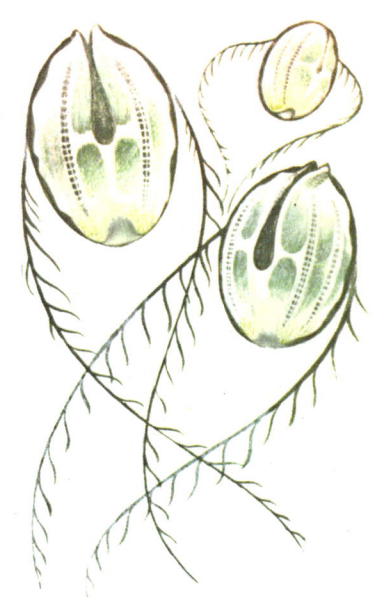

More examples of sea gooseberries with their branched tentacles fully extended.

Some colourful examples of sea anemones.

What are the 'flowers of the sea'?

Gaze into the rock pool at low tide and the gently waving tentacles of the beautifully coloured sea anemones will make it immediately apparent why these animals were once called 'plant-animals'. Anemones are not flowers, of course, and in fact they are greedy predators, catching and eating fishes, worms, crabs and any other creatures that touch their waving arms. Like the other members of the coelenterates, the tentacles of anemones bear stinging cells and their body plan is similar to that of the freshwater hydra. Anemones are more muscular, however, and have several rings of tentacles around the mouth. The stomach is divided by partitions to increase its surface area so that larger prey can be digested.

Anemones may look fairly static in the rock pool but if you could watch for long enough you would see that they are continually on the move, contracting and extending the body and slowly gliding about.

What is coral?

Coral, which people often collect as decoration, is the hard, dried skeleton composed mainly of calcium produced by colonies of small animals very similar to anemones. The polyps of living coral live in tiny cups in the skeleton and are continually adding to its mass. The coral grows into a variety of shapes. Some species produce numerous branches and in others the polyps are arranged in twisting rows on a rounded mass.

Coral thrives in warm, shallow water and it forms extensive reefs along tropical shores, particularly in the Pacific and Indian Oceans. The protection the reefs provide make them ideal habitats and they support crowded communities of fishes, many kinds of invertebrates and seaweeds.

The Great Barrier Reef off the north-east coast of Australia stretches for 1,200 miles.

(*Below*) These examples of coral skeletons illustrate the enormous variety of shape and colour that can be found.

How are coral reefs formed?

There are three types of coral reef: fringing reefs grow close to the shore in shallow water; barrier reefs grow parallel to the shore but are separated from it by a deep channel which may be several miles wide; and atolls which are circular islands of coral enclosing a lagoon, often hundreds of miles from any other land.

There are numerous theories to explain the formation of these types of reefs. The most popular is that one type developed from another in a gradual transition so that all three are different stages of the same process. If a landmass with a fringing reef begins to sink into the sea, as long as the coral can grow at an equivalent rate to the subsidence, the reef will grow further and further from the coast. Eventually a barrier reef is formed some way from the shore. If the process continues and the landmass disappears altogether, a ring of coral will be left forming an atoll. This is the simplest explanation for the formation of reefs; the actual processes involved are more complex.

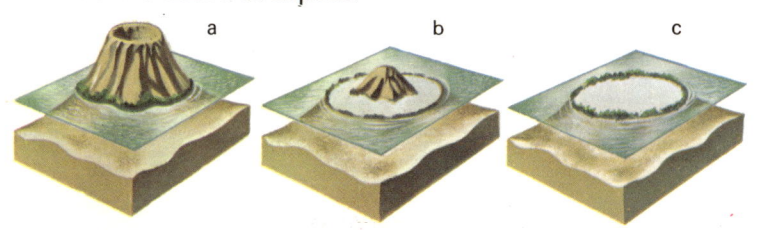

(*Left*) The three stages in reef formation showing (a) a fringing reef, (b) a barrier reef and (c) an atoll.

Why is a flatworm flat?

Flatworms represent a more advanced stage of development than the two-layered hydras, jellyfishes and anemones, because they have a third layer of cells. This middle layer has enabled different groups of cell tissues to become organized to form organs, or organ systems, with special functions. Thus the flatworms have a rudimentary digestive system, a primitive central nervous system including a small brain and simple eyes, an excretory system to help get rid of waste products, and complicated reproductive organs.

In spite of all these advances over the two-layered animals, the flatworms of the phylum Platyhelminthes are still extremely primitive and one of the things they lack is a blood system. The blood system in all higher animals is a transport system; oxygen and carbon dioxide gases are carried to and from all the tissues, together with nutrients from digested food and waste materials. The flatworms have solved this problem by being flat. This means that they are thin with a large surface area so that oxygen can easily pass through the body wall of the animal to all the tissues, and carbon dioxide can pass out. To transport the nutrients from digested food in the gut, the digestive system has developed an enormous number of small branches which carry nutrients to all areas of the body. Waste materials are carried back and passed out of the mouth.

(*Left*) Flatworms vary in size from the common species about half-an-inch long to the enormous tropical forms which can be up to a foot long. They are widespread in all ponds, lakes, streams and the sea and some even live on land in moist, warm woods.

Some flatworms reproduce by breaking off pieces of their body which then develop into new flatworms. They have remarkable powers of regeneration and experiments have been carried out to see how many heads of flatworms could form if cut repeatedly.

Where does this tapeworm live?

Tapeworms consist of segments and can reach lengths of up to 50 feet in the intestine of man.

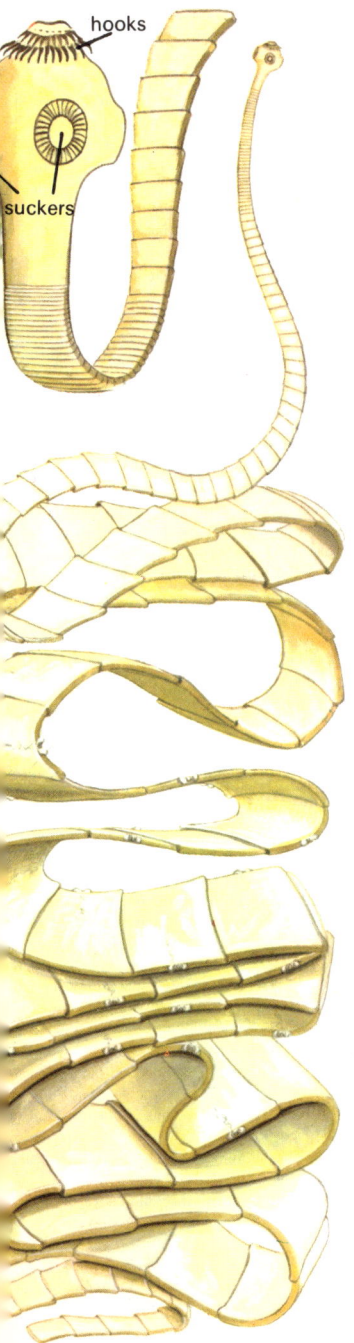

This tapeworm lives inside the intestine of a man. You may be puzzled as to how the worm manages to exist there.

Tapeworms belong to the same group of animals as flatworms but whereas the flatworms are free-living – they can move about and feed in streams and ponds – tapeworms are parasitic, which means they cannot live apart from the animals in which they live. Many features of the bodily structure of tapeworms reflect their unusual life.

Probably the most obvious is that tapeworms have no mouth or digestive system. Because they live in the intestine they are bathed in the food which their host is eating and digesting, and so they have no need for a digestive system of their own. All they have to do is simply absorb the food as it passes by them, and this is made easy by their flat, ribbon-like shape.

Living in this constantly dark, warm and very secure environment, the tapeworm has lost the need for a nervous system – there is nothing to react to – and so it is very poorly developed. Similarly it has a simple excretory system and weak muscles. The tapeworm does have a definite head, however, and this bears suckers and hooks to keep it anchored to the gut wall.

To compensate for the easy life the tapeworm lives it has the problem of ensuring that its offspring reach new hosts. The chances of this happening are slim and so the tapeworm produces masses and masses of eggs. The segments of the body are continually forming and contain both male and female reproductive organs. As the segments mature the eggs are formed. When the end segments break off they are passed from the human host. If a pig eats the eggs they develop into a larval stage and lodge in the animal's muscle. The cycle is completed when a man eats meat from the pig and the larval stage grows into an adult tapeworm.

The brain and the simple eyes of the flatworm are found at the head end together with groups of sensory cells sensitive to light, temperature and chemicals in the water. A flatworm gliding along moves its head from side to side 'tasting' the water. It quickly moves in on a food particle once it picks up its 'smell'.

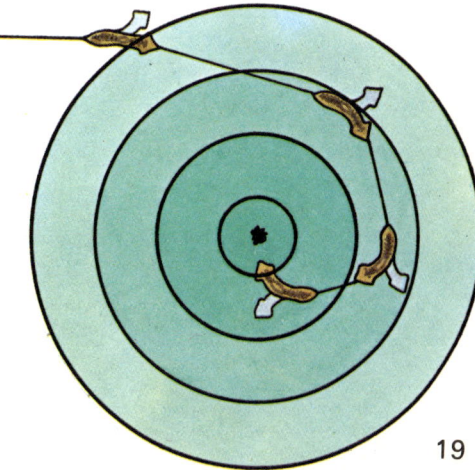

19

Why are ribbon worms significant?

Ribbon worms live along the seashore and although they are hard to see you can sometimes discover one under a stone. Another method of finding them is to place a bundle of seaweed in a bowl of seawater, whereupon the worms will usually crawl out. You will see then that they are normally under 8 inches long (although a giant 60 yards long was found in 1864) and can be brightly coloured.

Ribbon worms have two distinct improvements on the flatworm body plan. The first is that they possess a blood system. It is a simple one because it does not have a heart but nevertheless blood is circulated. This means that the problem of transporting gases and nutrients all over the body is solved. This in turn has meant that the digestive system is no longer complicated. It is developed for the more efficient straight-through passage of food during digestion, and exit of the waste through a special opening – the anus.

Ribbon worms are sometimes called 'proboscis worms' indicating a common feature – the long snout-like feeding tube which the worm can shoot out and coil round its prey.

Three types of ribbon worm, the one below showing its long, extended proboscis.

What are roundworms?

If you go out into your garden and dig up a spadeful of earth you will have just captured millions and millions of roundworms. If you could examine a sample of this soil under a microscope you would see the tiny thread-like worms, pointed at both ends, thrashing about in all directions.

Roundworms occupy practically every possible habitat you can think of; many cause economic problems by destroying fields of our plant crops and many are parasitic on members of every animal group. Some cause serious diseases like hookworm and elephantiasis in man.

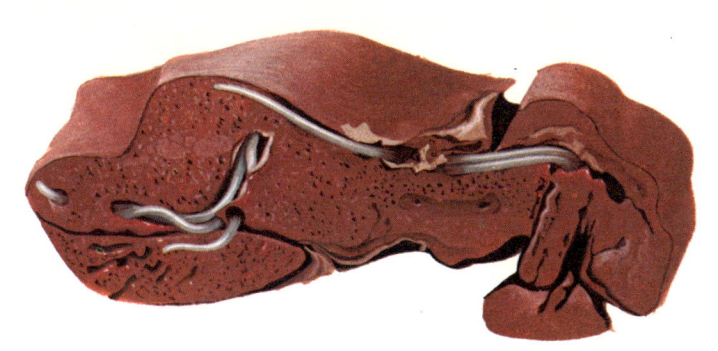

Many roundworms are parasitic on higher animals, some living in the liver of their host.

How do hookworms live in man?

Hookworm larvae live in the soil of countries with a warm and humid climate. They grow for a while and then stop feeding and become infective. If a bare-footed man steps on them they quickly enter the skin and bore through the tissues until they reach a blood vessel. Their development depends on reaching the intestine of their host, and they arrive there after a round-about journey. In the bloodstream they are carried to the heart and then on to the lungs. Here they bore into the lung tissue and are inevitably coughed up and swallowed again. They are now in the digestive system and soon reach the intestine, where they attach themselves to the wall and develop into adults. Thousands of eggs are formed and passed out from the host in his waste (faeces) to lie in wait as larvae in the soil for new hosts.

(*Below*) A magnified section to show how the adult hookworm attaches itself to the wall of its host's intestine.

(*Below left*) Hookworm larvae can enter the skin of their host either by crawling down hairs or by boring directly into the skin.

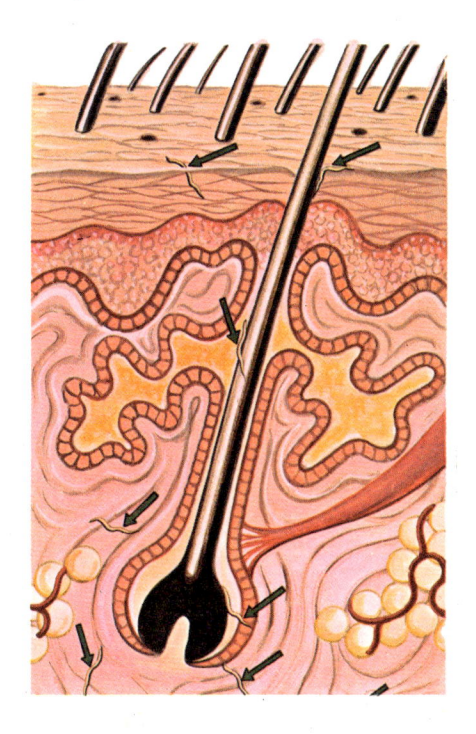

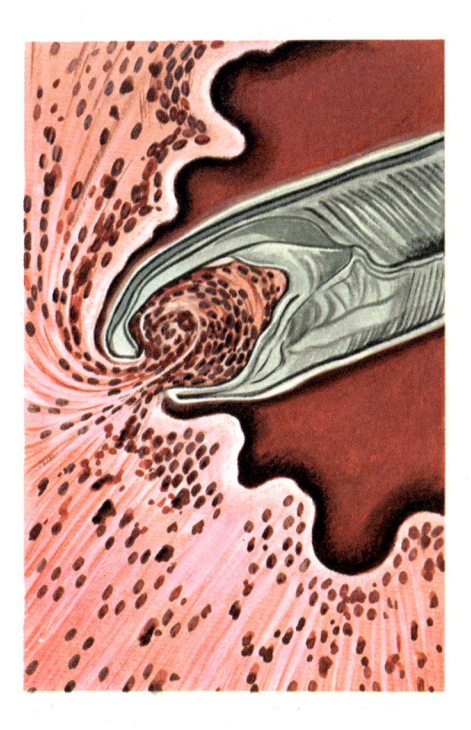

What is the most primitive mollusc?

Of the approximately 80,000 species of molluscs that exist, the most primitive is the humble chiton. The chiton shows all the typical characteristics of the molluscs. In the more advanced members like the slugs, snails, mussels, oysters, squids, octopuses and cuttlefishes, they are of course modified into a variety of forms – in the chiton they are very basic.

The soft body is divided into the head, which in higher molluscs bears the tentacles and other sense organs, the foot on which the animal creeps around, and the visceral mass which contains the body organs. A leathery skirt (mantle) covers the top of the body and forms a skirt around the sides. In the enclosed space (mantle cavity) the gills are found. The mantle secretes the shell which in the chiton is made up of eight plates.

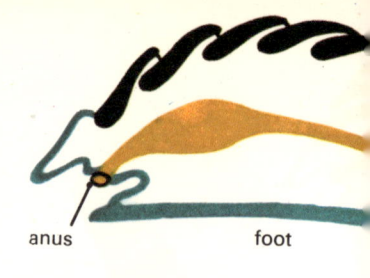

A simplified cross-section view of a chiton.

Chitons attached to rock at low tide are protected by the overlapping plates of their shell. They are not usually more than 2 inches in length.

(*Below*) The underneath and close up top view of a chiton and a single plate of the shell.

Where do chitons live?

It is quite difficult to spot chitons because they are usually small and often well camouflaged. A close examination of the rocks exposed at low tide will reveal them tightly gripping the rock with the plates of their shell overlapping to prevent them drying out. Their appearance and their habit of curling up when prized from the rock have given them two other names – coat-of-mail shells and cradle shells.

At night chitons move over the rock surface and graze on marine algae (simple single-celled plants) rasping them up into the mouth with a horny tongue covered in tiny teeth. This radula is a special feature of most molluscs. However far they graze chitons always return to exactly the same resting place. In time they wear a hollow in the rock in which they are well protected.

Large chitons, up to 8 inches in length, are found along tropical coasts of the Pacific and Atlantic Oceans.

mouth

Views of two kinds of tusk shell from the Pacific Ocean.

What are tusk shells?

Tusk shells, or more exactly elephant tusk shells, are another smaller group of primitive molluscs. It is quite easy to see how they came to have this name. The mantle completely encloses the body and the shell which it forms is therefore tubular and open at both ends – very similar to a miniature elephant's tusk.

As you can imagine, hollow shells like this, about 2 inches long, are just the right size for threading on a string to make a necklace. In the United States this is exactly how the Indians used these shells. In New Guinea, larger species of tusk shells are prized as decoration, and the natives adorn themselves by thrusting the shells through their nostrils or ear lobes.

Another species of tusk shell showing the animal's head with a ring of tentacles used for collecting food particles.

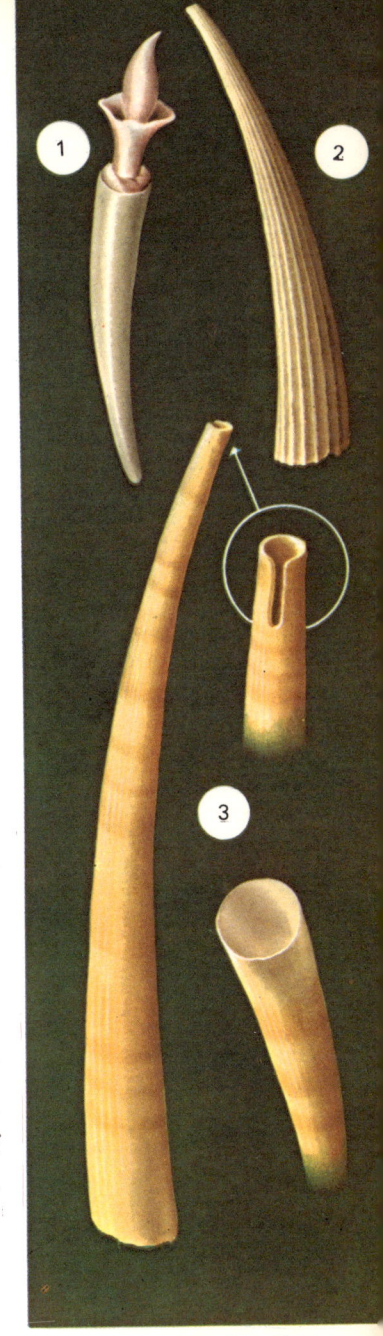

1. A tusk shell with the animal sticking out from the lower end. Tusk shells live on the sandy sea bottom, in contrast to chitons, and the lower end is embedded in the sand. 2 and 3 show tusk shells from the Red Sea and Japan respectively.

Two views of a typical bivalve mollusc. The left view shows the valves tightly shut while the right shows the siphons and foot extended.

siphons

foot

How do the bivalves move around?

A large group of molluscs have shells made up of two halves or valves, hence they are called the bivalves. A common feature of the bivalves is their large fleshy foot and this is used to move around in a way different from that of the chitons. The bivalves tend to be burrowers and they poke out the foot into the sandy or muddy bottom, the end swells to anchor the foot, and then the rest of the animal is drawn up and the foot extended again.

This is obviously a very slow process and not surprisingly the bivalves do not feed in the same way as the more mobile chitons. The mantle forms two siphons. Water is drawn through one into a large mantle cavity where it passes over the equally large gills before leaving by the other siphon. The gills not only extract oxygen from the water, they are modified to filter out suspended food particles which are then passed to the mouth and eaten. The bivalves have no head and no rasping radula.

Clusters of mussels are a common sight at low tide, clinging to pier supports, as well as to each other.

siphon

byssus threads

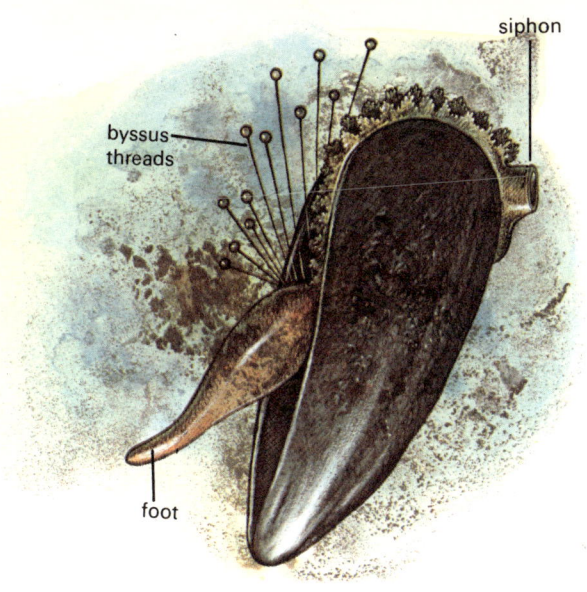

foot

A mussel showing how it attaches itself to surfaces using its byssus threads.

How do mussels fix themselves to surfaces high above the ground?

You may have wandered under a pier at low tide and glanced up to see masses and masses of mussels hanging high above you on the supports. In contrast to the chiton which 'sticks' itself to the rock surface, the mussels are actually hanging from surfaces of the pier on fine, strong threads. These are called byssus threads and are secreted by the foot. Mussels differ from burrowing bivalves in that they prefer to secure themselves in one place, 'hanging around' on rocks, piles and posts until the tide covers them again. Young mussels do move around a little by using the foot, but once they get older they settle down in one spot.

Many of the bivalves are of importance to us because we eat them in large quantities. Cockles, mussels, oysters and scallops are all popular as seafood.

A small green mussel from the Indian Ocean. A larger one (*below*) from Chile shows how attractive some shells become on polishing.

Which bivalves produced the 'cloth of gold'?

We have already seen how mussels anchor themselves to surfaces by byssus threads. In the warm waters of the Mediterranean area one mussel in particular secretes extra-long byssus threads in a bunch from one end. This mollusc is called the Noble Pen Shell or Fan Mussel and it is from the fine, silky-smooth golden threads of its byssus that in days past the 'cloth of gold' was woven. This material was very popular with seventeenth century noblemen in southern Europe; it was light and flexible and had a beautiful sheen.

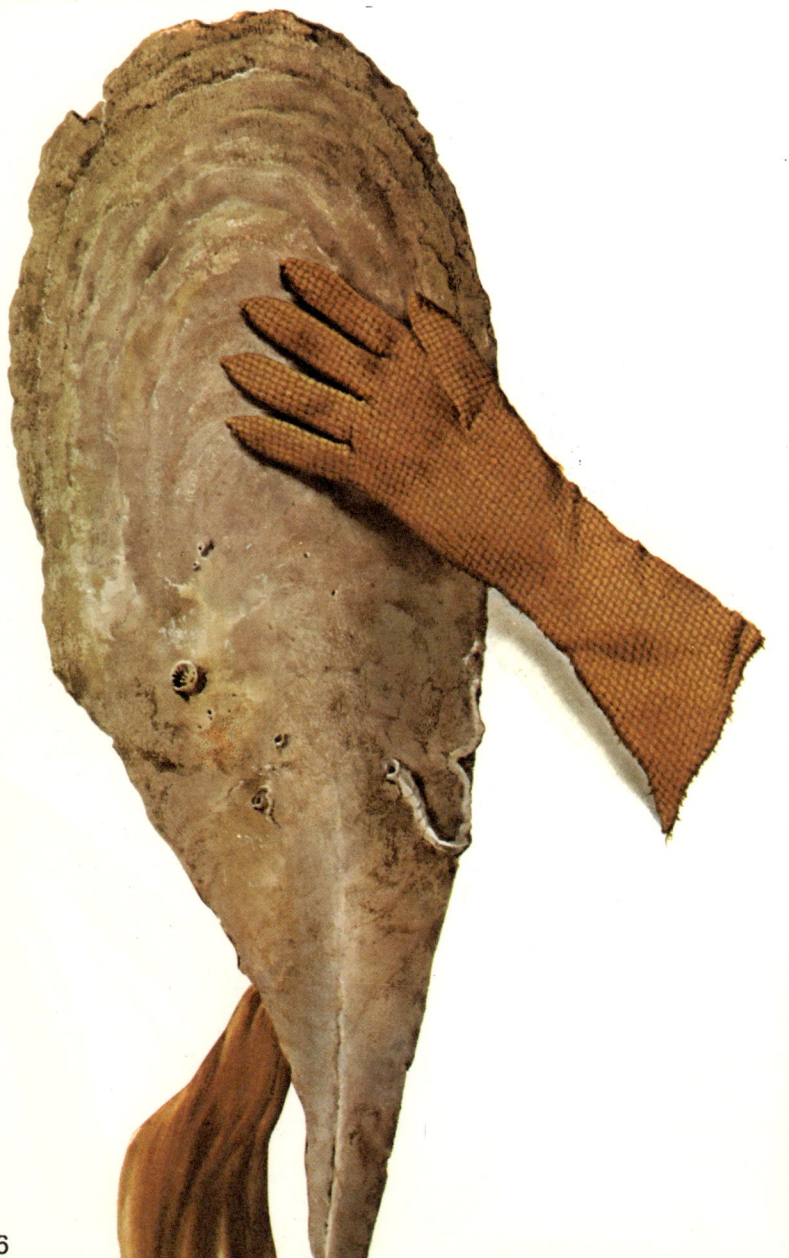

(*Left*) The Noble Pen Shell mussel showing its golden tassel of byssus threads and a glove woven from the threads. This mussel is about 16 inches long.

This diagram shows the early method of fishing for Noble Pen Shells required for the 'byssus weaving industry' of southern Italy.

A colourful tropical cockle from the Indian Ocean (1). A common European cockle (2) showing its extended siphons and foot. Cockles are a popular European seafood.

How does a cockle skip?

You can generally tell a cockle by its heart-shaped and characteristically ribbed shell, although cockles do come in various shapes and sizes. As you can see, cockles usually have short siphons with a fringe of tentacles around the end, and this gives us a clue as to how they live.

Enormous numbers of cockles are often found in sheltered, muddy estuaries. They burrow just under the sand until only the siphons protrude. Cockles have a long foot and if they are disturbed they give the foot a flick and kick themselves up from the bottom for about 8 inches. In this way they can skip away from enemies such as the starfish.

It is easy to see how razor shells gained their name. Their shape is very much like that of old-fashioned cut-throat razors and in addition the edges to the shells are very sharp. In America they are called 'jack-knife clams'.

How does a razor shell burrow quickly?

As the tide goes out you may notice depressions in the sand which mark the positions of razor shells just beneath the surface. If you decide you would like a better look at a razor shell and try to dig one up, you will be amazed to find that no matter how fast you dig the animal can burrow even faster. The smooth, streamlined shape of the shell and the powerful foot at one end of the animal enable it to burrow at an incredible rate. The foot is repeatedly extended, the tip swells, the foot contracts, and the animal is drawn down into the sand.

(*Left*) A giant clam on a coral reef.

Can the Giant Clam trap a man?

There have been many stories about Giant Clams closing on the arm or leg of an unwary diver and holding him until he drowned. However, no proof in the form of records has ever been presented to support them. In fact, the chances of such a thing happening are quite remote. The Giant Clam can grow to $4\frac{1}{2}$ feet in length, measuring 4 feet across, and weighing a quarter of a ton. It is found on the coral reefs of the Indian and Pacific Oceans. When the wavy edges of the shell are open, the brilliant purple and green mantle is revealed, making the large animal very conspicuous to a diver. Even if he poked a leg into the shell, the two halves would probably close slowly enough for him to realize what was happening and he could withdraw it in time. The Giant Clam is not adapted to be a man-trap – indeed it couldn't possibly eat a man if it did catch one. It feeds in the same way as smaller bivalve molluscs, by filtering food particles from the water, although it is unusual in that it also feeds on single-celled plants (algae) which grow along the edges of its mantle.

The animal is shown (*above right*) without its shell viewed from above, and, (*right*) the empty shell on its side is shown with a native to give an impression of its size.

Why does this bivalve have such a long siphon?

The long siphon of this bivalve mollusc has given it one of its common names, the Long-necked Clam. However, another feature is that it cannot close its shell because of the long siphon and so it is sometimes known as the Sand Gaper. It also has the names Soft-shell Clam and Otter-shell Clam, among others, but to avoid confusion its scientific name is *Mya arenaria*.

In contrast to the lightning burrowing speed of the razor shell the Long-necked Clam burrows very slowly and in fact prefers to live as deep in the sand as possible. It gradually works its way deeper and deeper as it grows. It must keep in contact with the surface, however, to draw in water for feeding and breathing and this is why its siphon is unusually long.

On the east coast of America these molluscs are relished as food and are very popular steamed, baked or fried and served with melted butter and cranberry sauce.

Two beautiful scallop shells from the Pacific Ocean (*left*) and the Red Sea (*right*).

(*Above*) The two siphons of the long-necked clam are encased in a single leathery tube.

(*Below*) The opening-and-shutting swimming action of the scallop.

Can scallops swim?

Scallops can swim very well and are one of the most agile groups of bivalve molluscs. You may look into a sea aquarium at the zoo one day and notice a starfish creeping up on a scallop. It is worth waiting to see what happens. Just as the starfish gets within reach the scallop will startle you by suddenly leaping up from the bottom in a cloud of sand, and by clapping its shell open and shut, it will swim jerkily away. It does this by drawing water into its shell and then forcing it out as the shell shuts, propelling itself along. The mantle does the job of funnelling the jet of water in various directions so that the scallop can swim forwards or backwards.

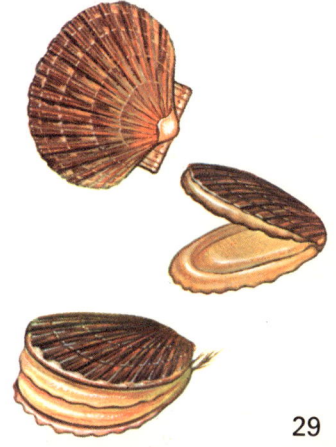

(*Left*) This sea hare is nearly a foot long and comes from the Indian and Pacific Oceans. Other species are found on European coasts which are much smaller.

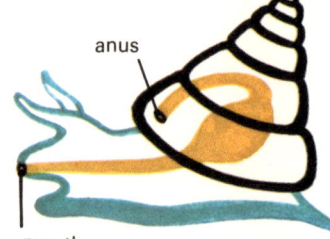

What are sea hares?

The sea hares introduce another large group of molluscs called the gastropods. These have a single shell (rather than one with two halves) and so they can all be described as univalves. Gastropods include snails, slugs, limpets and whelks.

The sea hares are unusual gastropods because their shell has become so reduced that you can scarcely see it under the large folds or wings of the mantle. These wings flap, circulating water to the gills and allowing the animal to swim quite gracefully. As you might expect the sea hare is vulnerable without a protective shell, but it has few enemies. This is because chemical secretions make it taste so horrible that no other animal will eat it.

You may wonder why the sea hare is so called. If you look closely at the second pair of tentacles you will see that these resemble the ears of a hare or rabbit.

(*Above*) The diagram shows the body plan of a typical gastropod mollusc.

Limpets can, in time, wear away hollows in soft rock by always returning to the same spot. The limpet (*above*) is called a key-hole limpet.

Does a limpet ever move?

Groups of limpets clustering together on rocks are a familiar sight at low tide. From curiosity you might have tried to pull one away from the rock surface and you will probably have been surprised at how tightly the limpet sticks there. It is easy to imagine that the limpet is stuck in the same position all its life. However, as soon as the sea returns to cover the limpets they come to life and begin to creep around on feeding expeditions. They graze on marine algae within a radius of 2 or 3 feet of the original spot and, strangely enough, they always return to the same 'home'. In time the limpet wears a slight depression in the rock in which it is even more protected from the crashing seas and from its enemies.

(*Above and below left*) Two attractive volute shells. The baler shell from Australia (*left*) is 6 inches in length.

Why are volutes highly prized?

Volutes are highly rated among shell collectors because of their exquisite beauty and the fact that a number of them are rare which, of course, increases their value. There are about 200 species and most of them come from tropical areas, particularly around the Great Barrier Reef of Australia. The large shell on this page is called a baler shell and this may give you a clue for one use to which it has been put. Natives in north-eastern Australia have used these shells to bale out canoes and for carrying water.

Some beautiful examples of cowries from the tropical areas of the world. The large pair (*right*) are golden cowries and are continually in demand by shell collectors for their delicate beauty.

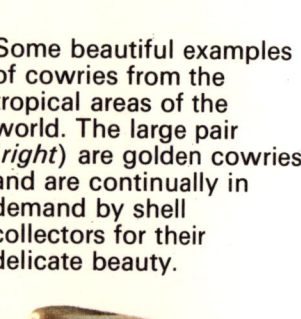

Why are cowries so shiny?

Cowries are noted for their beautiful colour, attractive patterning and, particularly, for their smooth, high-gloss finish. They look as if they have been carefully polished but in fact this flawless surface is produced naturally. When the cowry is alive two folds of the animal's mantle completely cover the shell and so it is very well protected from bumps and scratches throughout the cowry's life. This protective mechanism also deters attacks from the cowry's enemies, for example, starfishes, and of course helps to preserve the beautiful finish to the shell.

How does the whelk feed?

The whelk is an active and greedy carnivore continually moving around the sea floor scavenging for dead worms, crabs and fishes, but also preying on other molluscs. As it crawls around it holds its siphon above its head and apart from drawing water down this tube to the gills for breathing, the siphon is tasting the water. Any dead animal lying on the bottom, slowly decomposing, gives off unmistakable odours that taint the water and the whelk soon 'homes in' on any such carrion. The rasping radula is situated in the whelk at the end of a long extension from the animal's head called the proboscis. The whelk is quite partial to limpets and as we know (page 31) it is practically impossible to dislodge a limpet from its rock. The whelk's method is simple, the proboscis is extended and the radula quickly bores a hole in the limpet's shell, the proboscis pokes through and the radula begins rasping at its victim's flesh. The food is carried back within the proboscis to the animal's mouth. For bivalves the whelk waits until the two halves of the shell are slightly apart and then it quickly inserts the edge of its own shell to prevent the bivalve closing. The proboscis is inserted and the radula gets to work.

(*Above*) The round plate on the back of the whelk's foot serves as a door to seal up the shell opening when the animal is inside.

(*Top right*) The slug is really a snail without a shell although some slugs do have very small shells hidden within the body.

How are molluscs adapted to live on land?

Slugs and snails have quite successfully taken to the land although at a quick glance the garden snail does not look all that different from its sea water relative the Common Whelk. However, breathing air instead of water, the slugs and snails have no need of siphons and gills and in place of them the mantle cavity has become a lung. This opens to the outside through a hole which the animals can open and close – you may have noticed such a hole on a large slug on which it is quite conspicuous. Although living on dry land slugs and snails are still dependent on moisture and this is why they seek out dark, damp places to live, for example, under hedges. They produce lots of slime to keep themselves moist and this also helps them glide about easily. During the winter and dry spells they are forced to hibernate.

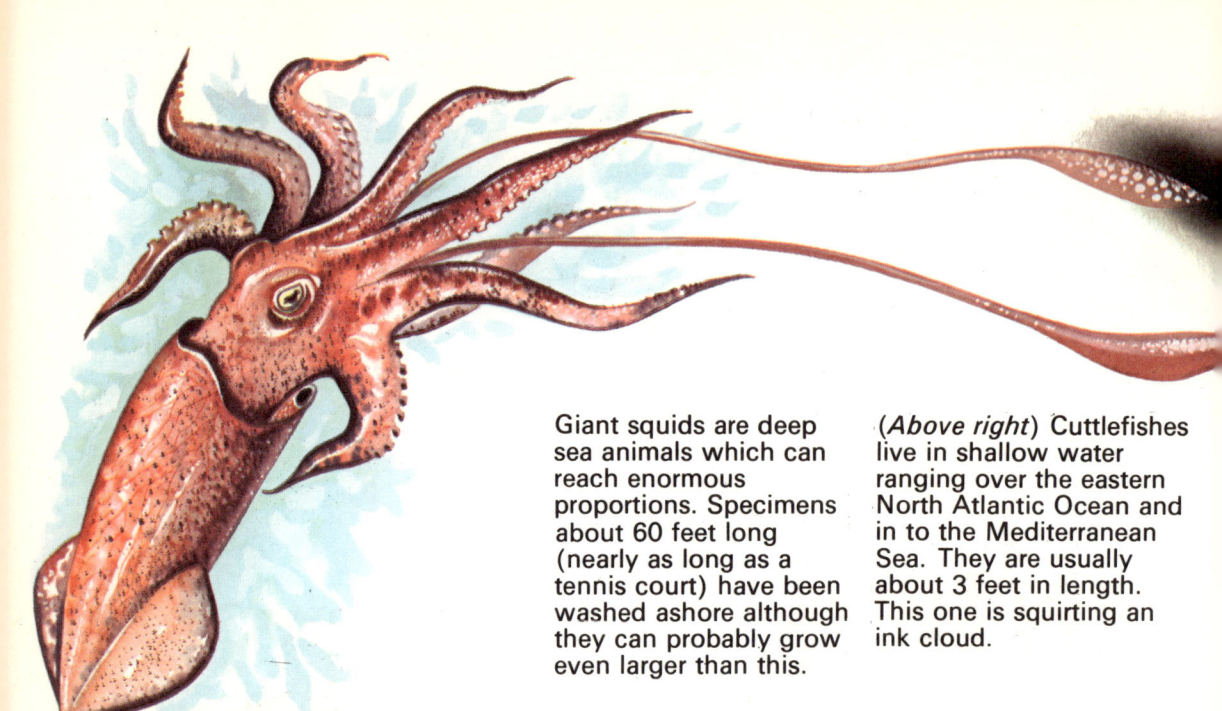

Giant squids are deep sea animals which can reach enormous proportions. Specimens about 60 feet long (nearly as long as a tennis court) have been washed ashore although they can probably grow even larger than this.

(*Above right*) Cuttlefishes live in shallow water ranging over the eastern North Atlantic Ocean and in to the Mediterranean Sea. They are usually about 3 feet in length. This one is squirting an ink cloud.

What is a cuttlefish?

You have probably noticed 'cuttlebone' pushed between the bars of a budgerigar's cage, or washed up on the beach. This 'bone' is not really bone at all but the shell of a cuttlefish, which is not a fish but a mollusc. The cuttlefishes, squids and octopuses belong to a group of molluscs called cephalopods and most are characterized by a very reduced shell or by not having one at all. The shell in the cuttlefish is completely enclosed by the mantle and, being very light, it helps to keep the animal buoyant.

The foot of all the cephalopods is modified to form either eight or ten tentacles which surround the head (cephalopod means head-footed). These bear suckers along their length and it is with them that the animals catch their prey. The edge of the mantle of the cuttlefish forms two flaps at the sides and by undulating these the animal swims about quite leisurely. In an emergency, greater speed is obtained by forcing out a jet of water from the mantle cavity through a funnel. The funnel can be directed in any direction and if suddenly attacked, the cuttlefish can shoot off out of danger.

Why does a squid squirt ink?

Another emergency tactic that can be adopted by cuttlefishes, squids and octopuses is the use of a smoke screen. All

These are deep sea squids which are illuminated by light organs.

these animals can swim rapidly by the jet propulsion method. If, however, a hungry shark or penguin gets too close it may be surprised to discover that it is in fact chasing a cloud of black ink, the squid having quickly squirted this out while travelling at speed and, swivelling its funnel, darting off in another direction.

Is an octopus dangerous to man?

There are stories of people being attacked by an octopus and frantically trying to detach the suckers of the encircling arms. This may happen very rarely and when it does the octopus is really investigating a new moving shape rather than attacking it. If the person could manage to keep perfectly still the octopus would soon let him go.

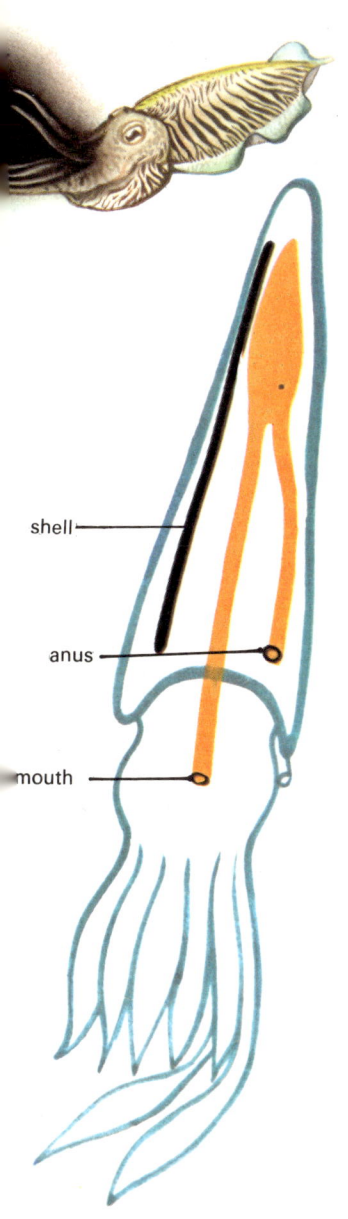

(*Above*) The body plan of a typical cephalopod.

(*Right*) Octopuses differ from cuttlefishes and squids in having eight arms rather than ten. They are also characterized by the absence of an internal shell.

A ragworm showing the paddles and bristles which project from either side of each segment.

What are the worms of the seashore?

Two common worms that you can find on the shore are ragworms and lugworms. Ragworms can be found under stones but lugworms live in burrows in the sand and have to be dug out.

The ragworm is about 8 inches long and swims in a characteristic side to side motion. As the waves overtake the worm, the side extensions in every segment push back like paddles, propelling the worm along. The paddles also serve as gills, being well supplied with blood vessels, and the tuft of stiff bristles from each helps support it and provides some protection to the animal. Ragworms are carnivorous and can give a bad nip with strong jaws so handle them with care.

The little coiled casts of sand on the beach at low tide mark the openings to the U-shaped tubes in which lugworms live. In the bend of the tube about a foot down lies the

(*Above*) The red tufts on the lugworm are gills. The U-shaped tube and cast of the animal are also shown.

(*Right*) Fan worms extend their feathery crowns to trap food particles in the water.

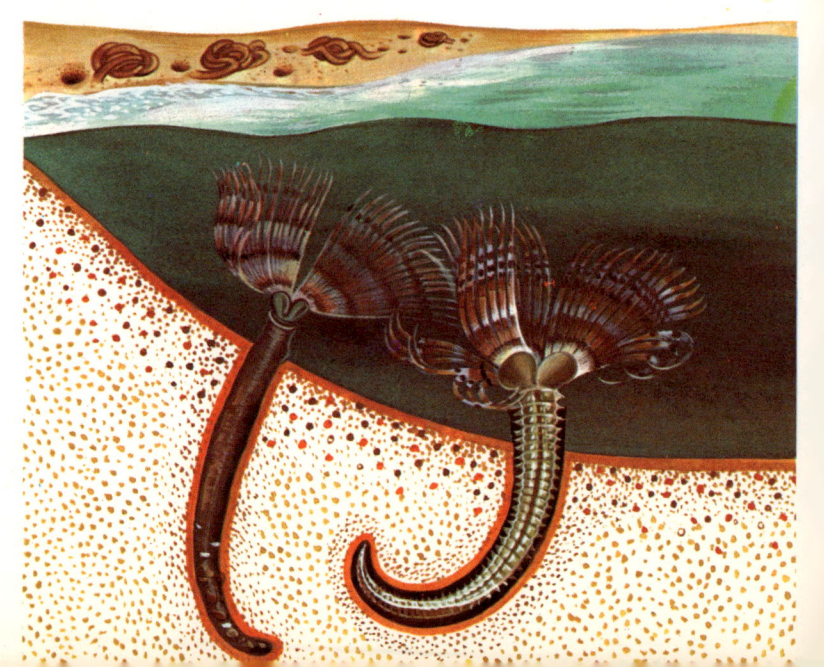

worm. By moving its head and swallowing sand the grains gradually sink above its head leaving a shallow pit on the surface. After feeding for about forty minutes the sand is passed from the worm at the open end of the tube to form the cast. By contracting its body the worm draws water into the tube from this end and this passes over its red gill tufts before flowing out of the other end. Both ragworms and lugworms are prized as bait by sea fishermen.

Other worms which live in tubes are the fan, or feather duster, worms. The tube projects from the sandy floor and from the end the worm spreads its beautiful crown of tentacles whenever it is covered by the tide. The tentacles sift out particles from the water, the smallest of which are eaten, those slightly bigger are used to extend the tube and the biggest are discarded. In some fanworms the tentacles act as gills.

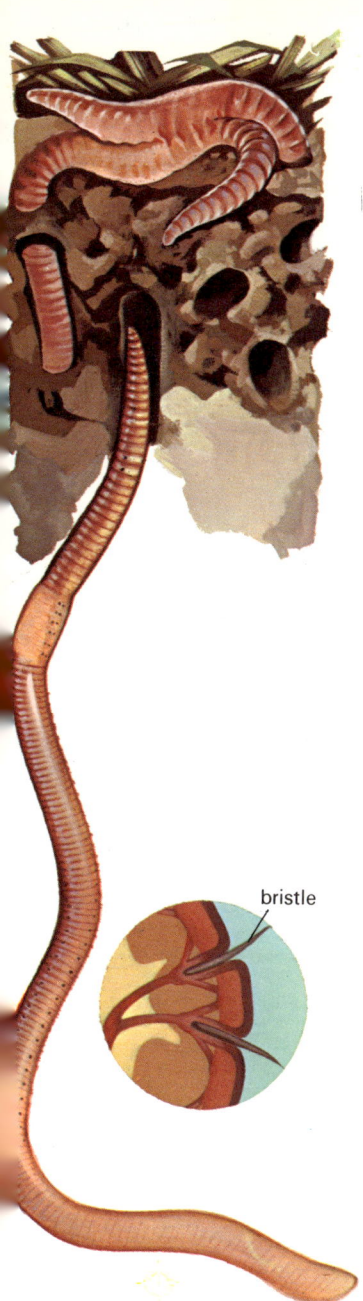

(*Right*) A normal-sized earthworm is shown next to a giant worm from Australia which can grow to 12 feet in length.

The bristles of the earthworm are shown in this section of the body wall, and can just be seen as two rows of paired dots along the length of the worm.

Why are earthworms good for the soil?

By their constant burrowing earthworms are forever turning over the soil, bringing fresh earth to the surface and covering it again. Their burrows allow air into the soil and water to drain from it. At night earthworms drag leaves and other plant remains into their burrows and perhaps eat only half, leaving the rest to decay in the soil. Humus mixed into the airy, well-drained earth makes it fertile and ideal for plant growth. Earthworms are adapted to an underground life by being streamlined; they have no projecting flaps or gills. However, if you listen to a worm crawling across a sheet of paper you will hear scratching noises. These are made by the short bristles (chaetae) projecting from each segment on either side. You can feel them by running your finger up the sides of the worm. It is these chaetae that help the worm crawl and prevent you from pulling it from its burrow head first. All the worms are characterized by their segmented bodies and they form the group called the phylum Annelida.

A typical peripatus about 3 inches long. These curious animals live in moist, dark places in the tropical forests of Australia, Africa and South America.

How does peripatus link the worms and the animals with jointed legs?

This insignificant looking creature excited zoologists in the nineteenth century when it was first discovered because it was unlike any other animal known at that time. It looks very much like a worm and yet it has rows of stumpy legs on either side and shows other features similar to animals of the phylum Arthropoda (animals with jointed legs).

The arthropods are the biggest and most diverse group of invertebrates and have successfully colonized the land and learnt how to fly. They include the crustaceans (barnacles, shrimps, lobsters and crabs), centipedes and millipedes, arachnids (spiders, scorpions, ticks and mites) and the insects. The feature that has been most responsible for the success of the arthropods is their tough external covering called an exoskeleton. This supports the animal's soft body on land and at the same time prevents it losing water by evaporation. It is light enough to allow easy movements and yet also provides good protection.

Another small freshwater crustacean related to the water fleas, called an ostracod.

(Right) Water fleas are about $\frac{1}{10}$ of an inch long and seem to spend their lives trying to stay in one position in the water.

Because peripatus has features which are both worm-like (thin skin, eyes), and arthropod-like (claws, breathing system), it is thought to be descended almost unchanged from the animals that gave rise millions of years ago to the worms and arthropods.

Are water fleas really fleas?

True fleas are parasitic insects. Water fleas are so called because of their erratic, flea-like swimming movements. The water fleas are common freshwater crustaceans and they are fascinating to watch in a pond or better still in an aquarium.

The folded shell which encloses the body is transparent and through it you can easily watch the workings of the water flea's body. The heart can be seen pumping away, and several pairs of feet are visible beating the water, filtering out single-celled algae and bacteria for food. You can even see the eggs and developing young on the back of the females. Watch how the water flea sinks a little and then frantically jerks its way back to its original position by thrashing the water with its two pairs of branched antennae.

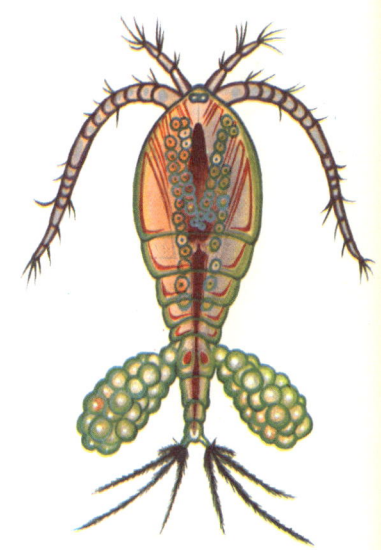

A selection of copepods — small crustaceans which form the main food of fishes in the sea.

What are copepods?

Copepods are another group of small crustaceans which live in the sea. They are better swimmers than the freshwater water fleas and use their legs as well as their antennae to propel themselves through the water. Copepods drift in enormous numbers in the upper levels of the sea. Together with other minute creatures they form plankton on which all other higher animals feed, either directly or indirectly. Thus they are a very important link in the food chain that ends with man himself.

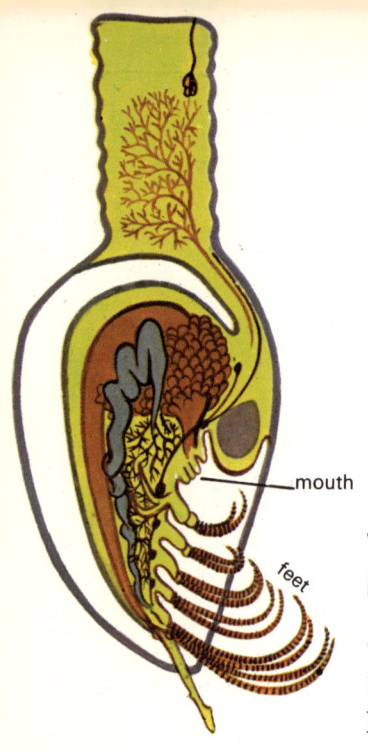

(*Left*) Goose or gooseneck barnacles often attach themselves by their long stalks to flotsam. Some even produce a bubble which acts as a float from which they can hang. Those shown here are attached to a piece of driftwood.

The body plan of a goose barnacle.

Which animals live on their heads and kick food into their mouths?

The animals that live in this extraordinary position are the barnacles. You must have noticed barnacles encrusting large rocks at low tide on the shore and you might be forgiven for mistaking them for limpets or some other kind of mollusc. In fact they used to be called molluscs until it was noticed that the larvae hatching from the eggs have several features in common with crustaceans. The larva swims around for a while feeding and growing. It eventually changes into a shelled form and chooses a suitable place on a surface on which to settle head first. A special secretion sticks it in position and it quickly encloses itself in a shell made up of plates. When the tide exposes the barnacle the plates stay closed to prevent loss of water from the animal. When the tide returns, however, the top pair opens and the feathery feet are pushed out to comb the water for suspended food particles.

Barnacles vary in diameter from $\frac{1}{4}$ of an inch to a huge type in North America which can grow to 1 foot across. There are a number of species. The one *far left* is feeding with its feet.

Where do barnacles live?

Barnacles will encrust practically any suitable surface on the shore. These include piles, pier supports, old tin cans and crabs which do not move fast enough to avoid the settling larvae. At one time they caused ships to slow down by settling on their bottoms but special paints are now used which inhibit the larvae from settling.

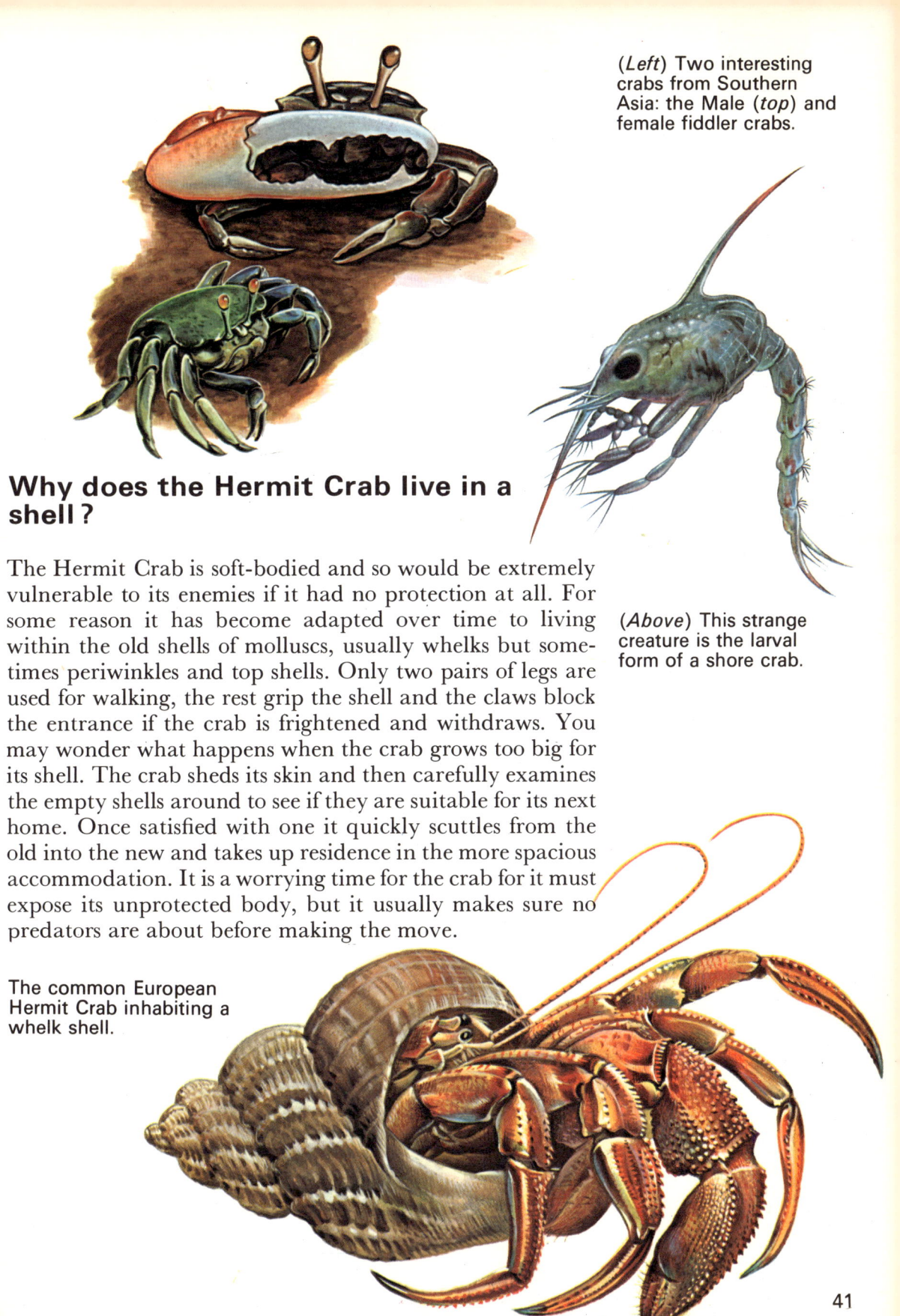

(*Left*) Two interesting crabs from Southern Asia: the Male (*top*) and female fiddler crabs.

Why does the Hermit Crab live in a shell?

The Hermit Crab is soft-bodied and so would be extremely vulnerable to its enemies if it had no protection at all. For some reason it has become adapted over time to living within the old shells of molluscs, usually whelks but sometimes periwinkles and top shells. Only two pairs of legs are used for walking, the rest grip the shell and the claws block the entrance if the crab is frightened and withdraws. You may wonder what happens when the crab grows too big for its shell. The crab sheds its skin and then carefully examines the empty shells around to see if they are suitable for its next home. Once satisfied with one it quickly scuttles from the old into the new and takes up residence in the more spacious accommodation. It is a worrying time for the crab for it must expose its unprotected body, but it usually makes sure no predators are about before making the move.

(*Above*) This strange creature is the larval form of a shore crab.

The common European Hermit Crab inhabiting a whelk shell.

Can prawns change colour?

There is one prawn that is particularly good at changing its colour. This is the Aesop Prawn. Normally it is pink but it can vary its body colour to match that of its surroundings. This usually occurs in times of danger when a predator is lurking nearby. If it takes refuge on a brown seaweed it gradually turns brown and on a green seaweed it turns green. Strangely enough at night it always turns blue, no matter what colour its surroundings happen to be. The colour is produced by pigment cells all over the prawn's body.

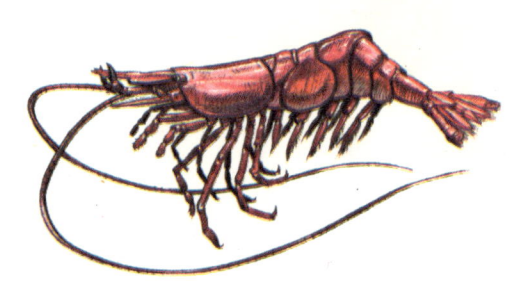

Can a lobster swim backwards?

If you look carefully at the rear end of a lobster you will see that it spreads out into a scoop-like structure called a tail-fan. Normally, of course, the lobster walks over the bottom or, if in a hurry, it can swim forwards using special swimming legs on its abdomen. If startled, however, it quickly bends its tail up underneath its body and paddles its way backwards out of danger at considerable speed. Shrimps, prawns and freshwater crayfishes also have a tail-fan and so all these crustaceans can swim backwards in this way. Another thing they have in common is that they are all enjoyed by man as food. Lobsters provide a lot of meat from the muscles in their large pincers and from the abdomen. The Spiny Lobster is found in both the southern Atlantic and Pacific Oceans. Europe produces the common European and the Norway Lobsters, the latter known as scampi.

(*Above left*) The Aesop Prawn matches its colour to brown and green seaweed. The normal colour is shown (*above*).

The European Lobster and the pot which is often used to catch it. Lobsters are scavengers and so the pot is baited with a choice piece of dead fish. The lobster climbs in easily enough but finds it practically impossible to find the narrow way out.

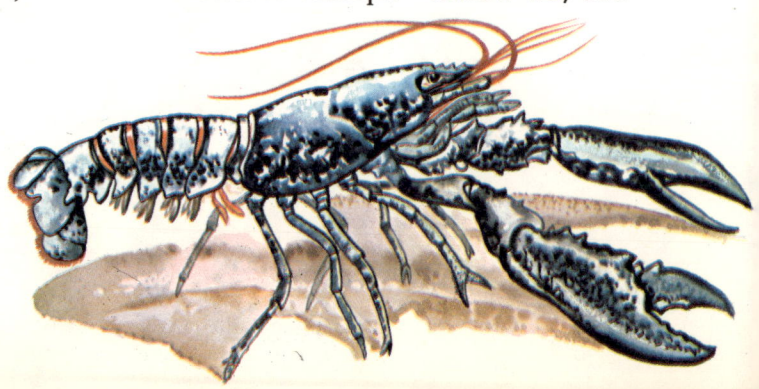

A giant millipede from Asia and a pill millipede walking and rolled up. Pill millipedes curl up when alarmed and some from the tropics are as large as ping-pong balls. Two centipedes are shown *below*.

How many legs has a centipede?

Centipede 'means 'hundred legged' but not many centipedes actually have as many as this. Some have as few as 15 pairs, others have as many as 173 pairs, but most sorts have about 35 pairs. Centipedes and millipedes form a small group of arthropods adapted for life on the land. With all these legs they run very quickly and although it has been discovered that the legs sometimes cross, the centipede never seems to trip up. Centipedes can sometimes be found in the home but usually live under the bark of fallen trees and under stones. They are generally about 1 or 2 inches long but species from North America can grow to 7 inches.

What is the difference between a centipede and a millipede?

A millipede does not have a million legs but it has twice as many as a centipede about the same length – two pairs to each segment. In spite of this the millipede moves more slowly than the centipede. It feeds on vegetation and often destroys valuable crops like potatoes, whereas the centipede is a carnivore and catches worms, spiders and insects, sometimes including flies.

Millipedes are interesting animals. At various times they have been known to swarm and once in France their seething numbers brought a train to a standstill. As they are blind their mating signals are highly developed. It has recently been reported that one type of millipede from Europe attracts a mate by banging its head on the ground.

The Cicada (*top*) and Bush Cricket are insects related to locusts well known for their strident 'singing' at night.

Why are there so many insects?

Of the animals with jointed legs, the insects form the largest and most diverse group and the group of animals that has had most success in adapting itself for life on the land. The first reason for this success is because they are small. On land their size is restricted for without the support of water their legs cannot bear the great weight of a large exoskeleton. Their muscles are generally well developed and so they are very active and do not have much difficulty in escaping from enemies. Another advantage of being small is that you do not have to grow much. Insects mature quickly and produce young several times a year. Large numbers of offspring have enabled insects to adapt to practically every sort of living condition and to practically every type of food.

How do insects develop?

Primitive insects lay eggs from which hatch young which look like miniature versions of their parents. Restricted by their hard exoskeleton the offspring are forced to shed their skins in order to grow, and this happens several times before they reach maturity. In other higher insects a larva completely different from its parents hatches from the egg. The caterpillar larva of the butterfly, for example, lives on plants and eats large amounts of leaves while quickly growing. Eventually it forms a hard case around itself and from this pupa an adult butterfly emerges. The butterfly hardly feeds at all and after mating soon dies. This more advanced insect development enables the larva and adult to concentrate on different aspects of the life cycle. The larva is the passive feeding stage and the adult the active reproductive stage.

The two types of Desert Locust found in dry areas of Africa. The green type lives a solitary life but the yellow and black type wreaks havoc in agricultural areas by swarming.

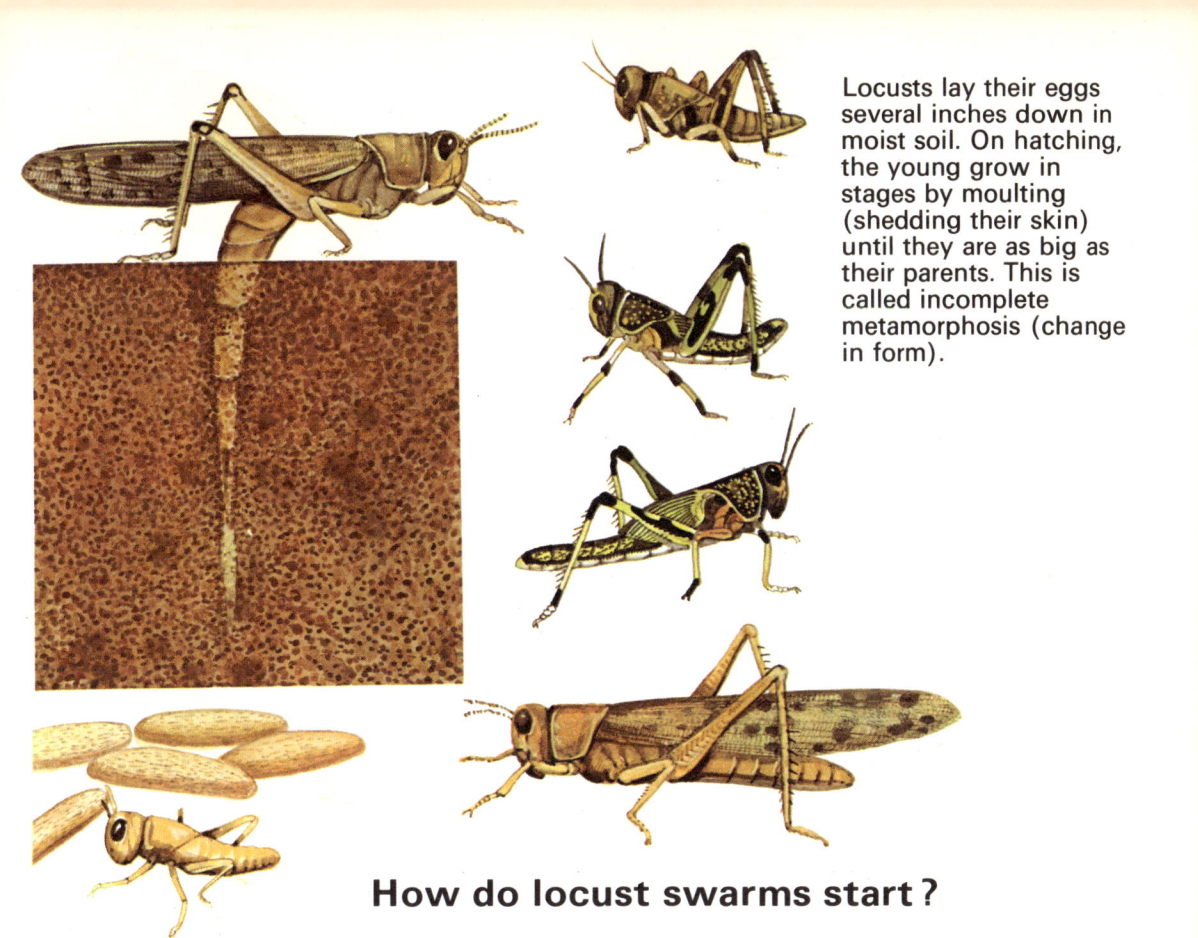

Locusts lay their eggs several inches down in moist soil. On hatching, the young grow in stages by moulting (shedding their skin) until they are as big as their parents. This is called incomplete metamorphosis (change in form).

How do locust swarms start?

One of the three types of locust that forms swarms in Africa is the Desert Locust. This locust usually lives like a grasshopper in what is called a solitary phase. Sometimes, however, all the solitary locusts from a wide area are driven together, perhaps by the weather, and they may find the conditions just right for feeding and mating. As locusts mate and lay eggs many times in a short period, enormous numbers of young locusts hatch and become stimulated by each other to form a swarm. They change colour and when all the available plants have been eaten they migrate in search of more.

The complete metamorphosis from larva to adult in the butterfly. The hard case from which the adult emerges is called the pupa.

How do these insects avoid detection?

The insects shown on these pages are mantids, a stick insect and a leaf insect. All live on vegetation and you will see that each has developed an appearance which blends perfectly with its surroundings. Mantids are usually coloured green or brown to match the colour of foliage and are often shaped to help the disguise, as well. Some are long and slender like twigs and others have a rough appearance to resemble bark. As they tend to keep very still for long periods during the day, these insects are very difficult to detect. The young stage of one species from Asia, the Flower Mantid, is even more adapted for concealment and bears a remarkable likeness to the pink flower of the plant on which it lives. It matches

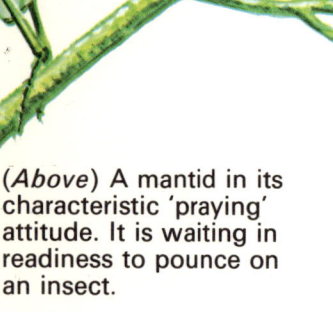

(*Above*) A mantid in its characteristic 'praying' attitude. It is waiting in readiness to pounce on an insect.

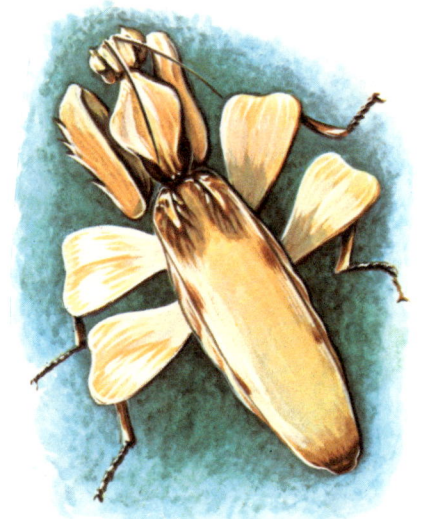

The young Flower Mantid (*below*) is remarkably camouflaged among the flowers of the plant on which it lives. Once it matures, however, it loses its pink colour (*left*).

its colour perfectly and flattened extensions from its legs give the impression of petals. This mantid has the double advantage of attracting insects such as butterflies which it can then easily catch, while remaining perfectly hidden from its enemies. In the same way the other well-camouflaged mantids are able to pounce on unsuspecting insects that wander by without having to move an inch to hunt them.

The camouflage of stick insects and leaf insects probably serves only to hide them from their enemies as both feed on plants alone. However, their ability to avoid being seen is just as good as the mantids. The stick insect has an elongated body and spindly legs and assumes an attitude which is exactly that of an extension of the twig on which it is resting. Unless it moves it is difficult to believe it is really an insect.

The related leaf insect bears an incredible resemblance to

a leaf, even down to the ribs on the wings which look exactly like the veins of a leaf. Some even go to the length of having marks to give the impression of fungal growths and bird droppings.

How does the mantid catch its prey?

The mantid stands completely motionless in wait for unwary insects. The head and upper part of its body are held in an upright position and the large front legs are folded, almost as if the insect was praying. (This is why they are sometimes called Praying Mantids.) The legs have sharp spines along their length and are jointed so that they can snap closed in a vice-like grip. Once an unfortunate insect strays within the long reach of these specially adapted forelegs, they lash out and fix the prey in a terrible embrace. It is then rapidly devoured. Mantids are greedy carnivores and feed on most insects including other mantids.

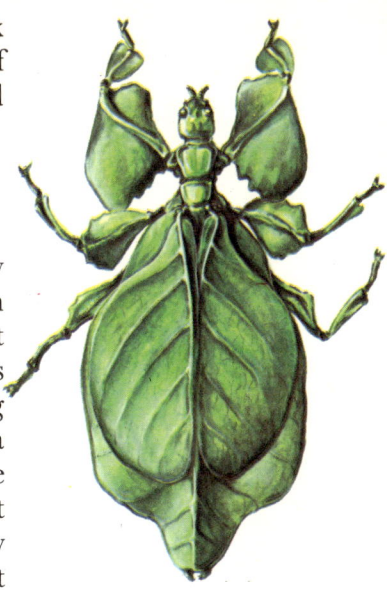

(*Above*) Leaf insects move slowly around on foliage in tropical forests. They bear an astonishing resemblance to the leaves on which they feed.

Where do mantids, stick insects and leaf insects come from?

Mantids are found in tropical and subtropical regions of the world. There is a European species which has been introduced into North America where it has become well established. The Flower Mantid of South-east Asia, sometimes called the Orchid Mantid, comes mainly from Malaysia and Indonesia, but species that resemble flowers are also found in Africa.

There are about 2,000 stick insects and leaf insects and most come from tropical Oriental areas. However, some types are found in both northern Europe and North America. The stick insects you may keep in your classroom as pets are probably from the Orient and would not survive outdoors during a cold winter.

Some stick insects from Asia can grow to 1 foot in length. Not surprisingly they are the longest insects known. Most stick insects are much shorter than this.

How fast can a dragonfly fly?

It is very difficult to estimate the speed of insects in flight but it is thought that some dragonflies can reach 30 miles an hour. Dragonflies are easily the most skilled fliers of the insects. You may have seen them on a summer's evening along the river bank, flitting and darting in vivid flashes of beautiful iridescent colour. You can see from their shape that they are well adapted for strong flight and acrobatic manoeuvres to catch other flying insects. They are equipped with two pairs of powerful wings. The very elongated body streamlines the dragonfly and helps to stabilize it in flight.

The aquatic dragonfly nymph extending its mask to seize a small tadpole (*right*). After several months the nymph is fully grown and crawls up a plant stem above the surface. The adult emerges from the final moult. When its wings have expanded (*bottom right*) and hardened it flys off to begin the second stage of its life.

As you might expect, a predatory insect that weaves and dives after its prey in the air must have good eyesight. The dragonfly's head is dominated by an enormous pair of compound eyes.

The dragonfly is another insect that develops by incomplete metamorphosis. This is to say that, on hatching, the larva resembles its parent with only slight modifications so that it can lead a life in a different environment. The female dragonfly lays her eggs in water. The larvae, or nymphs, lead an underwater life for two years before they finally emerge to change into adults. The nymph is as much a greedy predator as its flying parent although not so active. It creeps stealthily among aquatic vegetation and catches the fry of fishes, tadpoles and other insects. It seizes its prey using a specially extendable jaw called a mask. At rest this is folded up under the head and partly covers the face. Once a young fish swims within range the mask is flashed out and a pair of claws closes on to the prey to secure it.

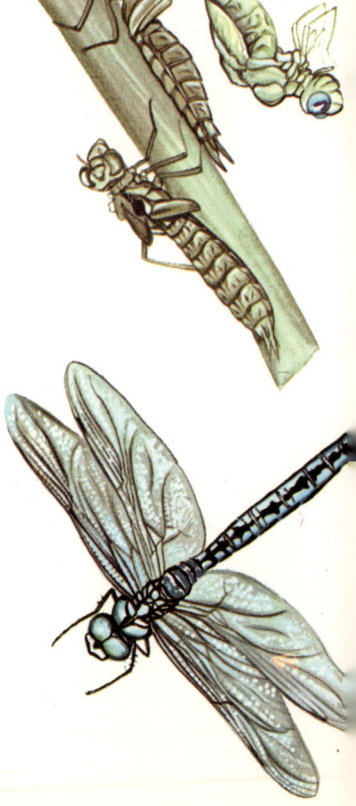

Which insects build enormous mounds?

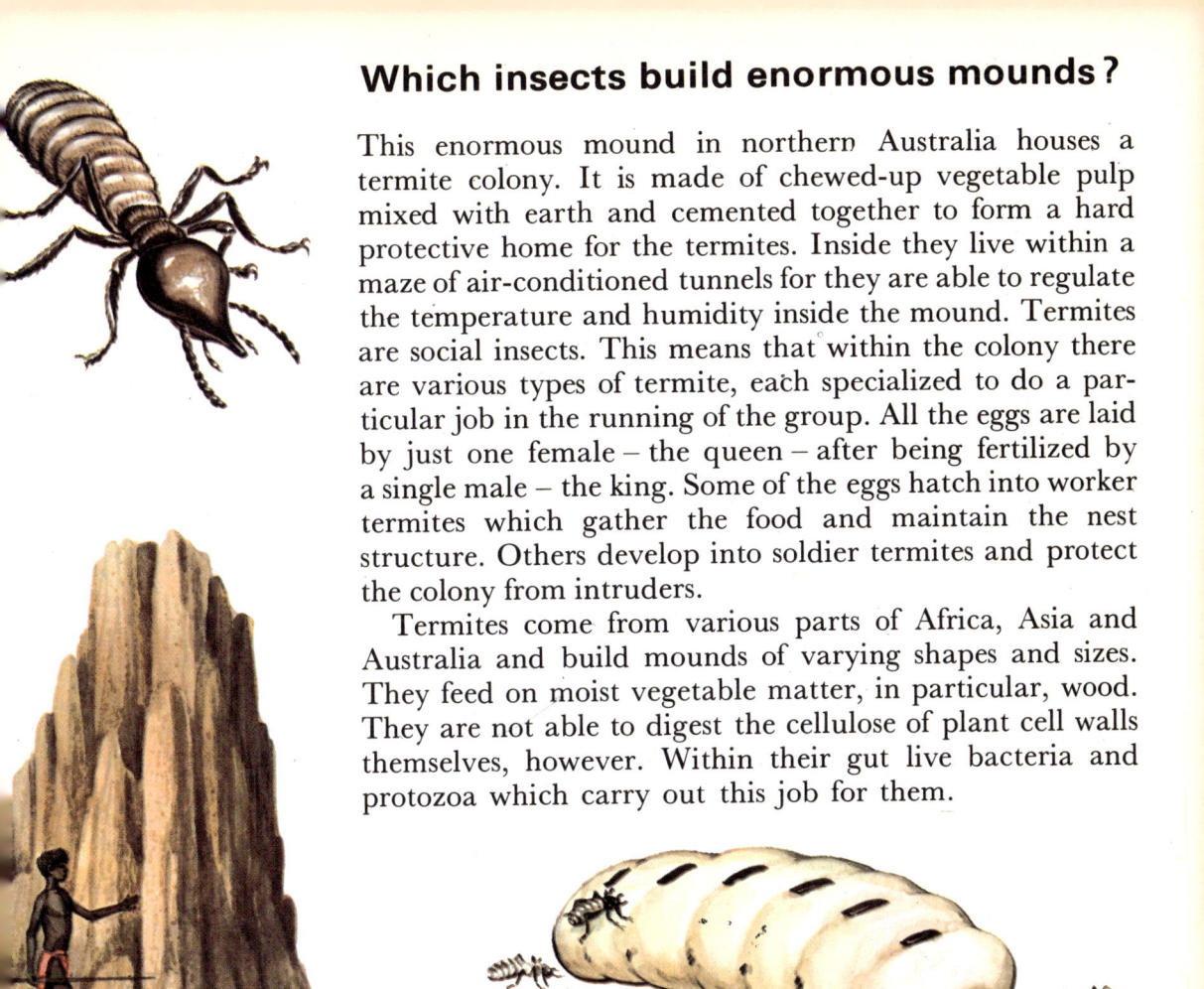

This enormous mound in northern Australia houses a termite colony. It is made of chewed-up vegetable pulp mixed with earth and cemented together to form a hard protective home for the termites. Inside they live within a maze of air-conditioned tunnels for they are able to regulate the temperature and humidity inside the mound. Termites are social insects. This means that within the colony there are various types of termite, each specialized to do a particular job in the running of the group. All the eggs are laid by just one female – the queen – after being fertilized by a single male – the king. Some of the eggs hatch into worker termites which gather the food and maintain the nest structure. Others develop into soldier termites and protect the colony from intruders.

Termites come from various parts of Africa, Asia and Australia and build mounds of varying shapes and sizes. They feed on moist vegetable matter, in particular, wood. They are not able to digest the cellulose of plant cell walls themselves, however. Within their gut live bacteria and protozoa which carry out this job for them.

(*Above*) The body of the queen termite becomes enormously enlarged so that her egg-laying capacity is increased. Two types of soldier termites are shown *top left* and *bottom right*.

How does a termite colony start?

When conditions are right special fertile winged termites hatch within the mound. They suddenly leave the rest in a dense swarm and disperse. After travelling a short way they drop to the ground and break off their wings which they no longer need. A male and a female pair up, choose a suitable home, perhaps in an old rotten log, mate, and produce young. The offspring are the pioneer workers and soldiers of the new colony. As more and more eggs are laid and hatched, and a nest built, the colony gradually becomes established. The original pair – the king and queen – remains within the nest for years and years, simply producing a continuing supply of new termites.

How do aphids damage plants?

You probably know how upset gardeners are to see aphids on their prize roses. They have good cause for anxiety since aphids do a lot of damage to many plants. They also do considerable economic harm to farmers. Their activities affect crops in two ways. By sucking the sap aphids soon cause the plants to weaken and die, and by moving from one plant to another, they can be responsible for spreading virus infections among crops.

The mouthparts of the aphid are modified to form a needlesharp tube which is inserted into the sap-carrying cells of the plant. The sap is thus diverted to the aphid and because it has a low nutrient value the aphid drinks vast quantities. Most of the sugary sap passes straight through the aphid and is excreted as honeydew. It is this that is so favoured by ants and by stroking the aphids with their antennae they stimulate a faster flow of honeydew.

(*Above*) Female winged aphids settle on fresh plants and produce generation after generation of wingless females without mating. In a short time a heavy infestation results. A winged female is shown *below*.

Why does the scarab beetle roll dung?

A fairly common sight in the drier areas of southern Asia, the United States and Africa, is a medium-sized black beetle scurrying backwards rolling a ball of dung. This is often several times the size of the beetle and can be as big as a tennis ball. Often a beetle will be helped in its labours by another, but if it is not careful the newcomer will make off with the dung himself. Once a suitable spot is found the beetle digs a chamber and feeds on the dung underground. Later in the year the beetles pair up and as before bury some dung. This time, however, the dung is intended for their young. The female shreds it carefully and refashions it into a pearshape in which the egg is laid. On hatching, the larva has a readily available source of food which it quickly eats before changing into an adult.

The scarab beetle parents go to a lot of trouble to provide a handy food supply for their young. The larvae have no worries about setting out on dangerous feeding expeditions and they are very secure and well protected in their own underground larders. A lot of effort is involved in providing for the young in this way but the method is very successful. The female does not usually lay more than four eggs in a year.

A scarab beetle rolling a dung ball with its back legs. In the United States these beetles are called tumble bugs. A goliath beetle is also shown. In Africa this enormous insect can grow to 6 inches in length.

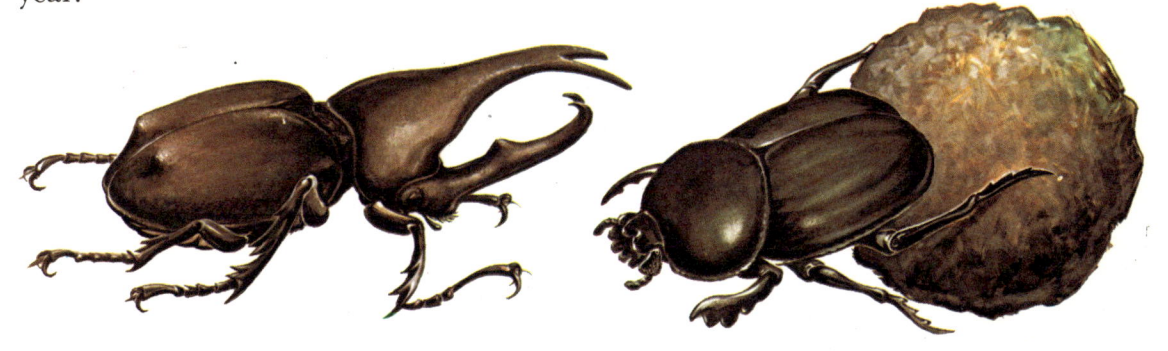

How does the ant lion larva catch ants?

In contrast to the graceful beauty of the adult insect, the larva of the ant lion bears a pair of cruel-looking jaws, and catches ants and small spiders in a most ingenious way. (It is the behaviour of the larva that gives the insect its name.) The small, fat creature carefully digs a steep-sided, conical pit in dry, sandy soil in a sheltered spot. The pit is about 3 inches in diameter and 2 inches deep and so forms quite a treacherous obstacle for any passing ant or other small insect. Alerted by dislodged grains of sand, the ant lion larva immediately appears from hiding at the bottom of the pit. It frantically scoops up sand on to its head and in a jerking movement flings it at its prey. The ant is usually bowled over by this onslaught and, losing its footing, tumbles down the sides of the pit to be pounced on and devoured by the ant lion. There are over 600 species of ant lions, several species occuring in the United States and some in southern Asia, but not all dig pits to trap their prey.

(*Below left*) The larva of an ant lion successfully ambushes ants by digging pits in sandy soil. The beautiful adult is shown (*below*) and can be from 1 to 3 inches long.

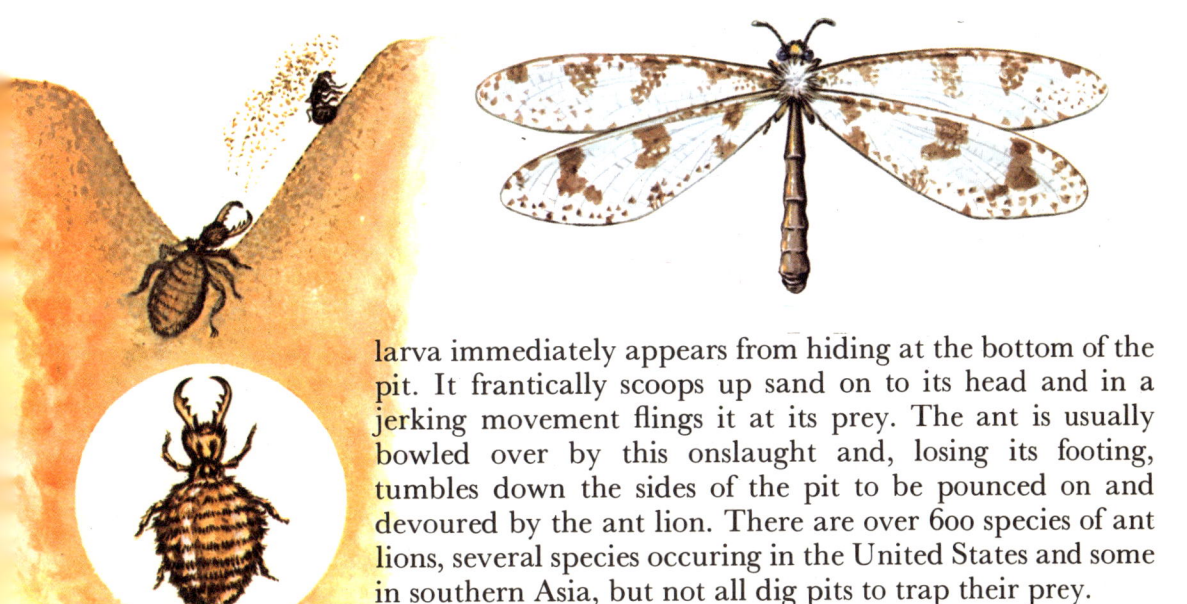

The Small Tortoiseshell Butterfly lays its eggs on the underside of nettle leaves. When the larvae hatch they will find themselves on a convenient food supply.

Where do butterflies lay their eggs?

Butterflies, and moths as well for that matter, are very particular about laying their eggs. Most butterflies leave them on only one sort of plant because this is the plant that the newly hatched larvae, called caterpillars, will feed on. So the female butterfly will spend some time finding the correct plant (the foodplant) before laying her eggs. You might think that for an insect this would be particular enough, but most butterflies even choose a particular place on the foodplant for the eggs and will leave them in no other. For example, one species of brimstone butterfly will only lay eggs on the topmost shoots of the buckthorn bush. You would never find them if you searched lower down the plant.

Further examples of butterflies' eggs magnified many times. Some butterflies lay their eggs on the undersides of leaves.

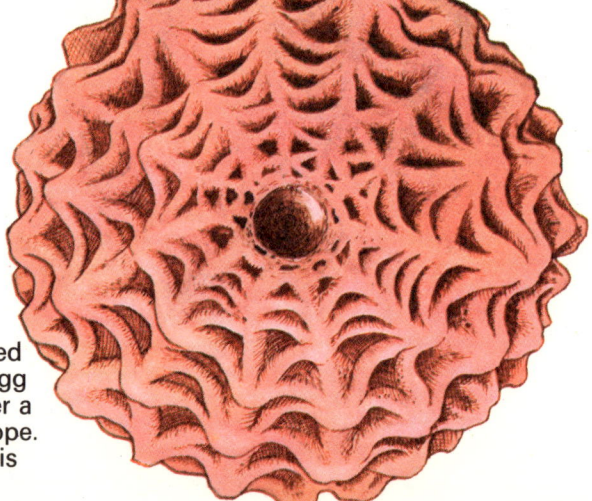

The attractive sculptured effect of a butterfly's egg as seen if viewed under a low-powered microscope. The hole in the centre is the micropyle.

What is the hole in the butterfly's egg for?

The hole in the butterfly's egg is called the micropyle. It is through this hole that the egg was fertilized in the female's body before it was laid. Once laid, it admits air to the developing larva inside, allowing it to breathe.

Some species of butterfly lay their eggs singly, others in small batches all over the foodplant, while yet others perhaps lay one large batch. All the eggs are varied in shape, size and colour, and viewed under a low-powered microscope, are beautiful to look at. They are so varied that it is usually possible to say from which group of butterflies a particular egg is from, if not the actual species.

A newly hatched caterpillar eating the egg shell it has just left.

Why does the caterpillar eat its egg shell?

Some butterflies' eggs are transparent and it is interesting to watch the development from the time the egg is laid to the time the larva hatches. The egg at first looks as if it is full of liquid but gradually the larva grows to fill it. As this happens the egg often changes colour several times. The eggs of some species hatch in a few days but with others it may be between two and three weeks before the larvae emerge. Their first meal is generally the empty egg shell and it is thought that this contains certain essential food substances that the caterpillar must have in order to survive.

The caterpillar grows quickly by shedding its skin about four or five times. The new skin forms beneath the old and in the caterpillar *above* the bump indicates the position of the new head capsule. A caterpillar like this is about to moult. By watching closely you will see the old skin split and the caterpillar wriggle out. The caterpillar *below left* has just moulted.

How many legs has a caterpillar?

Insects have three pairs of legs but in caterpillars these are increased to usually eight pairs. The first three pairs are called true legs and each leg bears a hook at the end to help movement. The other legs are called prolegs. These are more fleshy, do not have a hook, and serve only to support the caterpillar along its length.

Compared to the adult butterfly or moth it will eventually turn into, the caterpillar seems a slow and simple creature. This is because its main roles in life are feeding and growing. It spends its time crawling around on its foodplant, chewing as much plant material as it can with its strong jaws. It has no need of wings, large eyes or delicate antennae for such a life. However, this sort of lazy existence does mean that the caterpillar is quite vulnerable to its many enemies, other

(*Right*) The four stages in the change from a caterpillar to a pupa. Once secured by silk attachments the caterpillar moults and the pupal skin appears. The pupa is often camouflaged during the resting period.

insects and birds, for example. Many caterpillars are camouflaged to either make them difficult to see or to make them look as uncaterpillar-like as possible.

How do caterpillars change into butterflies?

This remarkable transformation, called complete metamorphosis (see page 44), takes place through a pupal or resting stage. When fully grown most caterpillars fix themselves to a suitable upright surface using silk from their silk gland. Some hang downwards but others spin a supporting girdle of silk around their middle and remain upright. The final moult then takes place but this time the new skin that forms is completely different from the old. The outline of the adult gradually appears and the position of the large eyes, wings and legs can often be seen. The skin hardens in a couple of hours and the pupa is then formed.

In this state the butterflies of temperate countries pass the winter. During this time a great reorganization of all tissues is going on. In warmer countries this period is shorter. The adults of some butterflies are formed within a week in some tropical countries.

When the adult is fully formed inside the pupa the colour of the wings is usually visible. The skin becomes soft, splits, and then the newly formed butterfly steps out. The wings are very crumpled and moist at first. The butterfly hangs upside-down for an hour to expand and dry them.

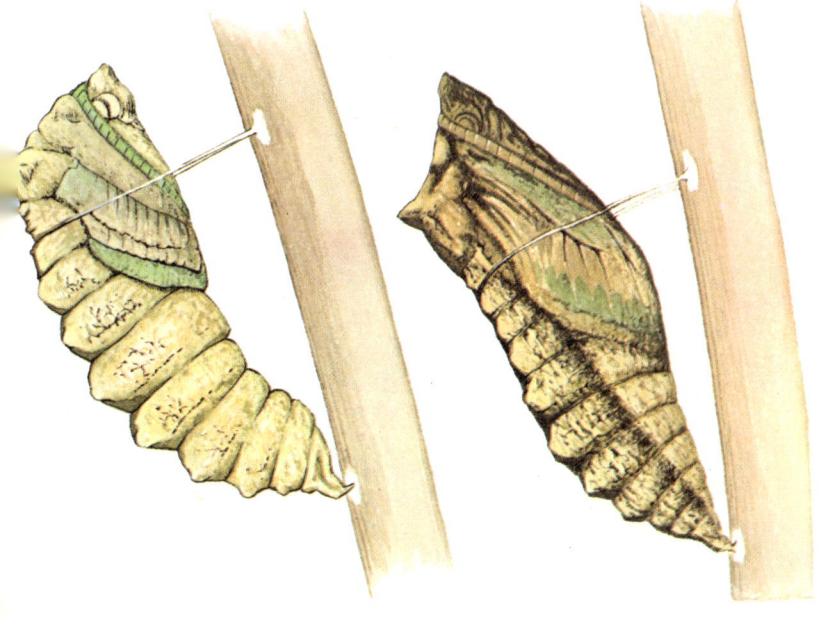

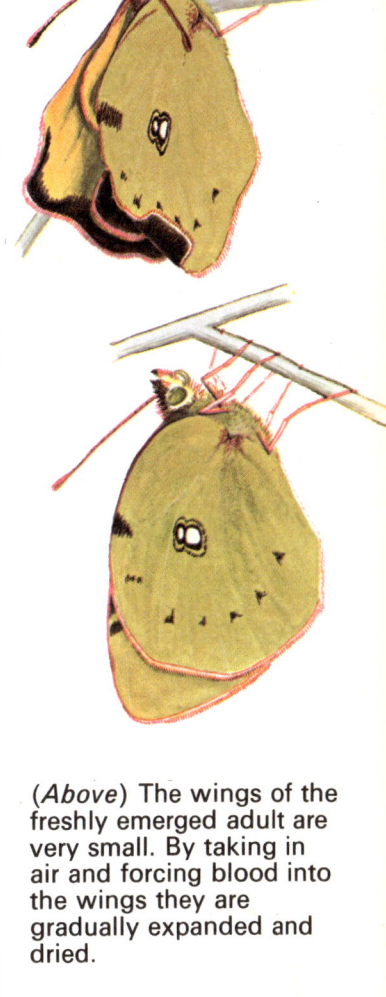

(*Above*) The wings of the freshly emerged adult are very small. By taking in air and forcing blood into the wings they are gradually expanded and dried.

How do bees communicate?

Honeybees, like termites (see page 49), wasps and ants, are social insects. They live in colonies and the work in running the colony is divided between the bees. Thus the queen bee does all the egg laying, the drones are males responsible for fertilizing the queens, and the workers are females that do all the work. In the wild, honeybees usually build their nests, composed of rows and rows of cells (combs), in hollow trees or caves. We keep bees in hives for the honey they make from nectar. They collect nectar from flowers and store it in the combs.

The worker bees are continually gathering nectar from flowers near the hive. If a bee discovers a good patch of nectar-yielding flowers it passes on the information to the other workers at the hive. It does this in the form of a dance. The distance from the hive, the direction and the kind of flowers, are all given during the dance, which is usually carried out at night.

A large queen honeybee (*top left*) surrounded by drones and workers. The larvae of new queens develop in the specially built large cells.

Bumblebees build their nests underground (*middle left*). The colonies of bumblebees do not survive the winter. Bees carry out the important task of cross-fertilizing many plants. They do this by unknowingly transferring pollen from one flower to another as they gather nectar and pollen for food.

(*Left*) Shown here are three examples of the dances performed by honeybees returning from good nectar sources. From the speed of the dance and the actual movements made, workers can tell exactly where these sources are.

Which ants form an army?

Army ants are unusual social insects. They live in a colony but for most of their lives they are continually on the move and have no permanent nest to return to. Each night they rest up from the day's march but press on again the next morning. Army ants have large appetites. Advancing columns disturb other insects which are promptly eaten. In fact, any larger animal, a snake or even a horse, for example, failing to move out of the way quickly enough, is promptly swarmed over by the ants and eaten alive.

(*Above*) Weaver ants at work using silk from a larval cocoon to join two leaves together.

(*Left*) A column of army ants on the march. Army ants are found in South America but also come from Africa where they are called driver ants.

How do weaver ants build their nest?

The tree nests of these ants, which come from India, Africa and Australia, are skilfully made from masses of living leaves. The leaves are arranged and secured by silk strands. The ants themselves do not have silk glands, but the larvae do and when they pupate they form a silk cocoon. When two leaves are to be joined, a team of ants holds the edges together while others pass a larval cocoon backwards and forwards along the join. The silk hardens on contact with the air and the leaves are woven together.

Which ants grow fungus?

Parasol ants from South America climb up into shrubs and trees and cut leaves into manageable sizes. These pieces drop to the grass where other ants pick them up and carry them back to the nest. The leaf fragments are not eaten by the ants themselves but fed to a fungus that the ants cultivate in the nest. The ants in turn feed on special bodies produced by the fungus.

A parasol ant carrying fungus food back to its nest. When a leaf fragment is too large it looks as if the ant is shading itself from the sun.

King crabs (*bottom right*) are found along the Atlantic coast of North America and on the coasts of China, Japan and the East Indies.

Two scorpions from southern Asia. Scorpions do not lay eggs but give birth to living young which promptly climb on to their mother's back.

What is the king crab?

The king crab, or horseshoe crab, is not really a crab at all. In fact it is not even a crustacean but a very primitive arthropod which belongs to a group of its own. From fossil evidence we know that king crabs were abundant in seas about 175 million years ago. The few species that survive today are virtually unchanged from those early ancestors and for this reason they are sometimes called 'living fossils'.

King crabs have some unusual features. They are about a foot across, have a heavy domed shell divided by a joint across the middle, four pairs of walking legs and a long spiky tail. The bony mouth extends between the bases of the legs which help in chewing up the food. These characteristics, together with their gills and mouthparts, tell us that the king crab is actually descended from the forerunners of another group of arthropods adapted for life on land – the arachnids. These include the scorpions, spiders, mites and ticks, and daddy longlegs or harvestmen.

Can a scorpion kill a man?

Scorpions are particularly ferocious animals, even to each other, and so they lead solitary lives. They live in dry, warm, areas of the world and in the wild hide themselves away in dark places, under logs or stones, for example, waiting for their prey. This normally consists of small insects and spiders. As scorpions cannot see very well they rely on these creatures brushing against them unawares. They are immediately pounced on when this happens, overpowered and torn apart by the scorpion's pair of large pincers. Only if resistance is met will the scorpion bring its deadly sting into action, usually held out of harm's way over its head.

The habits of scorpions make them particularly dangerous to man. They are attracted into homes and find ideal hiding places in shoes, beds and perhaps under carpets. Once disturbed they do not hesitate to use their sting over and over again. In the United States and Mexico it is said that more people die from scorpion stings than from snake bites.

Orb webs (*right*) of some spiders can be 8 feet in diameter and trap birds and bats. The enormous bird-eating spider (*far right*) from South America hunts its prey.

Do all spiders spin webs?

Most spiders spin webs of one sort or another but only some use the web to entangle their prey. The trapdoor spiders from tropical and subtropical countries are spiders that spin a tubular web in a hole in the ground. The hole the spider digs may be several inches deep and about an inch across. The web is spun to line the hole and once this is done the spider constructs a hinged trapdoor to fit the opening exactly. This is made from silk and small soil particles and is very often camouflaged with moss. This well-made retreat is a perfect home for the spider. If disturbed by its enemies it simply hangs on to the underside of the trapdoor, preventing it from opening. It is not fully known how the trapdoor spider catches its prey. It is thought that it peers out from the hole with the trapdoor ajar, and drags insects back into the hole as they pass by.

Male (*top*) and female trapdoor spiders from Australia. A trapdoor is shown (*right*) closed and open, as well as sections of three examples of trapdoors from different species. The thicker trapdoors are made by spiders living on the beds of old creeks to keep out floodwater.

What are the echinoderms?

Starfishes, sea urchins, sea cucumbers and sea lilies all belong to the phylum Echinodermata. Echinoderm means spiny skinned and all these animals have a spiky or leathery appearance. The echinoderms have a skeleton made up of small plates. In the arthropods the skeleton is external, enclosing the body in a case, but in the echinoderms it is internal and lies just below the skin. The spines are extensions from the plates and echinoderms are able to move them slightly as they are hinged at the base. The member of this

Starfishes have remarkable powers of regeneration. A lost arm will soon be regrown and the arm itself will sometimes survive as a new individual. Angry keepers of mussel and oyster beds used to dredge up the starfish pests, break them up and fling them back. This only increased their numbers of course and made the problem worse.

group that you are probably most familiar with is the starfish. If you pick one up from the beach it will feel quite hard and rigid and this is because it is probably dead. The plates of the starfish's skeleton are not joined together and so when alive it can bend its body and move its arms easily.

How does a starfish move?

The starfishes and sea urchins creep slowly around on hundreds of hydraulically operated tube feet. If you flip a living starfish over you will see rows of these tiny feet running the length of each arm. (If you leave the starfish upside-down, time it to see how long it takes to turn itself the right way up again. Some can do it in two minutes, others take over an hour.) Each tube foot is connected to a muscular sac embedded inside the arm of the starfish. All the feet are joined up by a system of tubes which draws in water from the sea. The whole arrangement is called the water vascular system. The sac contracts and pushes out the foot under pressure. A suction disc at the end grips the sea floor, the foot contracts forcing the water back into the sac, and the starfish is drawn along a fraction of an inch. Each foot would have little effect on its own but when the feet are used in relays the starfish has a speed of 2 inches a minute.

A starfish creeping up on an oyster. Starfishes are particularly fond of bivalve molluscs and cause a lot of damage on mussel and oyster beds.

(*Below*) A starfish using its tube feet to prise apart a scallop.

Starfishes can have from between four and fifty arms and there are many beautifully coloured species. They live in all the shallow seas of the world.

How does a starfish open a mussel with its feet?

Have you ever tried to prise apart the shell of a mussel or an oyster? It is practically impossible to do by just pulling, so how does the starfish manage it using only its tiny feet? The secret is that the starfish again uses its feet in relays. It hunches itself over the tightly closed shell and attaches its tube feet to either side. By resting some feet and pulling with others the starfish is able to exert a strong pull over a long period, and gradually the bivalve weakens until it gives up the test of strength. Once the valves open a fraction the starfish turns its stomach inside out and pushes it into the shell to digest the contents.

(*Below*) There are many species of sea lily. In some the stalk may be up to 2 feet in length. Fossil sea lilies have been found, however, with stalks as long as 70 feet.

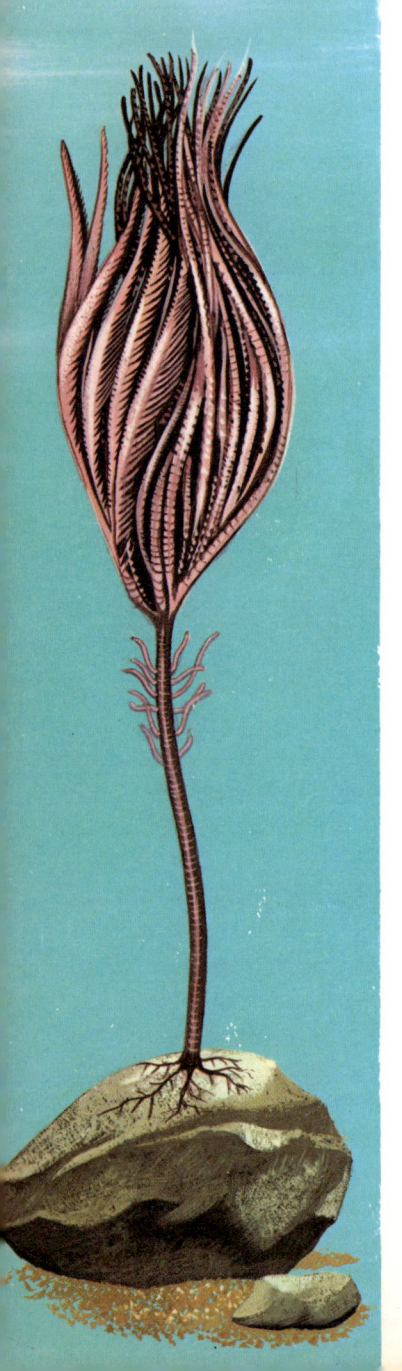

Is the sea lily a flower?

The sea lily certainly looks flower-like but it is in tact an animal. It is another echinoderm and so it belongs to the same group as the starfishes, sea urchins, and sea cucumbers, and has a basically similar body plan. The distinctive feature of the sea lily is its long stalk with which it fastens itself to the sea bottom, and the crown of feathery arms which arise from the top. In the depths of the oceans sea lilies spread these arms wide and catch food particles drifting down through the water from the upper levels. These are passed to the mouth and eaten. We do not know very much about sea lilies because most live only on the floors of very deep oceans and are therefore impossible to watch directly. They are very fragile animals and tend to break when dredged up from the sea bed, and will not survive in tanks. We do know that they belong to a very ancient group because many fossil lilies have been found which are 420 million years old.

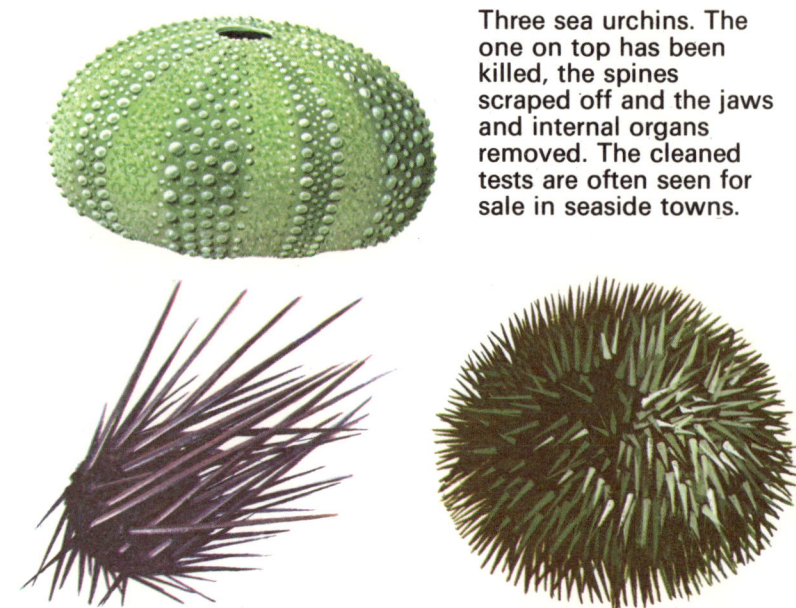

Three sea urchins. The one on top has been killed, the spines scraped off and the jaws and internal organs removed. The cleaned tests are often seen for sale in seaside towns.

Can you eat a sea urchin?

Many people do eat parts of these unappetizing spiny animals. They are popular in Mediterranean countries and the West Indies. It is the ripe ovaries that are roasted, fried or sometimes even eaten raw. Sea urchins are echinoderms with a box-like skeleton made up of tiny plates fused together. This 'test' as it is called, can be in many shapes: spherical, oval or flattened, and most have long moveable spines as extensions of the plates. Sea urchins have tube feet worked by the same system as the starfishes but they are generally longer, and project beyond the spines. The tube feet are arranged in five rows radiating from top to bottom of the test. Another feature in common with starfishes is the presence of tiny pincers on long stalks all over the sea urchin. These are gently waving all the time and pick off particles which settle on the urchin. This cleaning operation is important in slow-moving creatures that live on the sea floor because things are always dropping down on to them. Particles that are edible are passed round to the mouth in the middle of the underside. Urchins have particularly strong jaws to enable them to chew tough seaweeds.

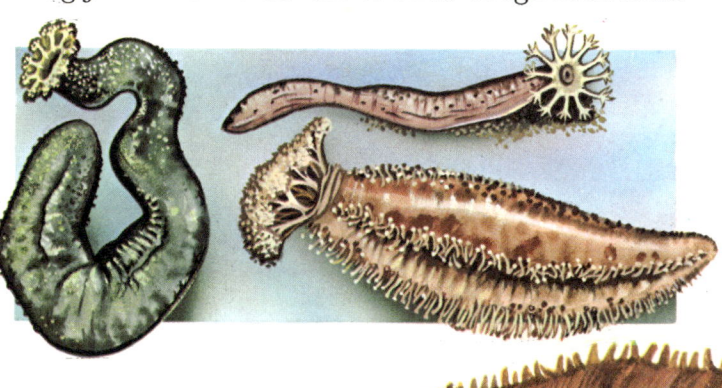

A variety of sea cucumbers. On most can be seen the rows of tube feet that enable slow movements.

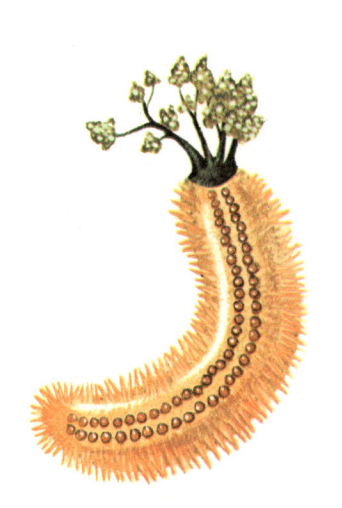

How does a sea cucumber avoid attack?

Sea cucumbers are echinoderms that have a tough leathery skin rather than a spiny one. Lying around on the sea floor in tropical and subtropical countries they look rather like long fat sausages with tentacles at one end. They feed by poking the sticky tentacles around and then placing them one by one into the mouth. All the food fragments are sucked off as the tentacle is removed, almost like licking marmalade from your fingers. To prevent being eaten by crabs, fishes and starfishes, many sea cucumbers produce a poison. Others when molested will eject long white sticky threads from the rear end to enmesh the attacker. More spectacular still are those species that partially turn themselves inside out when alarmed and rapidly shoot out their branched respiratory organs, reproductive organs and some intestine for good measure. This really confuses the attacker, allowing the cucumber to escape. It later grows a new set of everything that is missing.

Are these animals invertebrates or vertebrates?

So far in this book we have looked at animals without a backbone, the invertebrates. Now we are about to look at the animals which make up the phylum Chordata, that is, all those other animals that do have a backbone. These animals can be divided into the major groups: fishes, amphibians, reptiles, birds and mammals, and it is reasonably easy to see how these groups gradually evolved from one another. However, zoologists in the nineteenth century puzzled for a long time over how the backboned animals could have evolved from the invertebrates. A search was made for animals which might have descended from early forms that linked the two major groups. The animals shown here do not have a backbone but they have features which are shown by all other vertebrates.

(*Above*) An acorn worm showing its proboscis and collar at the head end and the row of gill slits opening from the intestine.

Some sea squirts live in colonies and encrust rocks in beautiful star-shaped patterns. Those shown here are growing in a cluster. A typical sea squirt larva is shown above the cluster and a cut-away diagram illustrates the internal arrangement of the adult.

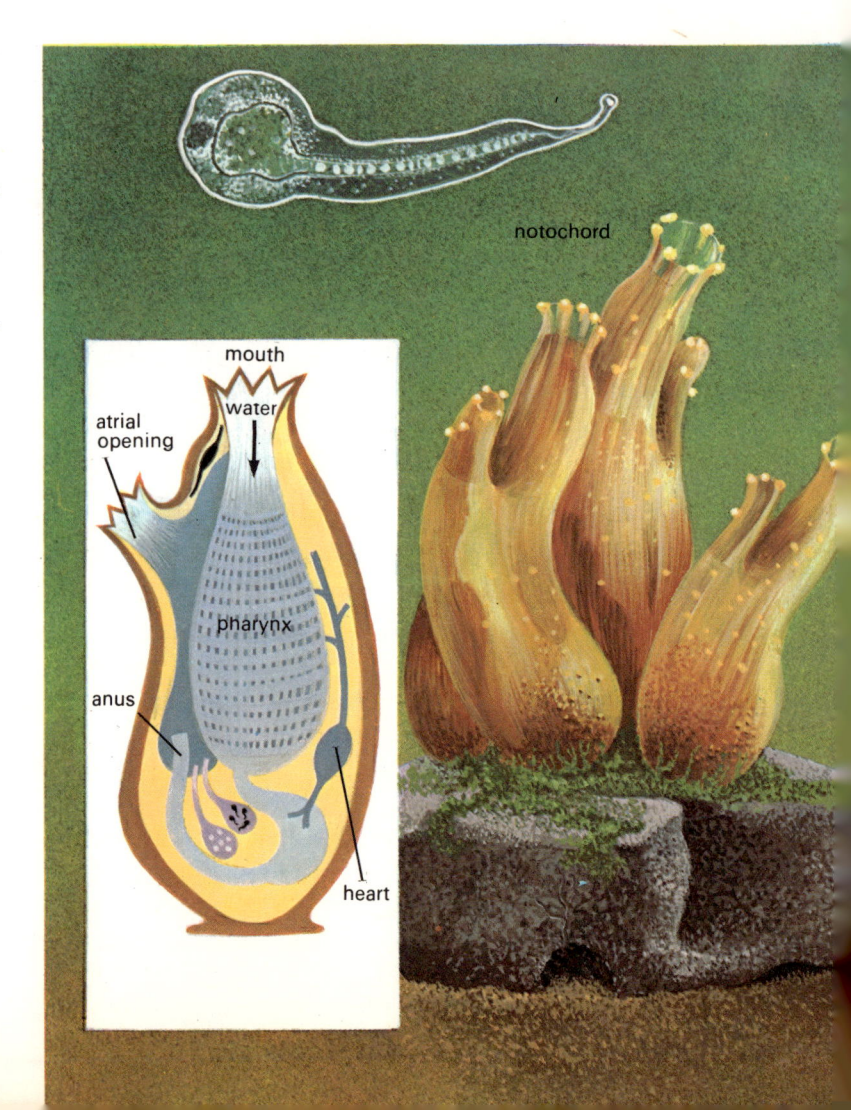

How do acorn worms and sea squirts provide the link between invertebrates and vertebrates?

Acorn worms are found buried in the sand along the shore and on the sea bottom. They look rather like earthworms but their structure is very different. At one end they have a swelling called a proboscis separated from the rest of the body by a short collar. The proboscis and collar have thick walls of muscle and are used for burrowing. Inside the proboscis the acorn worm has a short strengthening rod called a notochord. This is the beginning of the development of the backbone of the vertebrates and the acorn worm is one of the few animals that shows this. Other important vertebrate features are the openings from the intestine to the outside (gill slits) and the nerve cord in the form of a tube.

It is the free-swimming larva of the sea squirt that shows these important features rather than the fixed adult. The tiny tadpole-like creature has a long tail containing a notochord and hollow nerve cord. The pharynx of the intestine has the slits on the outside. When the larva settles it absorbs its tail and turns into a sac-like adult.

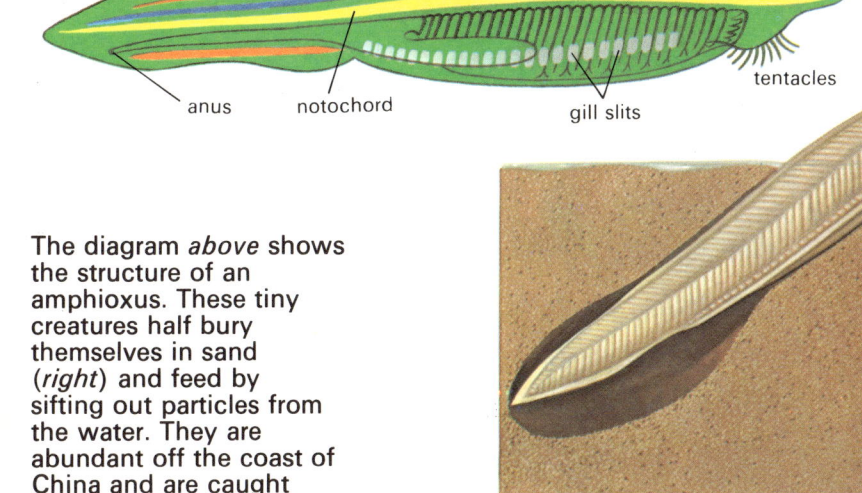

The diagram *above* shows the structure of an amphioxus. These tiny creatures half bury themselves in sand (*right*) and feed by sifting out particles from the water. They are abundant off the coast of China and are caught there for food.

What is amphioxus?

Amphioxus is a tiny fish-like animal that shows best of all the primitive vertebrate features we have seen in acorn worms and sea squirts. The long notochord extends along the length of the animal and supports blocks of muscles rather like those in the fishes.

FISHES

Are lampreys and hagfishes really fishes?

The strange eel-like creatures on these pages look nothing like typical fishes. They have no jaws and the mouth is a simple opening surrounded by rows and rows of sharp teeth. They have no proper bones and they have a smooth skin, unlike most other fishes which have both a bony skeleton and overlapping scales. However, as we have seen before, even the oddest looking animals can be of significance in the animal kingdom. Such creatures may be descended from ancestors that were important links in the evolution of one group from another, and they can tell us much about how this happened. So it is with the lampreys and hagfishes.

Most fishes have bony skeletons and jaws. However, some which are more primitive have a soft skeleton made of cartilage (sharks, rays and skates, for example) and some of these are even more primitive and lack proper jaws. These are lampreys and hagfishes and it is thought that all the more advanced fishes developed from fishes not unlike them, millions of years ago. The lampreys and hagfishes we see today are the survivors of this ancient group. Their characteristics help us to piece together the sequence of the development of the early animals from the primitive chordates, the descendants of which we have already looked at, to the bony fishes and all the other backboned animals we shall see in the rest of the book.

A typical lamprey with a close-up (*top*) of the sucker-like mouth and horny teeth. The gill openings which admit water for breathing can be seen just behind the head.

How many types of lamprey are there?

There are about thirty species of lamprey found today; some live in fresh water and some in the sea. Most are parasitic and attack fishes by attaching themselves by their muscular sucker-like mouth to the side of the fish. The rows of horny teeth rasp away at the skin of the fish and puncture its surface to make it bleed. The lamprey feeds on the blood and when satisfied allows the fish to swim off. It is usually weakened and is soon killed by a predator or by disease.

The marine lampreys enter rivers to reproduce and lay eggs in swiftly flowing stretches of water. The larval stage which hatches bears a striking resemblance to amphioxus

Lampreys attacking a salmon by attaching their heads to its side and feeding on its blood.

(see page 65) and leads a similar existence. It burrows in mud and silt and sifts out particles of food, eventually growing to about 5 inches in length. This takes up to six years before the larva is transformed into an adult lamprey, descends the river and takes up life in the sea.

(*Left*) Hagfishes are also despised by sea anglers because they will often attack a fish that has just been hooked. Here one is boring into a haddock.

How does the hagfish feed?

The hagfish has a particularly horrid way of feeding on other fishes. It is not a very fast mover and so cannot usually catch fishes that are good swimmers. However, what often happens, to the annoyance of fishermen, is that the hagfish comes across a netful of mackerel, haddock or flatfish which is just about to be drawn aboard. In the confined space of the net the fishes cannot avoid the hagfish and it is easily able to feast on them. The hagfish bores through the skin of its victim and actually rasps its way inside the body where it proceeds to digest all the flesh. Ultimately all that is left is a bag of skin and bones. Normally the hagfish feeds on dead and dying fishes, worms and crustaceans, and spends its time scavenging along the sea bottom. Where they regularly damage catches of food fishes they are a serious pest.

Hagfishes are sometimes known as slime eels because of the extraordinary amounts of slime they are able to produce. A bucket of water is soon turned into a slimy jelly if a hagfish is dropped in. The slime probably serves to protect the hagfish from the digestive juices of its host.

Some lampreys migrate from the sea to spawn in fresh water. Two lampreys are shown here spawning while attached to a rock.

Which is the most dangerous shark?

Sharks *from top to bottom*: the long sinewy Frilled Shark grows to 6½ feet in length; the Great White Shark has a man-eating reputation; the enormous but harmless Whale Shark; and the Blue Shark, which is found off European, African and American coasts.

Sharks are powerful, streamlined fishes with soft skeletons and proper jaws, and a reputation for being highly dangerous to man. However, of the nearly 300 types of shark known, only about a dozen have attacked human beings. One of those with the worst reputation is the Great White Shark or Maneater which grows to about 25 feet in length and is found in all warm seas of the world. Sharks are notoriously curious creatures and will eat anything that looks edible. Occasionally people are sampled by sharks but it is unlikely that sharks go out of their way to attack them.

(*Above*) Most sharks lay their eggs in horny capsules which get caught in seaweed by their long tendrils. Empty capsules can be found on the beach and are called 'mermaids' purses'.

Are the biggest sharks dangerous?

The two largest sharks are quite harmless to man and feed by filtering out tiny shrimp-like copepods (see page 39) found in plankton. As the 40-foot Basking Shark cruises along under the surface, water enters its huge open mouth and passes out through the long gill slits which almost encircle the head. Special 'gill rakers' strain out the planktonic organisms from the water and these are then swallowed as food.

The average length of the Whale Shark seems to be about 45 feet. In spite of its colossal size, the Whale Shark is quite docile, and has often been run down by ships at sea.

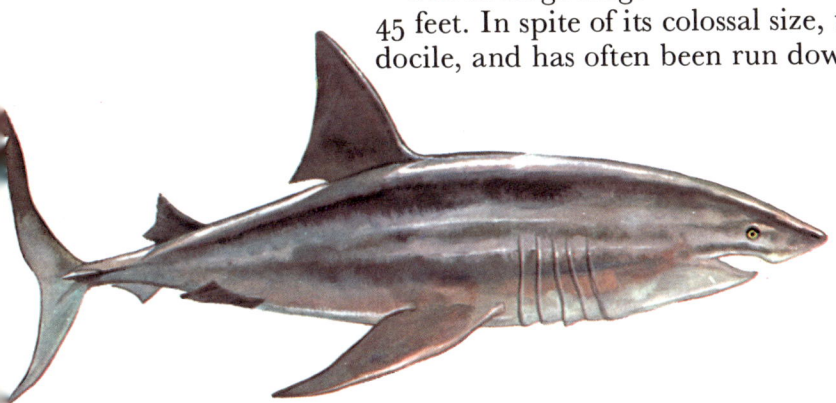

The Basking Shark is another harmless monster which cruises along feeding on plankton. It is common in temperate seas and particularly in the north Atlantic.

Which are the smallest sharks?

Two of the smallest sharks are the Dogfish and the Tope. These fishes are often caught by anglers fishing from piers. The Dogfish grows to about 2 feet in length and the Tope to 4 feet. You have probably eaten Dogfish as fish with your chips from fish-and-chip shops, for it is sold as 'rock salmon'.

The Dogfish (*top*) and Tope are small sharks but show the typical streamlined body. They live on the sea bottom and feed by scavenging.

How has life on the bottom changed the skates and rays?

The first obvious difference between skates and rays and more typical fishes is their shape. The skates and rays are bottom dwellers and they have developed this very characteristic flattened appearance. The pectoral fins, which in other fishes are situated just behind the gill cover on either side, are in rays enlarged to extend right round the head, rather like a pair of wings. By gently flapping these 'wings' up and down the skate or ray glides along very close to the bottom with the minimum of effort. The tail is hardly used at all and so it is very thin and trails behind, perhaps helping to steer.

Skates and rays, like the sharks, have a soft gristly skeleton made up of cartilage, unlike the more advanced bony fishes.

The skate's eyes are situated on top of its head as you might expect in a fish living on the bottom. This habit has also meant that the skate cannot breathe water through its mouth as other fishes do. If it did it would get a mouthful of mud and sand. Instead, water is drawn through two holes (spiracles) behind the eyes and passed out through the gills. Some rays that live in open water, however, breathe like other fishes.

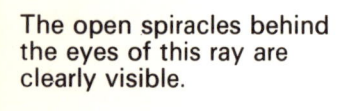

The open spiracles behind the eyes of this ray are clearly visible.

How dangerous is the stingray?

Natives from the Pacific region have been known to use the sharp spines of stingrays for the tips of spears and as knives. In Africa their tough skin has been used to make the heads of drums.

There are over one hundred kinds of stingray, widely distributed throughout the seas of the world. They all have longer and thinner tails than other rays and skates. Projecting from the top of the tail near the body end they have at least one but sometimes two sharp spines. These would be dangerous enough but the spines have poison glands, and stabs in the chest and abdomen have proved fatal on a number of occasions. When provoked the stingray can whip its tail round in a long, sideways thrust, or it can stab forwards over its head at its enemy.

Most rays lay their eggs in horny pouches rather like those of sharks. The eggs of some, the stingrays for example, hatch while they are still within the female, and are born alive.

What do skates eat?

The Common Skate (*top right*) and the Thornback Ray (*above*). Both are sought after by sea fishermen.

Living on the bottom the skate naturally feeds on the other animals it finds there – crabs, lobsters and oysters and other molluscs. It has strong crushing teeth to deal with these shelled creatures. To get at choice molluscs buried in the sand the skate will flap away with its pectoral fins and gradually work its way under the surface. It will then often sit there with eyes and spiracles above the surface.

From which fish do we obtain caviar?

If you have tasted caviar, did you realize that you were eating salted sturgeon eggs? If you have not actually tasted caviar you may have seen the black shiny eggs and wondered where they came from. Caviar is now an expensive luxury food because sturgeons are so rare.

Sturgeons come from central and eastern Europe and North America. They are large fishes. Many have been caught weighing over 2,000 pounds, and they have an armour-plated shark appearance. There are lines of bony plates along the scaleless sides and the mouth hangs underneath the head in an ideal position for grubbing along the bottom for food. Most sturgeons live in the sea and ascend rivers to spawn.

Sturgeons have poor eyesight but many taste-buds, and a bunch of sensitive tentacles help them to find food on the bottom.

Most of the fishes we know today are bony fishes and have hard bony skeletons rather than the soft cartilaginous ones of the primitive sharks and rays. The sturgeons have descended with little change from fishes intermediate between these two great groups, and so they represent a stage in the evolution of the bony fishes from the soft-boned fishes. They still have a mainly soft skeleton but show refinements which all other bony fishes also have. They have one gill opening (gill flap) and they have a swim, or air bladder. This gives them buoyancy and in other bony fishes it is used as an air-breathing lung (see page 95).

What use is the paddle of the paddlefish?

This extraordinary relative of the sturgeon has a long paddle-shaped nose extending for one-third of the length of its body. It was suggested that this was used for probing into

Only two kinds of paddlefish are known from widely separated regions of the world — the Mississippi River in North America and the Yangtse River in China. This suggests that this ancient group of fishes is on the decline.

muddy bottoms for food or stirring up the mud. This is unlikely as the paddle is very sensitive and easily damaged. A more likely theory is that as the paddlefish cruises slowly ahead, the paddle detects small organisms in the water by touch. In response, the huge mouth drops open and the food is drawn in and strained through the gills.

How ancient are the bowfin and gars?

Over 100 million years ago, bowfins and gars were widely distributed over both the continents of Europe and North America. Today they are confined to rivers and freshwater lakes of the eastern United States. Surprisingly enough, those few bowfins that exist have done so well in this area that they have become a nuisance. Bowfins really look like ancient fishes. Their heads are protected by heavy plates and they have large, bony overlapping scales. The swim bladder is adapted for use as a lung and so bowfins can live in stagnant water containing hardly any oxygen by gulping water at the surface. They can even live for up to twenty-four hours out of water.

(*Below*) Bowfins can grow to about 3 feet in length, and weigh up to 8 pounds, but most are 2 feet long.

(*Left*) There are about seven kinds of gars found in the eastern United States. The biggest grows to about 10 feet and comes from Mexico.

Gars are also very prehistoric in appearance. They have long, dangerous-looking jaws about twice as long as the head. Tightly fitting bony scales along the sides give them an armour-plated look. They will eat anything, and slash sideways at their prey with rows of sharp teeth. They have enormous appetites and so are not popular among freshwater fishermen who claim that gars eat more than their share of other fishes, and also steal the bait from their hooks.

Why do salmon leap waterfalls?

You may have been lucky enough to watch salmon jumping from the churning mass of water below a waterfall, trying to leap over it to continue their journey upstream. It sometimes takes several attempts but the salmon usually manage it in the end. What drives them to swim upstream in rivers with obstacles such as this?

Both Pacific and Atlantic salmon are hatched in freshwater streams but live for most of their lives in the sea. After several years of feeding and growing fat in the sea, the salmon instinctively try to return to the stream of their birth to spawn. Although they may be hundreds of miles from the mouth of their home river, they somehow find their way back to it. Zoologists have discovered that salmon have a well-developed sense of taste and so they may be able to recognize the smell of the water from their own river. They swim upstream, leaping obstacles on the way, until they find a suitable gravel bottom for spawning. Once this is done they are exhausted from the effort for they do not eat once they have entered the river from the sea. Pacific salmon die at this stage but Atlantic salmon drift back to the sea. Many die from fungus disease on the way but some survive to continue a marine life. After hatching, the young salmon live for about a year in the stream before descending to the sea where food is abundant.

The salmon (*below*) and the closely related trout (*left*) are probably the most popular fishes among anglers. They are sleek, powerful fishes which provide magnificent sport.

Big salmon have been known to leap as high as 10 feet in attempts to clear waterfalls. They sometimes swim up through the plunging water of really steep falls.

The marine hatchet fish (*right*) has a more striking appearance than the unrelated freshwater type (*left*).

To keep freshwater hatchet fishes in an aquarium you must have a cover to prevent them from flying out!

(*Below*) Arapaimas grow quickly to large sizes and have been known to live for eighteen years.

What are hatchet fishes?

It seems a strange name but some of these fishes really look like a hatchet or chopper. They are very thin fishes, flattened from side to side. The front half of their body is very deep and shaped like a blade. There are two groups of hatchet fishes, one that lives in the sea and one that lives in fresh water.

The marine hatchet fishes are small, ugly deep sea fishes. They have enormous eyes and flashing light organs along their sides. They hang motionless in the water and do not do much normal swimming. Instead they migrate to and from the surface each night to feed on plankton.

The freshwater hatchet fishes come from South America. They are said to be the only fishes that can truly fly. They leap from the water and propel themselves through the air for short distances by beating their enlarged pectoral fins.

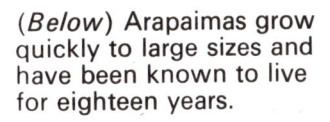

What is the largest freshwater fish in the world?

The Arapaima from South America is generally thought to be one of the largest freshwater fishes in the world. The biggest one found is said to have been 15 feet in length with a weight of over 400 pounds. Most are between 7 and 8 feet long with a weight of 200 pounds, but even this is a colossal size for a freshwater fish.

Which fish is the freshwater shark?

This sequence shows the embryo pike inside the egg; the young pike, immediately after hatching, with its yolk sac which is slowly absorbed as food; and successive growth stages to the adult fish.

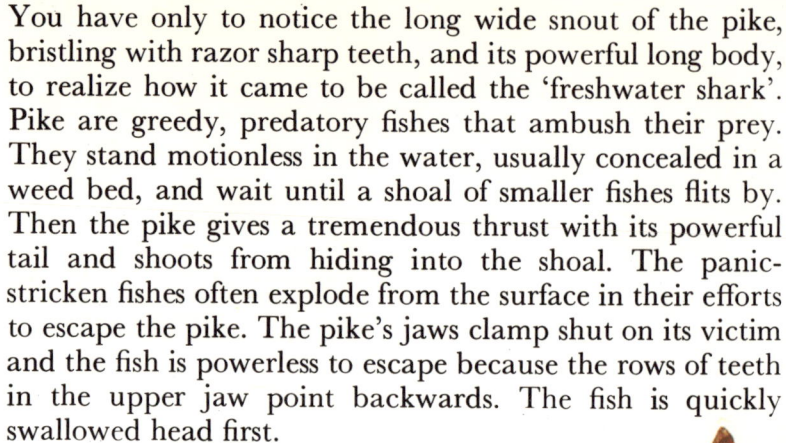

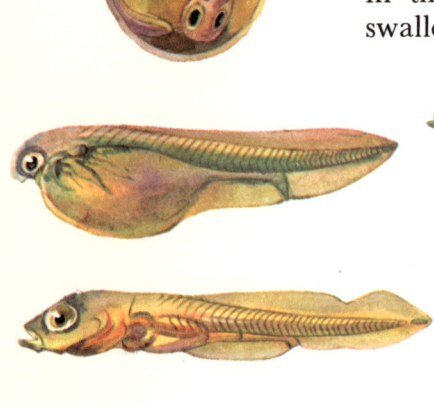

You have only to notice the long wide snout of the pike, bristling with razor sharp teeth, and its powerful long body, to realize how it came to be called the 'freshwater shark'. Pike are greedy, predatory fishes that ambush their prey. They stand motionless in the water, usually concealed in a weed bed, and wait until a shoal of smaller fishes flits by. Then the pike gives a tremendous thrust with its powerful tail and shoots from hiding into the shoal. The panic-stricken fishes often explode from the surface in their efforts to escape the pike. The pike's jaws clamp shut on its victim and the fish is powerless to escape because the rows of teeth in the upper jaw point backwards. The fish is quickly swallowed head first.

How savage are piranha fishes?

Piranhas are said to be savage enough to have once attacked a man on a horse fording a stream in South America, and killed them both. This is an old story and whether it is true or not is uncertain. What is certain is that these terrible fishes are feared through South America for their ferocity. They live in shoals – 'packs' is perhaps a better word – and they usually feed on other fishes. However, they will quickly strip the flesh from any animal falling into the water. They have been known to devour crocodiles and even cows in this way, leaving only the bones picked clean of any meat. There are about twenty species of piranha in South America but only four are really dangerous.

(*Below*) A piranha with a drawing of the head skeleton to show the powerful short jaws and razor sharp teeth. The teeth slice through flesh with ease.

Which fish keeps its eggs in its mouth?

The fish with this surprising habit is the Sea Catfish found in the Atlantic ocean off the east coast of America. Another surprising thing is that it is the male that takes on the job of looking after the future family, rather than the female. After the eggs have been laid and fertilized, the male quickly takes them up into his mouth. They form quite a mouthful as they can be the size of marbles and number up to fifty. They fill his mouth completely and prevent him from feeding. He carries them around for a month and all this time he is fasting, living off the stored food reserves he built up before spawning took place. His motherly role does not end when the eggs hatch. For another two weeks the youngsters swim into his mouth to hide when danger threatens.

All the catfishes have long fleshy extensions from around the mouth called barbels. It is because these faintly resemble whiskers that catfish were so-called. In fact they are used rather like whiskers. They are sensitive and they help the catfish feel its way around and find food in murky waters.

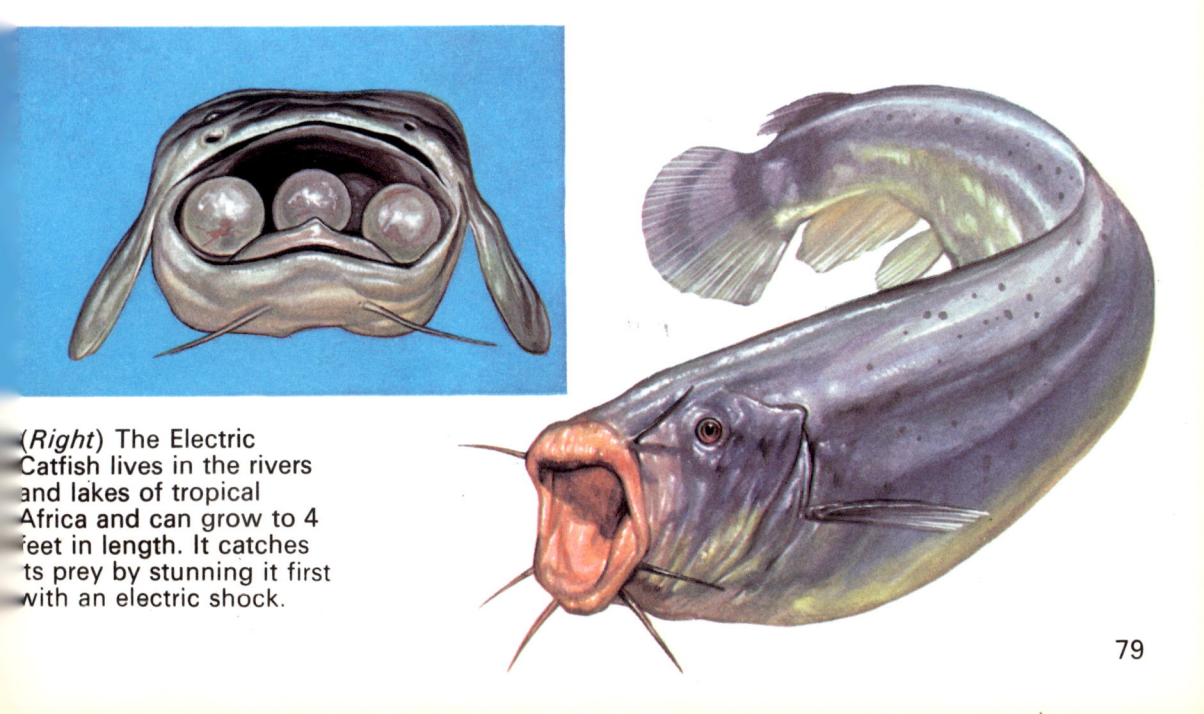

The Wels Catfish grows to huge sizes in muddy-bottomed lakes in central Europe. Specimens grow to 9 feet in length and some compete with the Arapaima's claim to being the largest freshwater fish in the world.

(*Below*) A male Sea Catfish displays a mouthful of eggs.

(*Right*) The Electric Catfish lives in the rivers and lakes of tropical Africa and can grow to 4 feet in length. It catches its prey by stunning it first with an electric shock.

A common member of the carp family is the Roach, a silvery fish popular with freshwater fishermen. Roach live in shoals in still, or slowly moving water. A good catch is a 2 pound specimen.

Which are the fishes of the carp family?

In this enormous fish family there are about 1500 species of carp and carp-like fishes. They are all freshwater fishes most of which have one or more barbels around the mouth.

Such a large family naturally contains fishes of great variety in size and colour. Besides the carp themselves most of the fishes we are familiar with in rivers and ponds belong to the family: minnows, Bleak, Rudd, Roach, Tench, Gudgeon, Barbel, Chub and Dace. In America there are other species called shivers, suckers, as well as many other minnows. Among the smallest members are the minnows which are rarely more than 4 inches long. At the other end of the scale the Common Carp grows to about $3\frac{1}{2}$ feet and can weigh up to 60 pounds. Even bigger is the enormous Indian Mahseer growing to 9 feet in length.

(*Left*) The Common Carp prefers still water and feeds by rooting around the muddy bottom. It is an important food fish in central Europe where it is reared in carp ponds.

Which goldfishes are freaks?

The wild goldfish is a very common fish from China, usually green or brown in colour. About a thousand years ago the Chinese noticed that red forms of the wild goldfish occasionally appeared. They started to keep these more attractive forms in ponds and bowls and managed to breed them. Since then, goldfishes have always been popular as pets and many different varieties and forms have been produced. Some of these are so bizarre they barely resemble fishes at all. The Lionhead Goldfish for example, has a large head grossly

Goldfishes bred for their long flowing tails and fins (*left*) are popular. Other strange forms include the Lionhead Goldfish and the Eggfish (*below left*). Goldfishes looking more like their wild relatives are shown *bottom*.

swollen with warty bumps. Other varieties, equally grotesque, have bulging eyes so distorted that the fishes can only look upwards. We can safely refer to such creatures as fish freaks because if such creatures were released into the wild they would soon die. They can only survive if man looks after them in ponds and tanks so that they have no worries about finding food or avoiding enemies.

How big does the Tench grow?

The Tench is another placid fish that prefers still, weedy waters with a muddy bottom. It is popular with anglers in Europe and a good fish would weigh 7 pounds. Like the carp, the tench can survive in water that has a low oxygen content. For this reason, a variety called the Golden Tench is also popular as a pond and aquarium fish.

(*Right*) The Tench is a characteristically shaped member of the carp family. In Germany it is popular as a food fish but its flesh tends to have a muddy flavour.

(*Below*) The larval stages and adult of the freshwater eel. The last stage but one shows the elver which enters European rivers in thousands after its journey from its birthplace in the Sargasso Sea.

Where do eels go to breed and die?

The life histories of the European and American freshwater eels are remarkable, and even today they are not completely understood. After living in freshwater streams, rivers and ponds for about ten years in the case of the females, and about six years in the case of the males, the eels fatten up, change colour from a yellowy-green to silvery-grey, stop feeding and begin a long journey. Those that are confined in ponds and lakes begin their migration at night by slithering across wet grass until they reach a stream. There they join other mature eels travelling downstream to the sea. Their journey does not end there, however. Both the eels from Europe and those from America head for one particular area of floating weed in the western Atlantic Ocean, called the Sargasso Sea.

For American eels the journey is moderate but for European eels it is immense. It takes them about a year to swim the 3,000 miles to their spawning grounds. On arrival spawning takes place, the eggs are laid and the eels die. Tiny, transparent larvae, called leptocephali, hatch from the eggs. Those of American eels head back towards the United States, while those of European parents drift along in the Gulf Stream towards Europe. During this journey they pass through a number of stages until, three years later, they

(*Left*) The Conger Eel, a large marine eel from the Atlantic and Pacific Oceans, also journeys to the Sargasso Sea to breed and die. It has another spawning ground in the Mediterranean, however.

enter the estuaries of rivers as elvers, miniature versions of their parents. Swimming upstream they eventually reach the home streams, rivers and ponds which their parents deserted four years ago.

This map shows the routes taken by the leptocephali of freshwater eels from the Sargasso Sea.

Is the moray eel as fierce as it looks?

The moray eel certainly looks dangerous and there are many stories of people being seriously injured by attacks from these large, sinewy fishes. The moray eel, however, is a shy, retiring animal and spends the day hiding away in nooks and crannies in coral. If an underwater diver disturbs a resting eel, it will naturally resent this, and when cornered it will not hesitate to lunge and bite to escape. Unprovoked attacks on people collecting shells on coral reefs are probably cases of mistaken identity on the part of the eel. The moray eel is partial to octopuses and could easily imagine a person's fingers to be the succulent tentacles of one of its favourite foods. But it may grab at the molluscs the collector is holding rather than his hand.

There are over 100 kinds of moray eel. They live in the shallows of tropical and subtropical seas and particularly on coral reefs. Some can grow to 10 feet in length.

83

(*Right*) Flying fishes' eggs are characteristically covered in long tendrils. The young fish has a different coloration from the adult and has a pair of long whiskers trailing from the jaw.

How do flying fishes fly?

In tropical and temperate seas, people on ships have long been fascinated by shoals of flying fishes bursting from the water to begin spectacular flights over the sea. Flying fishes have greatly enlarged pectoral fins which they keep folded against the body under water. Once in the air, however, these fins are extended as wings and allow the fishes to make flights over 400 feet across the wave tops. It has only recently become known exactly how the flying fish manages this. For a long time it was thought that the fish flapped its 'wings' like a bird, but high speed photography has revealed that the fins are held out straight, and the flying fish merely glides along. To make a flight it first gathers speed under water until it bursts from the surface at about 40 miles per hour. The fins are extended and the fish becomes airborne. It can prolong the flight by driving itself along with just its tail in the water until enough speed is reached for another take off. The lopsided tail is specially shaped for this purpose, the lower lobe being larger than the upper. It is not known why flying fishes developed this flying trick but it is certainly a convenient way of escaping from enemies.

(*Below*) Flying fishes are found in the Atlantic and Pacific Oceans and the biggest grows to about 18 inches in length.

(*Right*) The Three-spined Stickleback is the most widespread stickleback and it can live in both fresh water and the sea.

(*Below*) Another type of stickleback has fifteen spines and lives only in the sea. Other species have four, nine or ten spines. All are found throughout the northern hemisphere.

Which fish lays its eggs in a nest?

The female stickleback carefully leaves her eggs in an underwater nest which is built and tended entirely by the male. The male chooses the site, builds the nursery, and, like the male Sea Catfish (see page 79), takes very good care of the young until they are old enough to fend for themselves. The nest is built in the spring from fragments of waterweed woven around the stems of water plants. At this time the male develops a deep coloration offset by a striking red throat. When the nest is ready he attracts a female and lures her into it to lay her eggs. As soon as she leaves he follows her in to fertilize them, and then begins his period of care and devotion. He drives off strangers and aerates the eggs by fanning water into the nest with his pectoral fins. He also tends the young sticklebacks when they appear by keeping them all together in the nest area. Any youngsters straying too far are gently taken in his mouth and spat back into the family by the father.

Which male fish gives birth?

The female seahorse lays her eggs in a special pouch of the male. As they enter the pouch they are fertilized and for the

(*Left and right*) Seahorses are common throughout the Australian area of the Pacific Ocean. Other species live off the Atlantic coasts of North America, Africa and Europe.

next five weeks the male carries them around while his belly gets fatter and fatter as they develop. As they hatch inside him the male twists his body this way and that and eventually expels the babies one by one from the small opening to the pouch. Although the father looks as if he is giving birth, the young have actually hatched from eggs.

Swimming in an awkward upright position, seahorses are not very active and so have developed an interesting method of catching small crustaceans. Their mouths are long and tubular with muscular sides. By pointing the mouth at a shrimp, expanding the sides, and then suddenly opening the mouth, the crustacean is whisked into the mouth in a current of water. This happens too quickly for us to see.

The male dolphin fish has a blunt, square-shaped head. In the female the head is more rounded. Dolphin fishes are common in tropical seas and in some areas are popular as sport fishes.

Is the dolphin a fish or a mammal?

It is a confusing fact that there is both an air-breathing mammal called a dolphin that lives in the sea, and also a true fish of the same name. There are two kinds of dolphin fish. One is quite large and grows to about 5 feet in length, and the other is similar in looks but grows to only $2\frac{1}{2}$ feet. The favourite food of the dolphin fish is flying fishes and they chase them at speeds of over 35 miles per hour under water.

The archerfish lives in brackish water estuaries in places where vegetation overhangs the water.

Which fish spits at insects?

The archerfish from South-east Asia has the remarkable ability of shooting down insects from overhanging vegetation with water pellets. Its aim is quite accurate and it can usually dislodge a beetle or a fly about four feet away, so that it falls in the water. The archer fish then pounces on the insect and eats it. It is interesting to discover how the fish is able to project accurately drops of water over such distances. The roof of the mouth forms a long groove. If the fish suddenly closes its gill covers, water is forced from the gill chamber into the mouth. At the same time the tongue is raised so the groove becomes a long tube from which water squirts in a line of drops.

This Fire Clownfish has laid its eggs on a rock surface within easy reach of its sea anemone companion.

Why does the clownfish live among the dangerous tentacles of a sea anemone?

A beautiful and fascinating spectacle in a seawater aquarium is the vividly coloured common clownfish nestling in, and swimming among, the gently waving tentacles of a giant sea anemone. As we have seen, the arms of anemones are lined with thousands of stinging cells, and yet in some way the clownfishes seem unaffected by these. It is thought that the slimy secretion from the scales of the fishes probably helps to inhibit the effect of the stinging cells. The association between the clownfishes and the anemone is a symbiotic one, that is to say that both partners benefit from the arrangement. The fishes enjoy the luxury of a perfect hiding place from predators, which are probably occasionally lured into the anemone's arms, and the anemone also probably benefits from food brought to it by the fishes.

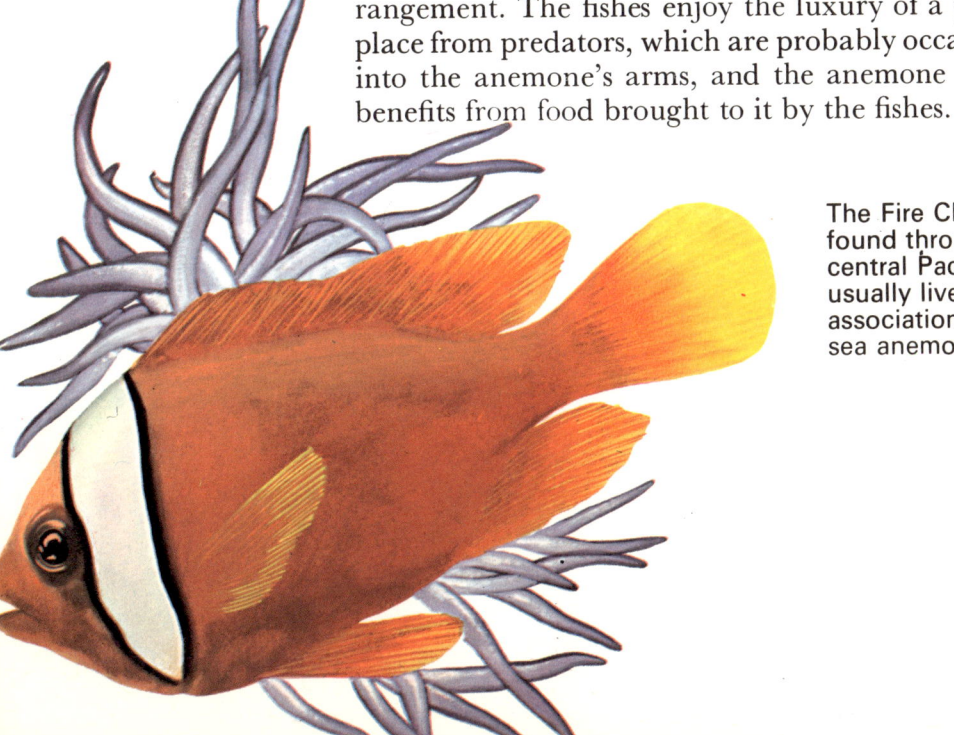

The Fire Clownfish is found throughout the central Pacific Ocean and usually lives in close association with a giant sea anemone.

Which fish is the 'reef barber'?

A small fish living on coral reefs throughout the tropics provides a useful fish-cleaning service for other fishes on the reef. This is the Cleaner Wrasse. The fish very carefully picks off parasites from the head and gill areas of larger fishes and sometimes even enters the mouth to finish the job properly. This tidying up service is greatly appreciated and fishes have been observed 'queueing up' for their turn of the 'reef barber'.

Which fish crunches coral?

It is difficult to imagine a more unappetizing meal than a hard mass of coral (see page 16), but parrotfishes seem to relish it. They bite off chunks with specially strengthened jaws shaped rather like a parrot's beak, hence their name. More strong teeth in the throat grind up the coral before it is swallowed. The parrotfish is actually feeding on algae and other plants growing close to the coral surface, and the only way to get at this food is to eat the coral as well.

(*Above*) The Cleaner Wrasse is shown here attending to the parasites on a Regal Tang. Other fishes provide a similar service for the reef community.

A parrotfish lurking in its coral cave. The inset shows the strong bone structure of the jaws which snip off pieces of coral with ease. Parrotfishes are common on tropical reefs and there are many brightly coloured species.

Mudskippers are shown here from the mudflats along the northern coasts of Australia. It is thought that mudskippers display to one another out of water by quickly raising and lowering the dorsal fin.

Which fish is just as happy out of water as in?

When the tide goes out from mangrove swamps and mudflats in Africa, Australia and southern Asia, most fishes go with it. The mudskippers, however, stay and are quite happy to skitter over the mud or sit quietly on mangrove roots. Every so often they have to dive into the pools left by the tide to renew the small amount of water they carry in the gill chamber. This water supply, and the fact that they also breathe air through a special area of the gill, explains how they are able to spend long periods out of water. Mudskippers are comical little fishes with 'pop-eyes' and large pectoral fins. They rest propped up on these fins or use them as crutches to scuttle around.

Mudskippers from southern Asia are shown here clustered on an exposed mangrove root. Their enormous bulging eyes are movable and allow the mudskipper to look in any direction.

Which fishes build bubble nests?

There is a whole group of fishes that constructs nests from bubbles. These are the labyrinth fishes from South-east Asia and Africa. Perhaps the most well known are the Siamese fighting fishes.

The male Siamese fighting fish blows bubbles, coated with a sticky secretion, just under the surface of the water. The bubbles cling together and eventually a nest several inches across and half an inch deep is formed. The female fighting fish joins the male under the nest and they spawn; the male twisting his body around the female to fertilize the eggs as they are laid. As each batch is laid the male retrieves the eggs from the bottom and blows them gently into the bubbles of the nest. When spawning is complete he drives the female away and tends the nest until the eggs hatch. He catches and replaces eggs that may fall from the nest and repairs any damage by blowing fresh bubbles. The eggs hatch within twenty-four hours.

Do fighting fishes fight?

Two male Siamese fighting fishes placed in the same aquarium instantly take up aggressive positions ready for a scrap. Their colours deepen, their long flowing fins become erect and they suddenly slash at one another at lightning speed. The fight is very dramatic and can last for up to an hour before one of the pair becomes too exhausted or injured to continue. The fight is such a spectacular sight that in Thailand contests are arranged before enthusiastic crowds and bets are placed on the outcome of the battle. For the aquarium market the fishes are bred for their beautiful flowing fins rather than for their fighting qualities. It is unwise to keep two males in a tank nevertheless.

(From top to bottom) The sequence of nest building, spawning and hatching of the fry of the Siamese fighting fish. The newly hatched 'fighter' is shown *bottom*.

(Above left) Only the male Siamese fighting fish has attractive long fins. Here a male and female are shown together.

What is dangerous about the scorpionfishes?

Their name may give you a clue as to why these fishes must be handled very carefully. These striking fishes are popular in marine aquariums. Drifting through the water with all their fins fully extended, they look wonderfully majestic. As you can see, the fins are composed of long, separate spines and it is eighteen of these that are potentially very dangerous. The spines have poison glands and if you are unlucky enough to be pricked, venom is injected in to the wound, causing great pain for several hours.

A Common Scorpionfish *(above)* and a Regal Scorpionfish. These fishes rarely use their spines in attack, merely for defence. There are several hundred types of these fishes including zebrafishes, dragonfishes, lionfishes and turkeyfishes. They all have tasty flesh and one species, the redfish, you may have eaten as 'fish fingers'.

Why does the plaice have a crooked face?

The gradual development from a normal-looking and normal-swimming larval plaice to the flattened adult with both eyes on one side of its face.

You must have noticed plaice and other flatfishes on fishmongers' slabs. Flatfishes are adapted for life on the sea bottom. Their flattened shape allows them to hug the sand or gravel closely in order to avoid detection by their enemies and also to find small crustaceans, worms and molluscs, on which they feed. We have already looked at other flattened fishes, the skates and rays (see page 72). Whereas the rays are flattened from top to bottom, the flatfishes are flattened from side to side, as you can see from the twisted appearance of their faces. On hatching, the young flatfish looks much the same as any other fish and swims about in mid water. When it is about half an inch long a strange thing happens. One of the eyes moves upwards over the top of the head and settles next to the other eye. The flatfish sinks to the bottom and comes to rest on one side with both eyes upwards. The mouth becomes bent to allow the flatfish to feed and so for the rest of its life the flatfish has a strange, lopsided face.

Why is the flounder left-eyed?

The flatfish group of fishes is quite a large one with about 600 members. It is interesting that in some of them it is the right eye that moves to the left side of the fish, and in others it is the left eye which moves to the right. Thus flatfishes are called either right-eyed or left-eyed. The flounder is left-eyed and so always comes to rest on the sea floor on its left side. In other flatfishes either eye moves to join the other, and in yet others the fishes are right-eyed or left-eyed according to where they live.

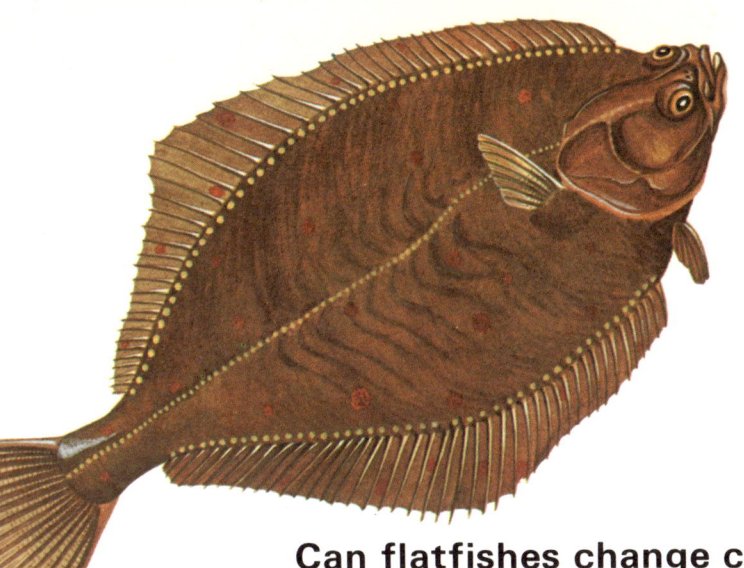

A left-eyed flounder. Plaice, flounder, halibut, turbot and sole are all flatfishes important to us as food fishes and can usually be seen on fishmongers' slabs.

Can flatfishes change colour?

For any fish living directly on the bottom, the ability to change colour is a great advantage. Flatfishes have developed this ability to a remarkable degree. You may look into an aquarium labelled 'turbot' at the zoo one day and wonder where on earth the fish is, so good is its camouflage on sandy or gravelly bottoms. The amount of light entering the fish's eye from its surroundings, and also from directly above it, appears to control the size of pigment-containing cells on the surface of its body. It is able to match the colour and pattern almost exactly and as it often lies half buried, it is practically impossible to see its outline.

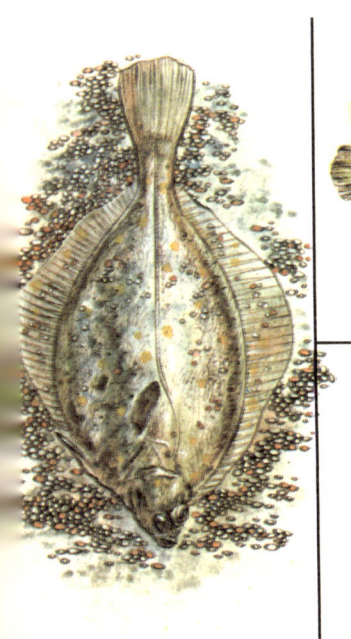

A plaice showing how well it can match its colour to the bottom. The underside of most flatfishes has no pigment-containing cells and is usually a pale creamy-white in colour.

The monster-like appearance of the coelacanth has remained unchanged for hundreds of millions of years.

Which 'fossil' fish is still alive?

For a long time zoologists studied the fossil forms of fishes which had obviously represented a stage in the evolution of the amphibians from the fishes. They could tell that they had been ugly fishes and very common about 300 million years ago. They called the fishes coelacanths. You can imagine the sensation that was caused when a coelacanth was caught by accident in the trawl of a South African fishing boat in 1938. For in fact the coelacanths had been living in the depths of the ocean while everybody assumed they were long extinct. It was almost as if a dinosaur had been discovered in the middle of a forest.

Unfortunately by the time this first specimen was examined someone had thrown away its internal organs so that it could be mounted. Rewards were offered for the capture of another specimen but it was not for another fourteen years that a further coelacanth was caught, this time near Madagascar. Since then a number have been studied but the sudden appearance of the primitive coelacanth is still called 'the great zoological discovery of this century'.

Both the African lungfishes *(below)* and the South American species *(below right)* have very reduced fins and paired lungs.

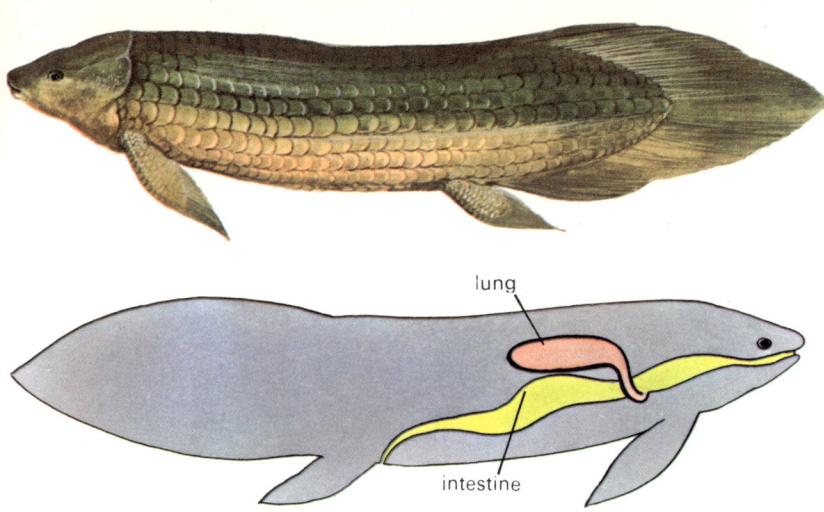

(Left) The Australian Lungfish. The drawing *below* shows how the lung is derived from the gut of the lungfish. In other fishes this extension is the swim bladder.

(Below) The fins of modern fishes *(top)* developed from the primitive limb-like forms *(below)* of the early fishes. This type of fin is still seen in coelacanths and lungfishes.

What are lungfishes?

The lungfishes are another group of fishes that are very similar to their ancestors of 300 million years ago. They are of great importance for they show us the characteristics of the fishes that eventually gave rise to early amphibians – the first vertebrate animals to colonize the land. There are only six species of lungfishes living today. Probably the most primitive one comes from Australia. It has paired fins at the end of leg-like extensions of its body and it has a lung. The lung enables it to breathe air directly on the surface. This means that the lungfish can live quite happily in stagnant water with a low oxygen content in which other water-breathing fishes would soon die. The other lungfishes come from Africa and South America. These types have two lungs and their fins are reduced to thin tentacles.

(Below) An African lungfish snug in its cocoon for the dry season. Lungfishes have been known to live for four years in cocoons.

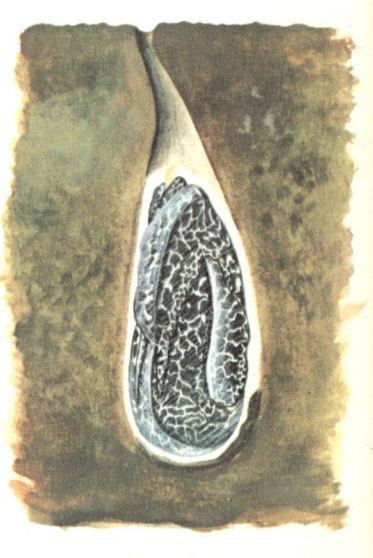

How do lungfishes survive the dry season?

The rivers, streams and ponds in which lungfishes from South America and Africa live, dry up every year. The lungfishes cope with this problem in an interesting way. As the water level drops and while the mud at the bottom is still soft, the fish digs its way down into the mud to form a chamber. The chamber is connected to the surface by a narrow breathing tunnel. Here the lungfish remains, slowly breathing air, until the rains fill up the stream or pond again. The African lungfish secretes large amounts of sticky mucus to keep itself damp in what is called its cocoon. It curls itself up inside in a characteristic upright fashion, with its tail covering its eyes.

AMPHIBIANS

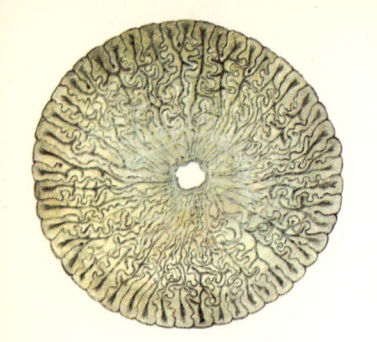

How were the fishes able to leave the water to begin life on land?

Many millions of years ago strange, fish-like creatures crawled from the fresh waters of ponds and lakes to begin life on land. These animals, which are known to us now only from fossils, were the ancestors of the amphibians, the first vertebrate animals to evolve which were capable of living on land. We do not know all the stages that must have taken place in this progression from life in water to life on land but we do have various clues. Study of fossil fishes and amphibians from this particular period, and of primitive fishes which we know have descended more or less unchanged from these fossil forms, provides these clues. It is obvious that the process was a very slow one and it was millions of years before the amphibians were well established on the land.

Eusthenopteron was a fish related to the early lungfishes which showed basic amphibian features. Its skeleton was similar and its teeth had the curious infolding of enamel *(top)* seen in early amphibians' teeth.

As you can imagine there were a couple of problems facing the vertebrates as they left the water. The first was that any animal living on land must be able to support the weight of its body and move around. For the fishes, the water provides support, and their fins and tail propel them along. We see the first step towards overcoming this problem in the curious limb-like fins of the lungfishes (see page 95). These soon developed into primitive legs for the early amphibians and the skeleton became stronger to bear the weight of the animal's body on land.

The second problem, of course, was that of breathing air. We have seen that the lungfishes of today are quite able to do this and so the problem was as easily overcome by their ancestors and related fishes.

Archegosaurus was a relative of *Icythyostega*. We can see from its jaws that it probably fed on fishes and so must have spent much of its time in the water.

Icythyostega was an early amphibian which still retained fish characteristics. It had well developed limbs in place of fins but its tail was still very fish-like.

Why did the amphibians colonize the land?

You may wonder why the vertebrate animals deserted the water at all and attempted to live on the land with all its problems. It is as well to remember that millions of years ago, conditions on the earth were very variable. Large bodies of fresh water would periodically dry up making life difficult, if not impossible, for the fishes. Many, of course, perished but others, better equipped with primitive lungs and stout fins, found they could survive being stranded and even move around a little. Eventually, from these early forms, animals able to spend most of their lives out of water developed. The amphibians were never quite able to live entirely without water, however. Most of those we know today lay their eggs in water and have a larval stage which develops entirely under water. These are the newts and salamanders, frogs and toads and the caecilians.

Archeria was another early amphibian similar in structure to *Icythyostega* with a long 'tail fin'.

(Above) *Aphaneramna* had an even longer snout than *Archegosaurus*.

How successful were the amphibians in adapting to life on land?

The success of the amphibians in colonizing the land was only partial. This was probably because the change in conditions of life in water to life on land was so great. We can understand this by studying the habits of the amphibians we find around us today. They certainly live for some of the time on land but they are forced to seek out dark, moist places under stones, logs or in dank vegetation. Although they have lungs, they do much more breathing through their skin and this must be kept moist to allow the efficient exchange of gases. Most amphibians go through a larval stage which develops in water. They return to water to mate and lay their eggs, and so could not survive only on land.

There are three groups of amphibians. Newts and salamanders still retain fish-like tails and probably spend less time on land. Frogs and toads have lost their tails altogether and are quite active on land. Caecilians spend their entire lives on land and have lost the use of their eyes and feet.

Crested Newt

Red-tailed Salamander

Red Salamander

Common Newt

(Left) The axlotl probably descended from a group of amphibians living in lakes and ponds which rarely dried up. They thus had no urgent need to develop into air-breathing adults and so evolved a mature larval stage.

Which amphibian never grows up?

The most famous amphibian which often never reaches adulthood is the Mexican Axlotl. This curious animal never leaves the water and can mate and produce young even though it is a larva. In all other amphibians the reproductive organs do not develop until the adult stage is reached. You might wonder why the axlotl is called an amphibian at all. Under certain conditions the axlotl will change into an adult – a salamander, actually. So it is an amphibian which is capable of developing and leaving the water, but which prefers to remain where it is.

(Right) Caecilians are found in soft earth in tropical areas of the world. This one is from South America.

(Below) Caecilians lay their eggs in burrows near water. The larvae hatch, then wriggle into the water to complete their development.

What are caecilians?

Caecilians are curious, limbless amphibians which spend their entire lives underground. Their feet have completely disappeared and their eyes are small and ineffective. Caecilians have descended from the earliest amphibians to have appeared on land. They are, therefore, an important link in the evolution of the later amphibians and reptiles, from the air-breathing fishes. They appear to have been the first vertebrate animals to live entirely on land.

How do frogs develop?

During the spring, probably in May, you may hear a noise rather like the quacking of ducks. If you investigate this strange sound, the chances are that you will discover a frog pond in which the males are croaking for all their worth to attract the females. A male clambers on to the back of a female and as she lays eggs in batches, he fertilizes them. A female can lay several thousand eggs in a season. A ball of protective jelly swells up around each egg as it is laid, sticking them all together into the familiar frogs' spawn. If you can find some frogs' spawn it is worth keeping a dozen eggs in an aquarium at home to watch their development. The eggs hatch in about ten days and the larvae hang from the leaves of water plants until their mouths open. They are active then and feed by scraping microscopic plants from the surfaces of plants and stones. Look carefully and you can see little tufts on either side of the head. These are the gills with which the tadpoles first breathe. As the

The male frog fertilizes the eggs as they are laid by the female *(above)*.

(Right) The circle shows the life cycle of the frog from spawn, to newly hatched tadpole, to the final stage of tadpole development, to adult. The cycle usually takes about three months.

tadpoles develop, these gills shrivel up and a flap of skin grows over them. After about two months the legs appear, first the hind legs where the body joins the tail, and then the front legs. The tadpole gulps air from the surface into its newly formed lungs and starts to include meat in its diet. It is important to feed your tadpoles on small pieces of cooked meat dangled in the aquarium on cotton threads at this stage. The tail gradually shortens, the tadpoles stop feeding, and eventually emerge as miniature frogs ready to feed on small insects. At home, don't forget to provide a surface for your tadpoles to clamber on to. Once their lungs are fully formed they will soon drown if they cannot leave the water.

What are these frogs looking for?

Certain ponds and streams are used by frogs for breeding year after year. They travel overland from a wide area to these particular places during the breeding season, and meet up to find mates and lay their eggs. Sometimes these favourite spots are filled in and built over during the construction of housing developments. This is the reason hordes of frogs are occasionally seen entering new estates in the spring.

(Above) Some interesting frogs. *(From top to bottom)*: the African Hairy Frog develops rows of thin gill filaments along its body and thighs during the breeding season; a tiny frog known as the Glass Frog from South America; the Three-striped Arrow Poison Frog used by South American Indians to tip their arrows; and an African Arrow Poison Frog.

(Right) Frogs habitually seek out communal breeding places each spring.

The Water-holding Frogs survive droughts by storing water in their bodies. It is said that Aborigines dig them up and squeeze the water from them when they are thirsty.

How can frogs live in the desert?

It is hard to imagine frogs living in the parched desert areas of central Australia. The rainfall in such regions is very light and every year the streams and ponds dry up completely in the periods of drought. This means that amphibians must not only be able to survive the drought, but must quickly lay their eggs and prepare themselves for the next dry period, too.

Wallace's Treefrog *(left)* from Malaya and another gliding frog *(right)* from Java.

One frog has overcome these problems admirably. As the pond dries up, the Water-holding Frog takes in water through its skin, swelling up to look very bloated indeed. It digs down into the mud while this is still soft, and lies dormant in a sealed cocoon for the period of the drought. When the rains soften the mud again the frog breaks out of its cocoon, replenishes its water supply and breeds. The eggs hatch quickly and the larvae turn into frogs in a couple of weeks while the water is still available. The young frogs grow rapidly, feeding on the insect life that also flourishes during the rainy period. At the onset of the next drought the young frogs also begin to store up a water supply to last them through the dry period. Water-holding Frogs also occur in the south-west United States.

Can frogs live in trees?

Another surprising place to find frogs is among the branches and foliage of bushes and trees. Frogs have been quite successful in adapting to these surroundings, and there are about 500 sorts of treefrogs widely distributed in the world. Some spend most of their time in water but others prefer to clamber and jump among branches and twigs in pursuit of insects, their favourite food. They are entertaining to watch while feeding for they are very agile and leap and swing in spectacular displays of aerial acrobatics. A modification of their feet gives them a good grip and helps them to hold on to branches after particularly long jumps from branch to branch. At the ends of the fingers and toes of the treefrog there is a small disc. These are tiny suction cups that enable the frogs to land and cling securely to the smooth surfaces of leaves and branches.

Many treefrogs are green in colour and this has an obvious value as camouflage among the foliage of their homes. Some treefrogs show startling patches of colour as they jump. These are not visible when the frog is crouching and the sudden flash of orange, red or yellow might temporarily distract an enemy to give the frog time to escape. These 'flash colours' as they are called are usually found on the inside of the frog's arms and legs.

Treefrogs *(from top to bottom)*: Hylambates maculatus from Africa; the Common European Treefrog; The Green Treefrog from North America; and the Smith Treefrog from South America.

Can frogs fly?

A species of treefrog from Malaya is even more adapted for scrambling and leaping after flying insects. This is Wallace's Treefrog and it has webbed feet with specially long fingers and toes. When the frog launches into a leap it stretches the fingers and toes wide apart, and the increase in surface area enables it to glide downwards for considerable distances. It does not fly so much as glide, but the advantage is that the frog can catch insects which it would otherwise be unable to reach by jumping normally.

Which frog prefers water to land?

The Clawed Frog spends most of its life underwater. It is well adapted for a mainly aquatic existence with a smooth skin, a powerful streamlined body, and muscular hind legs with enormous webbed feet. It rarely ventures on to land and if you caught one and placed it on the ground, it would flop clumsily back to the water.

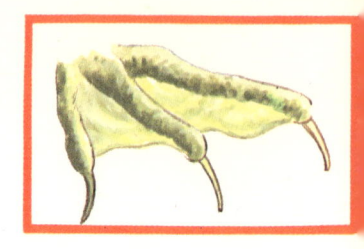

The inside three fingers of the Clawed Frog's hind feet have short black claws. These may help stir up the bottom when the frog is rummaging around for insect larvae, and they may also help grip the prey when the Clawed Frog discovers something edible. The claws are shown *(top)* and a Clawed Frog tadpole *(above)*. The Clawed Frog lives in swamps, rivers and ponds of South Africa.

Which frog keeps its tadpoles in its mouth?

We have already discovered a fish which looks after its young in this strange way (see page 79). Darwin's Frog does the same thing. When the eggs are about to hatch the male frogs scoop them up with the tongue and slide about seventeen into specially enlarged vocal sacs. The tadpoles are carried about inside the male throughout their development into froglets, and they are thus completely protected during this hazardous period. The male can still feed while supporting his family in this way, but understandably, he cannot croak.

Darwin's Frog is only 1 inch long and hops about energetically in the beech woods of Argentina and Chile.

Despite its colossal bulk, the Giant Frog is well camouflaged and is quite difficult to spot squatting on moss-covered rocks next to waterfalls.

Which is the biggest frog in the world?

Even larger than the South American Bullfrog is the Giant Frog from West Africa. Specimens of this monster amphibian have been reported as being 2 feet long and weighing 13 pounds. The Giant Frog is also found tasty to eat by the natives of the areas in which it lives. Unfortunately it is becoming increasingly rare.

Who eats this fat frog?

The South American Bullfrog is a colourful, fat frog and makes an attractive pet. Its spawn and **tadpoles** are shown *below*.

This enormous frog, which comes from the swampy areas of South and Central America, is relished by the local people as food. The flesh of its muscular back legs apparently tastes delicious and the frog is so popular for dinner that large specimens are difficult to find. The South American Bullfrog can grow to $8\frac{1}{2}$ inches long and weighs several pounds.

The European Common Toad is a welcome visitor to gardens and may make its home in a broken flowerpot.

(Below) Toads' spawn is laid in long strings which stick to underwater plants. The larvae are not unlike frog tadpoles.

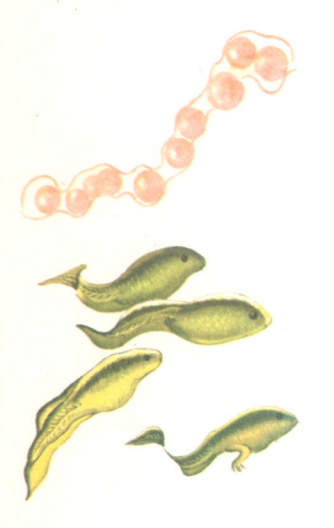

What is the difference between frogs and toads?

Most people recoil in horror at seeing a toad in the garden. Toads are certainly more ugly than frogs. They have large flattened bodies with dry, wrinkled and pimply skins. The head of a toad is blunter than a frog's and its arms and legs are shorter. The toad spends most of its time on land and it is a slow mover, unlike the active frog. It likes to establish a home for itself in some secluded spot to which it returns each evening after its leisurely feeding crawls. If you find a toad in your garden you might persuade it to stay by setting up a superior toad home – an old flowerpot is ideal. If it takes up residence your toad might stay for years. The flowers and vegetables should benefit by the toad's presence for it will feed on slugs, beetles and many other insect pests. It is often called the 'gardener's friend' for this reason. Don't worry about catching warts from your toad because this is just an 'old wives tale'.

(Right) The South American Toad grows to 7 inches in length and makes a splendid pet.

(Right) The male Midwife Toad takes care of the fertilized eggs. He carries them around on his back until the tadpoles hatch.

The Surinam Toad is another amphibian that sifts through mud to find its food. It has long, slender fingers for this purpose and each has a cluster of sensitive tentacles at the tip. These help the toad to detect its food by touch in thick mud or particularly muddy water.

Which toad hatches young on its back?

A Western Toad calls for over a minute using the air contained in its large vocal sac.

Another remarkable amphibian breeding habit is seen in the Surinam toad from South America. The female lays the eggs which are fertilized immediately by the male in the normal way. As the female lays them, however, he manoeuvres them up on to her back and presses them into her specially thickened skin. They sink in and after a short time the skin grows over them. The female then swims about her business quite unconcerned with the enormous lumpy load of about sixty eggs on her back. The eggs hatch and the tadpoles complete their development while still carried in the skin of their mother. A tiny lid on the top of each bump eventually pops open and each toadlet is released and swims up to the surface. As few eggs are laid the method is usually very successful.

A fat, colourful toad from Brazil. The Brazilian Horned Toad is known for its aggressiveness and has sharp teeth in its upper jaw. It will even pounce on and devour a toad of its own kind if given the chance.

109

REPTILES

Why did this early reptile have a 'sail'?

This prehistoric reptile, called *Dimetrodon*, lived about 280 million years ago. The reptiles evolved from the amphibians and were enormously successful in colonizing the land. We have seen that although amphibians were the first vertebrate animals to emerge on land, they were still dependent on water for reproduction (see page 102). For the reptiles this problem was solved by the evolution of a shelled egg which enabled them to produce young independently of water. The shell protected the developing reptile inside from drying up, but at the same time allowed it to breathe. A food supply was provided by yolk, and special membranes enclosed the embryo in fluid, carried oxygen to it, and stored its waste products. The egg gave reptiles a big advantage and they quickly evolved to become the dominant group of animals for 150 million years. Reptiles were, and still are, unable to control their body temperature. It is thought that *Dimetrodon* coped by turning its large skin 'sail' to the sun to absorb heat when it was cold, and away from the sun when it was hot.

Which were the biggest dinosaurs?

The first dinosaurs appeared on the earth about 200 million years ago and were no bigger than chickens. They ran and hopped about on their hind legs, a feature of the huge dinosaurs that followed. The biggest dinosaurs weighed 50 tons although they fed on water plants in lakes, and so much of their weight was supported by water. Other dinosaurs lived on land and were ferocious carnivores.

Tyrannosaurus (above) was nearly 50 feet long (as long as two buses end to end) and 19 feet high. Mummified scaly skin *(above left)* has been found from dinosaurs, and nests containing up to thirty eggs *(above right)* discovered.

How did the prehistoric reptiles fly?

The prehistoric reptiles were so successful they even conquered the air. The front legs of those that moved around on their back legs soon developed into primitive wings. A long bony wrist and finger supported a leathery flap of skin which stretched from front to back legs. These pterodactyls became increasingly clumsy on land. They hung about in trees and on cliffs, gliding and flapping to the ground to feed. They probably fed on fishes which they snatched from the surfaces of lakes.

Reptiles are unable to control the temperature of their bodies. *Dimetrodon* used the enormous surface area of its 'sail' to absorb the warmth of the sun. Today you may see lizards basking in the sun in exposed places.

(Right) Three types of pterodactyls are shown. These early flying reptiles had long pointed jaws and teeth which suggests they fed on fishes. Later on reptiles again took to the air. This time they were more successful and from this group the birds evolved.

Is the Tuatara a prehistoric reptile?

The Tuatara certainly looks as if it stalked around the ancient landscapes of 200 million years ago. The long crest of spines running from its head along the length of its body gives it a very prehistoric appearance. Today the Tuatara is a very rare reptile and is found only on a few scattered islands lying off the New Zealand coast. It is another of those animals we call 'living fossils'. Creatures very much like the one species that exists today roamed around prehistoric landscapes millions of years ago. They formed a large and successful group called beak-heads and many fossil forms have been discovered widely distributed throughout the world. Together with many other successful reptile groups, such as the dinosaurs, the beak-heads suddenly declined in numbers. We still do not know why the age of reptiles suddenly ended but all Tuataras but one became extinct. Somehow this species managed to survive conditions that caused so many reptiles to disappear from the earth, and has lived unchanged up until the present day. It is a unique animal and represents a whole vanished order of reptiles. The other surviving remnants of the great prehistoric reptile disaster are the turtles, crocodiles, lizards and snakes.

Tuataras have lived for up to fifty years in captivity and it is claimed they may live up to 100 years in the wild. They are about 2 feet long.

The Leatherback Turtle is the largest reptile found today. It has discarded a bony shell and instead has a streamlined, smooth, leathery skin. It grows to 7½ feet in length and weighs up to 1500 pounds.

When is a turtle a tortoise?

Turtles and tortoises form a large group of reptiles characterized by a heavily armoured shell. The protection this shell gives probably accounts for their survival, but it is not known exactly how this peculiar structure evolved.

Although the shell provides complete protection, it makes movement on land very slow and cumbersome, and most members of the group in fact live in the water. With the support of water the turtles have become good swimmers in both fresh and sea water. In America all members of this group are called turtles, whereas in Britain this name is reserved for those that live in the sea. Those that live in fresh water are usually called terrapins and those that live on land are called tortoises.

The Green Turtle *(right* and *below)* is the turtle we use to make soup. The eggs are also prized for food and the turtle has seriously declined in numbers recently due to heavy depredation by man. Attempts are being made to build up stocks again, however.

Why is this Green Turtle crying?

The Green Turtle hauls its enormous 300 pound bulk up out of the sea to above the high water mark and digs a large pit in which to lay its eggs. Its long powerful flippers, so efficient for swimming at sea, are not very suitable on land and the female has to drag the huge weight of her body along. Every few yards she stops for breath and with a huge sigh lifts the heavy shell from her body so that her lungs can fill with air. While on land her eyes are continually streaming and it has been suggested that she is reduced to tears by the exhausting task of laying her eggs! This is, of course, not true and the tears are actually a way of removing the extra salt the turtle takes in while feeding and drinking at sea. They are not seen until it comes ashore.

This ridiculous-looking South American turtle is called the Matamata. Its extended neck bears flaps of skin that wave in the water and attract fishes. The Matamata then quickly opens its enormous mouth and the fishes are swept in.

Do terrapins make good pets?

Most pet shops sell terrapins. They look like small, flattened tortoises and are usually kept in shallow dishes of water. The flattened shape is, of course, an adaption to life in water and the terrapins can therefore be termed amphibious. They can live both on the land and in the water but should not be confused with amphibians. Terrapins are reptiles and so lay their eggs on land although they can swim and catch their food in water. Amphibians are basically aquatic animals that can spend part of their life on land. They must return to water to breed.

The Greek Tortoise *(below)* is here drawn to scale against a Giant Tortoise *(right)*.

The terrapins *(middle)* are the female *(left)*, male *(right)* and young *(below)* Elegant Sliders.

Terrapins are sometimes called water tortoises, cooters or sliders. The cooter *above* is from North America.

Most terrapins come from warm countries and, as pets, should be kept warm in temperate or cool countries. You can use an aquarium to keep them in. Fill it with only a couple of inches of water and arrange surfaces for the terrapins to climb on to. You can keep the temperature in the tank constant either by using an aquarium heater or by hanging a light bulb over the tank. Terrapins will eat a variety of foods but do require careful attention, and you should consult an expert if you are seriously considering keeping them.

How long can tortoises live?

Probably the most popular reptiles kept as pets are tortoises. An enclosed garden is an ideal place, for then the tortoise is prevented from wandering away. From old records of people keeping tortoises in the past in this way we know that they can live for many years. Some of the records are conflicting and give figures of 62 and 92 years for one tortoise. One undisputed claim gives the age of a particular tortoise as at least 182 when it died on the island of Mauritius in 1918. This specimen is preserved in the British Museum (Natural History).

Almost forty sorts of tortoise come from tropical and subtropical areas of the world. We can see how they are most obviously adapted for life on land by comparing their feet with the flippers of the turtles (see page 115). The tortoise is supported on short, stubby feet with claws, and on these it plods laboriously along, carrying its domed shell with it. Tortoises are herbivorous and so if you keep one in your garden, make sure it cannot get near your seedlings.

The Greek Tortoise *(above)* is the tortoise most commonly kept as a pet. The Radiated Tortoise *(far right)* is an attractively marked species. The cut-away drawing *(centre)* shows how the backbone of a tortoise is fused to the shell and its ribs flattened to give support.

Which are the biggest tortoises?

The largest tortoises in the world are those that live in the Galapagos Islands and on islands in the Indian Ocean. These monsters, which are appropriately called Giant Tortoises, can grow to more than 4 feet in length and to over 400 pounds in weight. They are rare today. During the nineteenth century the crews of sailing ships on long voyages in the Pacific and Indian Oceans realized that these abundant tortoises were a ready supply of fresh meat. Many thousands were slaughtered in a short period.

A large African Nile Crocodile about to enter the water. Crocodiles are protected by a thick, scaly skin which is prized for making items such as handbags and shoes. Nile Crocodiles are now rare as a result of hunting for this trade and the sale of crocodile products is discouraged.

What is the difference between alligators and crocodiles?

The crocodiles, alligators, caimans and the gavial make up a group of about twenty reptiles. They all have the same basic appearance and, like the turtles and terrapins, they are all amphibious. The alligator differs from the crocodile in having a shorter and broader snout although there is yet another, more definite difference. In both animals the fourth tooth of the lower jaw is enlarged. The teeth in the narrower upper and lower jaws of a crocodile are in line and so this tooth fits into a groove of the upper jaw, and can be seen when the crocodile closes its mouth. The teeth in the broader, upper jaw of an alligator overlap those in the lower. The enlarged tooth this time fits into a pocket in the upper jaw and cannot be seen when the mouth is closed.

(Below) The ugly snout of the man-eating Salt-water Crocodile. This species comes from India, the Philippines and northern Australia, and is notorious for attacking man.

The long, powerful tail of the crocodile indicates that it is a good swimmer. The ears, eyes and nostrils are all in line on top of the head so that it can lie practically submerged waiting for its prey. It is also quite agile on land and leaves the water to breed and bask in the sun.

(Left) The American Alligator is another animal that has become rare due to hunting for its skin and for sale to tourists. Alligators do not make good pets, however, because they soon grow to an unmanageable size.

How dangerous are crocodiles?

All crocodiles are meat eaters and feed in water. They are particularly successful in catching smaller animals because they can float up very close to their prey without being seen. They catch animals at water holes in this way and, holding them under water, they back off into deeper water until the prey drowns. Crocodiles tear pieces from their victims by gripping with the teeth and turning over and over. Crocodiles mysteriously attack man in only some areas of Africa. They are probably more aggressive when protecting a nest or when the water is drying up. Older 'rogue' specimens perhaps become used to catching domestic animals in a particular locality and eventually attack the men who tend them.

A baby caiman hatching from its egg. Crocodiles from South and Central America are generally called caimans.

Why does this crocodile have a long snout?

If you take a stick and sweep it through water you may be surprised to find that little effort is needed to part the water. The stick does not offer much resistance and so slices through very easily. The gavial is unlike other crocodiles in that it feeds almost exclusively on fishes. You may be beginning to realize why it has such a long, narrow snout. Powerful strokes of its strong tail propel it quickly through the water after its prey, and long sideways slashes of its mouth soon render the fishes helpless. The gavial is a shy crocodile and does not attack man.

(Below) The Gavial lives in the rivers and estuaries of India.

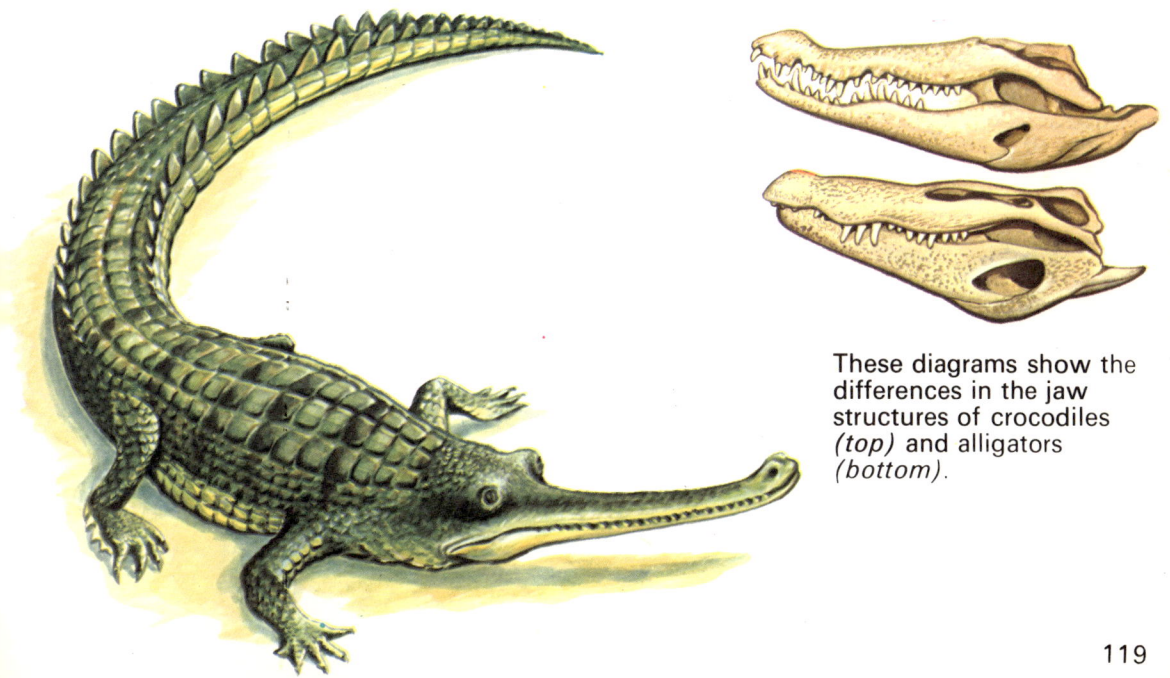

These diagrams show the differences in the jaw structures of crocodiles (top) and alligators (bottom).

How can a gecko run up the wall?

(Above) These geckos show the curiously shaped toes that enable them to cling to surfaces in impossible positions. Geckos belong to the enormous lizard and snake group of reptiles.

Visitors to tropical countries are usually introduced to the acrobatic antics of geckos on their first evening. As the lights go on and insects begin to cluster around them, the geckos appear from their daytime hiding places. To reach the insects they think nothing of scampering up the wall and sometimes even across the ceiling. A close examination of the gecko's foot reveals how it is able to carry out these gravity defying movements. The toes are fat and flattened and the underneath of each consists of rows of soft, folded skin bearing thousands of tiny hooks. These catch in any irregularity, however small, in the wall or ceiling, and support the animal's weight.

What use is the Frilled Lizard's frill?

As the Australian Frilled Lizard bounds away from danger (above) its frill lies folded along its neck. When cornered, however, it turns and opens its frill at its enemy in a dramatic bluff display (above right).

The Frilled Lizard grows to 3 feet in length in dry and sandy areas of north-eastern Australia. It lives in trees but often comes down to feed on the ground. If you come across one in the open and chase it you will soon discover why it has a frill. When disturbed the Frilled Lizard at first takes to its heels, sprinting across the ground on its hind legs, with its long tail acting as a stabilizer. If there is no tree to climb and it finds itself cornered, it turns and tries to frighten its enemy away. The long frill is suddenly erected around its neck and the mouth opens wide in a defiant, aggressive gesture. The sudden flash of colours from the frill and inside the mouth, together with angry hissing noises, usually changes the attacker's mind. If you were chasing a lizard that suddenly turned on you with a head several times bigger than it was a moment ago, wouldn't you have second thoughts about catching it?

How can a chameleon look at two things at once?

If you see a chameleon in the zoo you may notice that although it sits on a branch with one bulging eye on you, the other eye may be looking in a completely different direction. The eyes are very curious. Each has a thick conical lid which covers nearly all the eye apart from a small peephole at the tip. Each of these lids can revolve independently of the other and they look very much like

(From top to bottom) The Indian Dwarf Chameleon, Jackson's Chameleon and the Common Chameleon. Chameleons are well adapted for living among foliage. Their toes are joined into two groups so that their feet grip the branches like pairs of tongs. The tail is also used for gripping and, of course, Chameleons can change their colour and usually match their surroundings.

turrets as they swivel around focusing on objects. The objects they focus on most are insects. Chameleons live in trees and their roving eyes probably give them a better chance of spotting their prey among the foliage without being seen themselves. They are very stealthy creatures and stalk along the branches after insects extremely slowly. They can look all round them on either side, without turning their heads. Once an eye sees an insect, the other swivels round to focus on it as well. After carefully judging the range, the chameleon suddenly darts out its tongue and snatches the insect into its mouth. This happens more quickly than we can see but the chameleon's aim is deadly and it rarely misses.

What is the American Chameleon?

The American Chameleon is really an anole lizard. The anoles are a large group of tree-lizards that come from North and South America and the West Indies. The American Chameleon became so called because it can change its colour – a well-known characteristic of chameleons. There are no chameleons in the New World and so the anole lizard is the creature that most resembles them. Anoles change their colour a lot more slowly than chameleons and in response to more than just their surroundings. The temperature, light intensity and how the anole is feeling at the time, all affect its final colour.

The female American Chameleon *(below)* is drab compared to the splendid throat sac of the male *(right)*. He can expand this to show off its bright colours either to attract a mate or warn off a rival.

Which lizard squirts blood from its eyes?

The horned toads come from desert areas of North America and Mexico. They are insect eaters and bury themselves in the warm sand each evening as night falls. They can grow up to 5 inches long.

Nobody knows quite how or why the Horned Toad (which is really another lizard) squirts blood from its eyes, but we know for certain that it does happen on occasions. Naturally there are a number of theories to explain this strange phenomenon. Somehow the lizard is able to increase the blood pressure in its head, rupture the membranes of tiny blood vessels in its eyes, and squirt drops of blood for several inches. It is said that this action is usually defensive and that when squirted into the eyes of an attacker, the blood of the Horned Toad acts as an irritant.

Which big lizards eat seaweed and cacti?

The Marine Iguana and the Land Iguana come from the Galapagos Islands in the Pacific Ocean. They are both enormous lizards. The Marine Iguana grows to 4 feet in length and the Land Iguana to $3\frac{1}{2}$ feet.

The Marine Iguana is the only lizard to have adapted to life in, or at least next to, the sea. It lives on the cliffs and rocks of the coast in large colonies and feeds on the beds of seaweed exposed at low tide. It can swim well, however, using its long, vertically flattened tail, and sometimes dives under the surface to feed.

The Marine Iguana *(left)* and the Land Iguana *(below)* are large lizards of the Galapagos Islands.

The Land Iguana, as its name suggests, lives inland from the coast and leads a more conventional lizard life. It is also mainly a vegetarian but, instead of seaweed, feeds on a variety of plants including shoots and fruits, but particularly cacti, spines and all. Larger Land Iguanas have been known to eat small mice and rats.

The large iguanas of the Galapagos were once very abundant. When man settled on these islands, however, he brought with him many domestic animal competitors for the iguana habitat, and today the iguanas are very reduced in numbers.

How can skinks see with their eyes closed?

The skinks make up a large family of fairly small lizards found in all the warm countries of the world. There are about 600 species and many of them come from Africa where they are the most common lizard. Despite their abundance most people are not at all familiar with skinks and this is probably because they are shy and retiring. If you did see one you would not think it a particularly remarkable lizard, for skinks have no fancy frills or striking coloration.

The majority of skinks live on or actually in the ground. They crawl among stones, fallen logs and leaf litter. They are not fast movers on the ground but many are very accomplished at burrowing. They are well adapted for this sort of movement being slender, smooth-skinned and having a small, pointed head. Another skink characteristic which is designed to help this worming, squirming movement through the soil is the reduction in size of the limbs. In some skinks the feet look ridiculously small for the body and in others they have disappeared altogether.

In addition to their streamlined appearance some skinks have another adaptation to their subterranean way of life. To protect its eyes when burrowing or grubbing through ground debris, the skink will close its eyes. In lizards the lower lid closes over the eye. The lid of some skinks has a small, more or less clear 'window', so that its vision is not completely cut off.

A group of skinks: *(top left)* the Western Greater Skink, *(bottom left)* the European Skink, and *(top right)* the Five-lined Skink.

Which is the most beautiful reptile?

The reptile awarded this title is the European Green Lizard. It is the second largest lizard to be found in Europe, the male reaching a length of 16 inches, 10 inches of which is its tail. (The largest European Lizard is the Eyed Lizard which reaches 2 feet in length.) Green lizards are found widely throughout Europe although they do not occur naturally in Great Britain. Attempts have been made to establish colonies but it is believed that the climate is not really warm enough for them.

Two members of a large lizard family which is found across Europe and Africa: *(top)* the European Sand Lizard and *(left)* the European Green lizard. The Uta Lizard *(right)* is from the New World.

You may find a Green Lizard for sale in a pet shop, for their elegant reptile shape and vivid colouring make them popular as pets. They are not difficult to look after but do need proper conditions, so take advice before you buy one. You can feed them on insects, spiders and worms.

Why do lizards shed their tails?

Confronted by an enemy many lizards snap off their tails to distract the attacker while they scamper to safety. In some skinks the brightly coloured tail twitches and jumps for a time to add to the confusion. The lizard soon grows a replacement.

The Komodo Dragon *(left)* comes only from the Indonesian island of Komodo and three other islands. It belongs to a group of lizards called monitor lizards all of which have a similar appearance. *Below* is the Grey Monitor from the Middle East and north-west India.

What is the largest lizard in the world?

Can you imagine a lizard 10 feet long and weighing 300 pounds? There is a monster lizard of this size called the Komodo Dragon. It is easy to see how it came to be called a dragon. Its long neck supports a large head with cruel-looking jaws and its powerful, thick tail accounts for half its length. Short legs with clawed feet and a stout body complete the picture, but the final dragon-like touch is the forked tongue which the Komodo Dragon flicks out as it trundles along.

Altogether this is a thoroughly frightening lizard. It is said that the tail is fairly ineffective against man, but the terrible jaws would make a serious wound if they clamped on to an arm or leg. The Komodo Dragon is a ferocious carnivore and will kill and eat any smaller animal it can catch. Some have even been reported eating small deer and pigs.

(Below) Gould's Monitor is found in Australia as is the Perentie *(below left)* which is the second largest lizard in the world, growing to 8 feet in length. These two are fighting.

Some lizards are very snake-like in appearance. The skink *(above right)* has a slim body with small limbs and the Slow-worm *(below right)* has lost its legs altogether.

Differences between lizards and snakes: *(below)* lizards have several rows of belly scales *(left)*, whereas snakes have only one *(right)*; and *(far right)* lizards usually have eyelids and a visible ear drum *(above)* whereas snakes' eyes are protected by a transparent scale *(below)*.

Are snakes really modified lizards?

Several features of the monitor lizards are not found in other lizards but are found in snakes. For example, the monitor lizards are the only lizards to swallow their prey whole, or if it is too big, pieces of it. Other lizards chew and crush their food before eating. Another snake-like characteristic is the monitor lizard's forked tongue, again unknown in other lizards. Finally, monitor lizards are unable to shed their tails, a typical lizard characteristic unknown in snakes. These clues indicate that monitors and snakes probably descended from the same ancestor way back in prehistoric time.

Other lizard families also have snake-like features and we have already seen that the burrowing skinks have long, streamlined bodies with reduced limbs. One lizard often mistaken for a snake is the Slow-worm. You can tell the Slow-worm is a legless lizard, however, by the several rows of scales along its belly (snakes have only one row), by the presence of eyelids (snakes have none), and by its notched tongue (snakes have forked tongues).

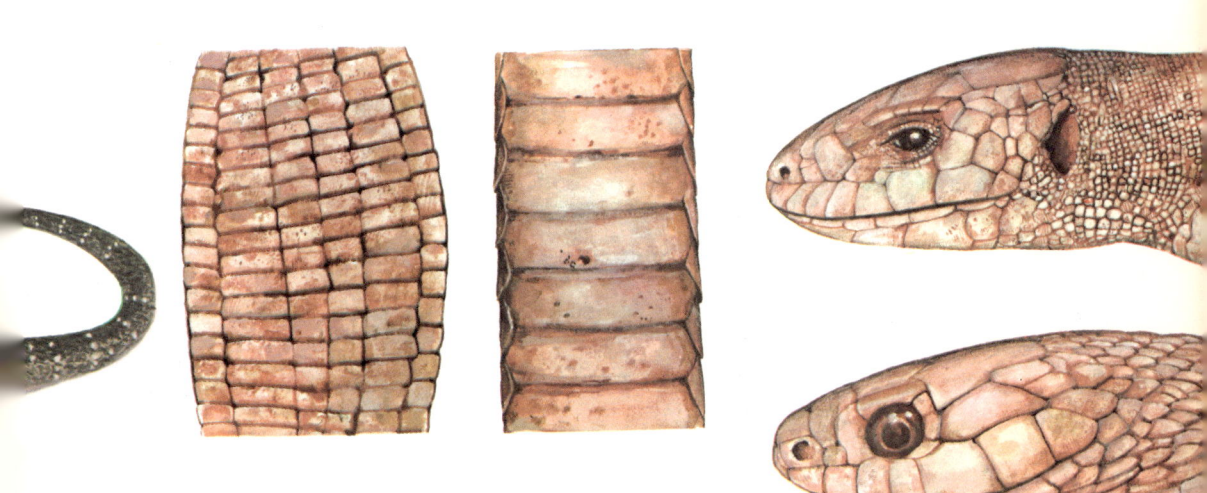

How do snakes slither?

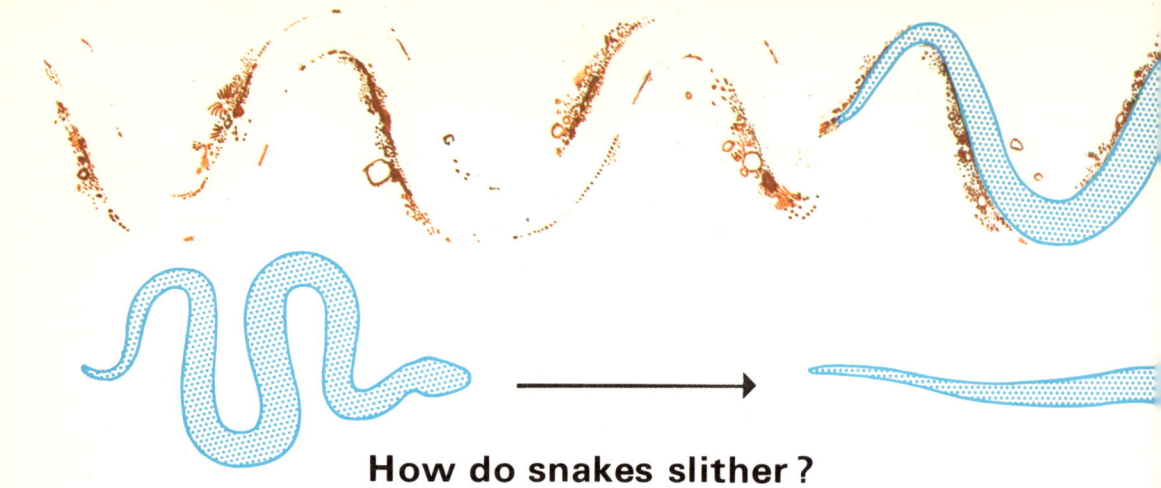

You might think that, without legs, snakes would have difficulty in moving. However, snakes have developed the art of slithering to a fine degree and grass snakes, for example, can slither as fast as a man can walk. They move along sending waves of contractions alternately along the muscles of either side of the body. This results in horizontal curves or waves passing from the head of the snake down to the tail. The rear edge of each wave pushes backwards, and so if the passage of waves down the snake is checked by bumps and stones on the ground, the snake moves forward. A snake crossing a sandy patch leaves a trail with sand heaped up at the rear of each wave, showing where the thrust was made.

Some snakes move by a variation of this method called 'concertina locomotion'. The snake throws the front half of its body into waves, grips the ground and draws up the rear half. The rear half then forms waves which push the straightened front half forward.

Heavy, fat snakes tend to creep forward in a straight line. They do this by sending a wave of contraction down the narrow row of overlapping scales on their belly. These scales move forward slightly and then back, and their continued action along the snake push it forward slowly.

How does a sidewinder move?

If you place a snake on a very smooth surface, the waves passing down its body will not grip and the snake will not move forward. Loose, shifting sand has much the same effect on conventional snake slithering, and so we find a different method of movement in desert snakes. A sidewinding snake throws its head into a sideways loop. It places its neck on the sand and twists the rest of its body off the sand and through the same spot, pushing downwards at the same time. As the body spirals through this point the head makes a new loop and again touches down in front and to the side. These actions leave a line of parallel 'J' shapes in the sand. The curved bottom of the 'J' is made by the head touching down, the stem by the body looping through and forwards, and the cross by the tail thrusting off. A sidewinder travels forward even though it is spiralling sideways.

How does a snake shed its skin?

Slithering along the ground tends to wear out the snake's skin so it replaces it from time to time with a new one. The new skin grows underneath the old and when it is fully formed, fluid is secreted between the two to keep them apart and lubricated. The fluid behind the transparent eye scale clouds the eye and prevents the snake from seeing for a few days. It hides away and then splits the old skin at its lips by rubbing its head. The old skin is turned inside out as the snake wriggles out.

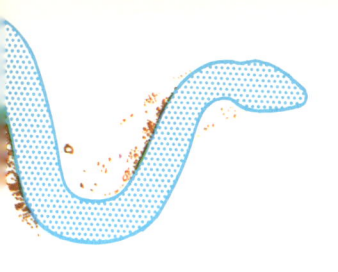

(Above) The normal slithering action of a snake leaves a characteristic trail with sand heaped up at the edge of each wave (top). The 'concertina' method of movement is shown bottom.

(Far left) The sidewinding action of snakes in deserts leaves a series of 'J' shapes in the sand.

(Above) A snake turns pale and its eyes go cloudy when it is about to moult. The old skin is pushed back from the head and turns inside out as the snake emerges (right).

Why is this snake seeking the shade?

If you feel chilly you begin to shiver and if you feel warm you begin to perspire. Both these actions result in you controlling the temperature of your body independently of the temperature of the air. Birds can also do this but reptiles cannot. This is why birds and mammals are spoken of as warm blooded and reptiles as cold blooded. A snake's blood is not always cold, however. It is true that a snake has no insulating fur or feathers to prevent heat loss from its body, but it does have a limited amount of control over its temperature. Its method of control is simple: in the morning it warms up its body by basking in the sun. Once it is warmed up it can begin the day's activities. If the snake then becomes overheated it will seek the shadow of a rock or bush in which to cool off. The body temperature of a snake is therefore always more or less that of its surroundings.

What is a hibernaculum?

In temperate countries the temperature in the winter months remains low over a long period. Snakes and other reptiles would soon die if they were exposed to such cold and so they hibernate. By hiding themselves away in underground holes and burrows made by other animals they escape the low temperatures and pass the winter in a torpid state. This means that all their bodily actions are slowed down so that hardly any energy is used up. Some snakes hibernate on their own but others return each autumn to a communal hole or hibernaculum. Forty snakes have been found sharing the same winter quarters, and a popular hole is often used by more than one species.

(Above) A snake cannot control its body temperature as well as birds and mammals. If it becomes too warm it must seek the shade.
(Right) In a hibernaculum several snakes will share the same winter quarters.

How does a snake swallow its prey?

Snakes catch live animals and eat them whole. They can swallow prey several times larger than their head. This is made possible by very loosely jointed jaws which enable the mouth to be opened wide. Backward pointing teeth grip the prey while the mouth is worked over the animal. Lots of saliva helps the meal to slip down the snake's throat.

A snake can catch and swallow whole an animal several times wider than its head. The jaws of a snake are especially mobile and its skin is capable of being stretched taut over bulky bodies.

How does a snake find a mate?

The snake has poor eyesight, no voice and it is deaf to sounds in the air. Snakes lead solitary lives and the male snake looks very much like the female snake. You might wonder how a couple ever meets in order to mate. A snake's tongue flickers in and out. Somehow it looks dangerous but all the snake is doing is smelling the air. The tongue picks up particles from the air and passes them into two special 'smelling organs' in the roof of the mouth. These are called Jacobson's organs and are pits lined with sensory cells.

Smelling its way along in this manner the snake can track down its prey and also follow the movements of a female. During the breeding season the female lays down a trail of scent produced in some snakes from glands in the tail, and in others from the skin. The male quickly recognizes the scent of a female and is soon able to find her.

In most snakes, elaborate 'courtship' gestures are made before mating takes place. Here a pair of rattlesnakes face each other with their tails curled together.

Eventually the male throws a loop around the female to bring their reproductive organs together, and mating takes place.

Why are snakes' eggs usually white?

Most snakes' eggs are oblong in shape, and white or pale cream in colour. They are usually laid in some sort of nest although the snake's nest is nothing like a bird's nest. The snake covers its eggs in a shallow depression in the ground, or hides them in a pile of leaves, or buries them in manure. Apart from one or two exceptions, snakes do not incubate their eggs because they are unable to generate their own body warmth (see page 130). The nest sites are therefore chosen to insulate the eggs as much as possible from sudden drops in air temperature. Manure and decaying vegetation generate heat and so eggs laid in such nests usually hatch faster than those on the ground. In all the nests, however, the eggs are concealed and so do not need protective colouring to camouflage them, as do certain bird's eggs.

The eggs of a snake are characteristically oval in shape and white in colour. This Blue Racer will soon cover up her eggs to prevent them from becoming chilled and to hide them from enemies.

The drawing *(below)* shows the egg-tooth with which the snake *(bottom)* has just torn a rent in its shell.

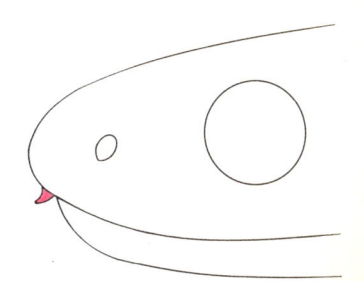

How does a young snake escape from the egg?

When fully formed the young snake lies tightly coiled up within the egg. In order to escape the confines of the tough shell it is equipped with a tiny 'egg-tooth' which projects from the end of its nose. This is quite sharp and with vigorous slashing movements the snake rips an opening in the shell. After resting from this effort, the young snake wriggles through the hole it has made and soon afterwards the egg tooth drops off.

Not all snakes lay eggs. Some give birth to live young and although these offspring have no need of an egg-tooth, it is usually present, bent back out of harm's way. The eggs of these snakes are retained within the female's body for the incubation period and the eggs hatch as they are laid.

(Left) The Tree Boa is a particularly attractive boa from tropical South America. When resting it stacks up the loops of its body along a branch, with its head inside the outer coils. Its coloration makes it difficult to see among the foliage.

Does a Boa Constrictor crush its prey?

The boas and pythons are giant constricting snakes. Many people imagine this means they coil themselves around their prey, and squeeze and squeeze until the victim is crushed to death. This is, in fact, not so. A Boa Constrictor, or any other boa or python, strikes at its prey with an open mouth. Backward-pointing teeth grip the animal while the snake quickly throws loops of its body around its prey. The snake may secure itself by coiling its tail around a fixed object, such as a tree, and then tightens two or three of the coils around its victim. This prevents the animal's ribs from moving so that it stops breathing and quickly suffocates. As soon as the victim ceases struggling the boa unwinds itself and starts to swallow it. Boa Constrictors eat reptiles, birds and small mammals.

The Royal Python *(above)* and the Rubber Boa *(below)* both curl up into balls when threatened.

The Boa Constrictor is found in Central and Southern America and can grow to 15 feet in length.

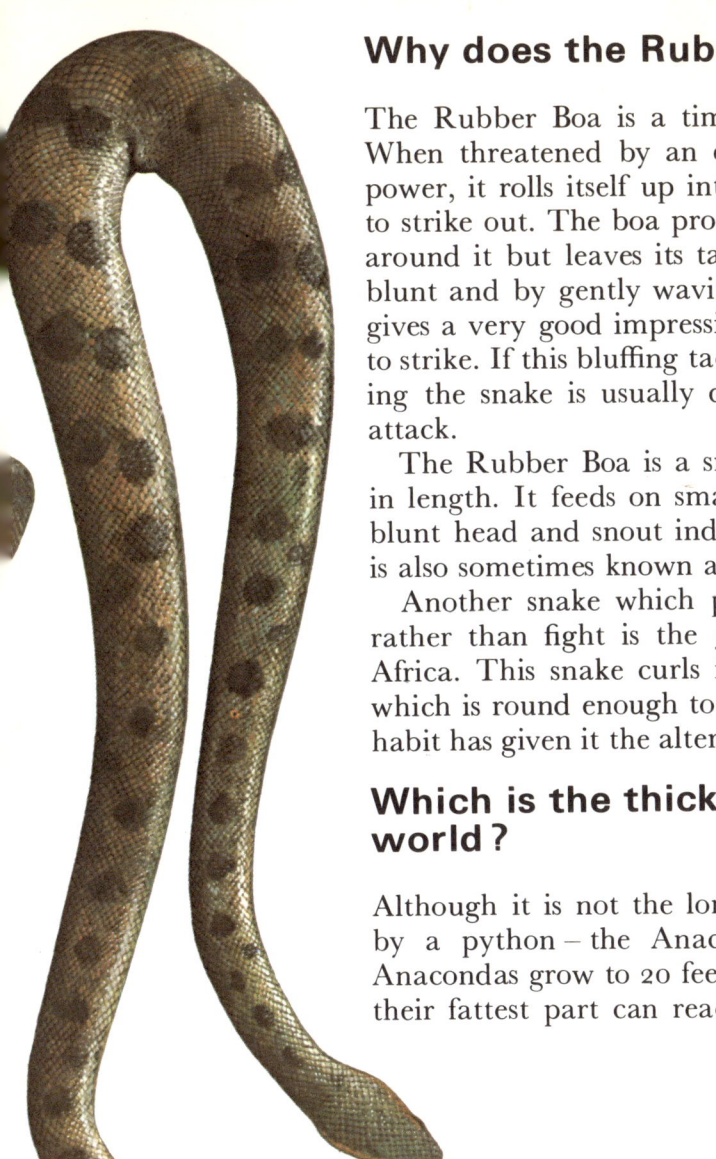

Why does the Rubber Boa wave its tail?

The Rubber Boa is a timid snake from North America. When threatened by an enemy it knows it cannot overpower, it rolls itself up into a ball rather than attempting to strike out. The boa protects its head by coiling its body around it but leaves its tail out. The tail is both stiff and blunt and by gently waving it backwards and forwards it gives a very good impression of the head of a snake about to strike. If this bluffing tactic succeeds, the animal disturbing the snake is usually deterred from pressing home an attack.

The Rubber Boa is a small boa growing to only 2 feet in length. It feeds on small mammals and lizards and its blunt head and snout indicate a burrowing way of life. It is also sometimes known as the Silver Boa.

Another snake which prefers to roll up out of danger rather than fight is the 5-foot Royal Python from West Africa. This snake curls itself up very tightly into a ball which is round enough to be rolled for some distance. The habit has given it the alternative name of Ball Python.

Which is the thickest snake in the world?

Although it is not the longest snake – this title is claimed by a python – the Anaconda is certainly the thickest. Anacondas grow to 20 feet in length and measured around their fattest part can reach 3 feet in diameter. Naturally such a colossal snake (weighing about 17 stone) cannot move swiftly and so the Anaconda relies on lying in wait for its prey. One favourite place is in the trees that overhang river banks and swamps, and another is in the shallows of the water itself. As animals come down to the water to drink the Anaconda pounces from its hiding place and overpowers its startled prey. The Anaconda is sluggish on land, but it can swim and it can climb up the branches of trees to rest and sunbathe during the day. Although there are stories of it being a man-eater, these are doubtful, no reliable evidence ever having been produced to prove them.

By lying in wait near water, the Anaconda surprises and overcomes mammals as large as the Agouti *above right*, shown to scale.

The 3-foot Flying Snake from South-east Asia, India and Ceylon flattens its body and glides from tree to tree. Both the tree-snakes illustrated here are venomous, killing their prey with poison injected through their fangs.

Do snakes live in trees?

(Above) The African Vine Snake puffs out its throat when alarmed to reveal the more brightly coloured skin of its throat.

Many snakes live in trees. One in particular, the African Vine Snake, shows most of the tree-snake characteristics. It is only about 4 feet in length and nearly half of this is the snake's long and slender tail. The slim shape of the Vine Snake is ideal for climbing quickly through the branches of trees, and its mottled colouring provides a perfect camouflage among the foliage. The Vine Snake lies along branches with about one third of its body extended into space. It remains like this for long periods, carefully scanning the area for birds, frogs, chameleons and geckos. It has very good eyesight for a snake. Its eyes are situated on the front of the head and grooves along the snake's nose give uninterrupted vision. The tongue of the Vine Snake is brightly coloured. The constant flicking in and out is thought to attract prey.

Can snakes fly?

Snakes cannot fly but one or two have become very good at gliding. A snake with this ability launches itself into space from high up in a tree. As it falls it flattens its body and draws itself in underneath to an almost concave shape. The increased surface area cushions the snake's fall and enables it to prolong its descent through the air. It either glides into another tree in this way, or all the way to the ground. One flying snake is also good at leaping across wide gaps in the branches. It coils itself up, then suddenly unwinds, shooting itself across the gap in a stiff, upright position.

Do snakes eat snakes?

King snakes are particularly fond of eating other snakes although they do not go out of their way to track them down. A chance encounter with another species usually results in the king snake overcoming the other by constriction. King snakes are immune to the venom of poisonous snakes and so even such deadly species as rattlesnakes and copperheads are not safe from them. King snakes are protected in some areas, for their snake-eating habits are considered useful.

A king snake *(right)* constricting a copperhead snake. King snakes are common in the southern United States.

How does the Egg-eating Snake eat eggs?

The Egg-eating Snake lives in trees in Africa and spends most of its time gliding along branches in search of birds' nests. Once it has found an egg the snake carefully examines it to gauge its size, and by flicking out its tongue it can tell whether the egg is bad or not. If all is satisfactory the snake yawns once or twice, practising for the task ahead, and then holds the egg steady with its body while it starts the swallow. The jaws of snakes are especially hinged to enable them to open very wide but, nevertheless, it takes the Egg-eating Snake about twenty minutes to work its jaws around the egg. Once the egg is swallowed it immediately comes up against a row of sharp projections sticking through the skin in the roof of the throat. These are extensions from bones of the spine. The snake arches its neck and with a quick sawing movement the egg is rubbed against this row of 'teeth', collapsing the egg and releasing its contents. These pass into the stomach and a valve immediately closes to prevent their return while the snake spits out the shattered shell.

How do snakes eat snails?

If snakes can swallow eggs you might think they can easily swallow snails. They can, of course, but a snail's shell is much tougher than that of an egg. Thirst snakes have overcome this problem by having a short upper jaw and an

(Above) The sequence of events in the consumption of an egg by an Egg-eating Snake. The red point indicates the sharp projections in the throat.

(Right) A thirst snake extracts a snail from its shell by hooking it out with the teeth of its long lower jaw.

In contrast to the might of the pythons, the slender thread snakes live inconspicuously underground, feeding on termites.

elongated lower jaw. While the upper jaw holds the snail, the lower jaw reaches in and long teeth grip the snail's soft body. With a quick twist, the snail is withdrawn and eaten.

Could a python kill a leopard?

There is a widely quoted report of the remains of a leopard being found in the stomach of an Indian Python. This particular python was 18 feet long and had apparently suffered little damage in the tremendous struggle it must have had to suffocate such a large mammal. A large meal of this size lasts a python a long time.

The Indian Python feeds on mammals, birds and reptiles of considerable size. The specimen that managed to kill a leopard must have been particularly powerful.

What is the largest poisonous snake in the world?

Imagine strolling along a jungle path and suddenly meeting a 14-foot King Cobra rearing up to head height with hood spread and fangs bared. A terrifying experience but one that could easily happen if the path happened to pass near the nest of the snake. King Cobras are very aggressive, venomous snakes and all too keen to attack if their nest is disturbed in any way. The record length for a King Cobra is 18 feet and this makes it the longest poisonous snake in the world. It comes from India, southern China and South-east Asia.

Cobras are well known for rearing up from the ground when annoyed and spreading their impressive neck hood. The venom is produced in glands situated just behind the cobra's eyes. Ducts carry the poison to the hollow fangs at the front of the mouth. When the snake bites a victim, muscles squeeze the glands and force the venom down the fangs and into the wound. Once the victim has been paralyzed by the venom, it is quickly devoured.

The magnificent King Cobra *(below)*, and the Indian Cobra *(below right)* showing its characteristically marked hood.

Do cobras dance for snake-charmers?

You have probably seen pictures of cobras emerging from baskets and swaying to the music from a snake-charmer's flute. The erect head and spread hood of the snake is merely a reaction to its sudden emergence from the dark basket into bright sunlight. The snake cannot hear the music, of course, because it is deaf (see page 132). It cannot see very well either and its movements are the result of following the first object that it sees – the snake-charmer's flute. The Indian usually sways in time with the music himself and so it certainly looks as if the snake is dancing.

These drawings show the position of a cobra's venom glands and the duct through the fang to its tip.

Which cobra 'spits' at its prey?

(Below) The Ringhals is a cobra that sprays venom at an attacker. The small drawing shows the passage of venom down the hollow fang and out at the front.

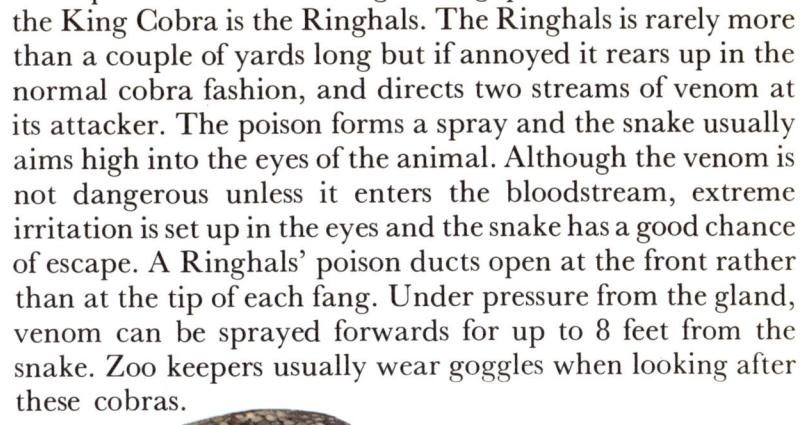

Perhaps an even more frightening poisonous snake than the King Cobra is the Ringhals. The Ringhals is rarely more than a couple of yards long but if annoyed it rears up in the normal cobra fashion, and directs two streams of venom at its attacker. The poison forms a spray and the snake usually aims high into the eyes of the animal. Although the venom is not dangerous unless it enters the bloodstream, extreme irritation is set up in the eyes and the snake has a good chance of escape. A Ringhals' poison ducts open at the front rather than at the tip of each fang. Under pressure from the gland, venom can be sprayed forwards for up to 8 feet from the snake. Zoo keepers usually wear goggles when looking after these cobras.

How do these two snakes differ?

At first glance the strikingly coloured snakes below look identical. If you look again you will see a slight variation in the colour banding between the two. Venomous coral snakes come from North, Central and South America, Africa and Australia. Wherever they occur, other species are found with markings practically, but not quite, the same. The bright colours are a warning to predators that the coral snakes are poisonous, and so the mimics also benefit from this protection, although they are not venomous.

(Left) A true coral snake (top) shows a slightly different sequence of bands from a mimicking false coral snake (bottom).

Seasnakes are found in the warm, coastal waters of the Indian and Pacific Oceans. Most are about 4 or 5 feet long.

The drawings *below* are of the large venom glands and fangs of a viper. The fangs are shown folded into the mouth and then erected just before striking a victim.

Which snakes live in the sea?

There is one group of snakes that is so well adapted for life in the sea that most of them never leave it. If you caught a seasnake and placed it on the ground it would flop around and show no sign of the efficient slithering of its land relatives. In the water, however, seasnakes are excellent swimmers. Their bodies are flattened from side to side towards the rear end, and the tail is often paddle-shaped to help drive the snake forward. Other adaptations of the seasnakes include nostrils on the top of the head and valves in the nostrils which prevent the entry of water when the snake is diving.

Seasnakes are extremely venomous but surprisingly they are among the least aggressive of poisonous snakes. They are particularly fond of eels which succumb within seconds to their venom. The quick-acting venom presumably prevents the prey escaping into awkward holes and crevices once it has been bitten. Seasnakes rarely bite man and fishermen disentangle them from their nets by hand with little fear.

Which snakes have folding fangs?

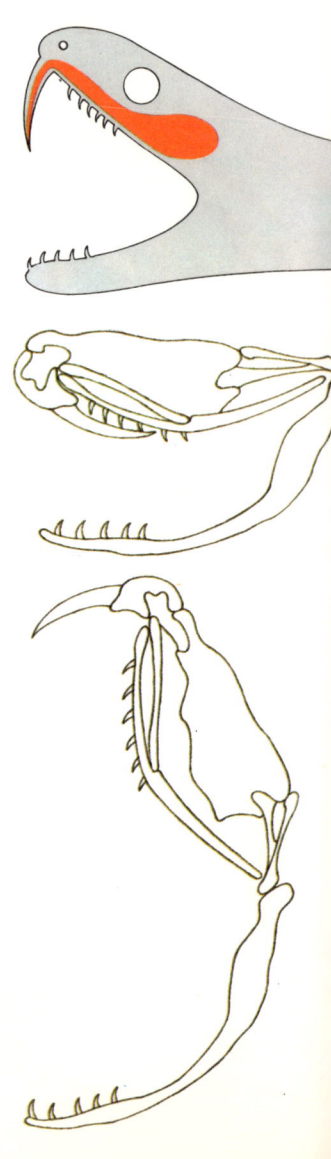

The snakes with the most advanced venom injection system are those with folding fangs – the vipers and rattlesnakes. These snakes have large venom glands and long fangs which are folded into the mouth when not in use. When about to strike, the snake erects its fangs and then plunges them deep into its victim. Unlike other venomous snakes which hang on to their prey, the viper immediately withdraws its fangs and waits for the deadly venom to do its work. In a short time, depending on the size of the prey, the animal dies. Because they have such an effective striking action, vipers do not bother to pursue their prey. They merely lie in wait for a victim and then trail it for the short distance it manages to cover after being bitten.

How dangerous is the Adder?

Unless you are a young child, you need have no real fears about the effects of an adder bite. Adders are vipers and so have an efficient venom, but it is only really effective on small prey – lizards, mice and shrews. Adders rarely bite humans unless they are frightened by being trodden on or deliberately provoked. Many people try to kill them on sight but this is hardly necessary for they are actually quite useful in killing rodents. If someone is unlucky enough to be bitten, he may feel ill for a day or two but the chances are he will recover.

The Horned Asp *(top)* and the Adder *(above)* are both vipers. The Horned Asp lives in North African deserts. You can recognize an Adder by the V-shape on its head and its zig-zag markings.

What makes a rattlesnake rattle?

The distinctive rattle from a rattlesnake is actually more of a buzz. The sound is a warning to an unwary animal or person that the rattler is nearby, and does not want to be trodden on or interfered with in any way. A series of hollow interlocking scales produces the noise. In most snakes the last scale is a cone fitting over the tail. When the snake sheds its skin this scale drops off before being replaced. The young rattler loses its last scale at the first moult but underneath there is a thicker scale – the first rattle. This is loosened at the next moult but remains attached to the snake's tail. After subsequent moults new end scales form and a series of loosely attached cones is gradually built up. These make the characteristic sound when rattled together.

The Eastern Diamondback Rattlesnake is one of the largest rattlers of North America.

(Far left) A close-up view of a rattlesnake's rattle. The rattle does not grow indefinitely. The end segments tend to wear and eventually drop off and so the rattle usually comprises no more than fourteen rattles. The diagram *(left)* shows a cross section through the end of a rattle. It illustrates how each segment has two constrictions. The segments interlock and are held together by one being bigger at a certain point than its predecessor.

Which are the biggest rattlers?

The rattlesnakes are confined almost entirely to North America. The two largest are the Eastern and Western Diamondback Rattlesnakes. The Eastern Diamondback averages more than 5 feet in length, but the record is a specimen over 8 feet long. It lives in undisturbed brush country and feeds mainly on rabbits. The Western Diamondback averages about $4\frac{1}{2}$ feet in length and is rarely more than 7 feet. It lives in prairies and deserts. Rattlers as big as this can have fangs nearly an inch long.

Which is the Horned Rattlesnake?

We have already met the Horned Rattlesnake under its other name when we discovered how snakes moved (see page 128). The Horned Rattlesnake is another name for the Sidewinder. You will remember that this snake has evolved a special method of moving over loose, shifting desert sand. Such unstable terrain slows down the normal slithering action of other snakes, and so the Sidewinder has a considerable advantage in its particular habitat. The two scales enlarged to form horns probably protect the snake's eyes from the glare of the sun. They may also prevent sand from drifting into the eyes when the Sidewinder lies half buried to escape the sun's heat.

The Horned Rattlesnake from the desert areas of the United States is also known as the Sidewinder.

BIRDS

Archaeopteryx had a lizard-like head, teeth, claws on the wings and a long reptile-like tail. It would have been classed as a reptile had it not been for its feathers. Feathers differentiate all birds from reptiles (and other animals). Modern birds retain scales on their feet.

How did birds evolve from reptiles?

As we have seen (page 113), pterodactyls were the first reptiles to master the air. They made clumsy gliding flights on wide flaps of skin. Pterodactyls proved an unsuccessful group of animals, however, and while they were dying out other reptiles experimented with flight. These were probably long-tailed lizards that ran on their hind legs. They became attracted to life in trees either to find food or to escape enemies, and eventually they too started gliding. In their case the scales on the front limbs gradually changed into feathers to form a light, expanded wing surface. We

Prehistoric running birds are shown from *far left* to *right*: the 6-foot *Phororhachos* and the 7-foot *Diatryma*. A rhea is shown next – a modern South American representative of running birds – and then *(below)* an enormous 12-foot Moa.

have a good idea of how some of these 'feathered reptiles' looked from the famous fossil *Archaeopteryx*, which has both reptile and bird characteristics.

Which birds were the first true birds?

The fossil record of bird evolution is incomplete because birds do not make good fossils. They are light and fragile and so are not easily preserved. The chances of the ancestors of modern birds falling into the right sort of mud and silt for good fossilization were remote. Those that died on land, of course, were quickly eaten up, as they are today. However, after *Archaeopteryx* we know of two kinds of prehistoric seabirds that were true birds. *Ichthyornis* was small, rather like a gull or tern of today, and was probably a fish eater. *Hesperornis*, on the other hand, was a much larger diving bird that had lost the power of flight.

(Left) Ichthyornis was 8 inches tall and may have been an early gull. It could fly well.

(Left) Hesperornis was about 5 feet long and had powerful legs and feet for swimming. It might have been an early diver or loon.

Which were the giant running birds?

One group of early birds evolved in areas free from carnivorous predators. They therefore spent much of their time on the ground and eventually developed into giant running birds. On the prehistoric plains of North America *Phororhachos* and *Diatryma* roamed. These were enormous birds with powerful legs, and heads as large as those of horses. They were carnivorous but others, like the Moas, were inoffensive grazers although still huge. Moas became extinct not many centuries ago and were wiped out by Maori tribes in New Zealand through overhunting.

149

Which are the modern running birds?

The flightless Australian Cassowary *(below)* is built like a bird battering ram, in contrast to the chicken-sized kiwi *(right)* which probes the ground for earthworms and grubs.

There are several groups of birds alive today that are unable to fly. These are the ostriches, rheas, emus, cassowaries, kiwis and penguins, and it is worthwhile considering why they cannot fly. You might think that enormous birds like the cassowary, emu and ostrich are too heavy to lift themselves into the air. This is, of course, a factor, but it is not the real reason why these birds have tiny wings and are unable to take to the air. It was at one time thought that the modern flightless birds evolved separately from the animals that eventually gave rise to the flying birds. The flightless birds were assumed to have not yet developed the power of flight because their wings are still evolving. This view is no longer held. It is now realized that the modern running birds did have flying ancestors, but that they lost the power of flight through disuse of their wings. Living in areas free from predatory enemies, the running birds have had no need to fly away from danger, and so have developed powerful legs and bodies for running about instead.

Why does the cassowary have a bony crest?

The bone 'helmet' of the Australian cassowary can be directly related to its habit of charging through dense undergrowth at speeds of up to 30 miles an hour. This stocky, flightless bird comes from northern Australia and New Guinea and may be up to 5 feet high. It is rarely seen for it prefers to live in the middle of impenetrable rain

At 5 to 6 feet high the emu is the second largest bird in the world. It lives in most undeveloped areas of Australia.

forests and so not much is known about its habits in the wild. It is fairly obvious, however, that with its protective horny crest, powerful, wedge-shaped body, and long, flexible feathers, the cassowary is well equipped for forcing its way through thick jungle at speed. A cassowary in a zoo once charged through the netting of its cage, leaving a clear outline of its body in the wire.

What is the largest living bird?

Standing 8 feet high and weighing 300 pounds, the ostrich is easily the largest bird in the world. On African grasslands it has adopted the habits of a grazing animal and groups roam about feeding in the company of zebras and gazelles. It is well adapted to this sort of habitat. Good eyesight and a long neck enable it to spot danger from a long way off. Powerful thighs and long legs can carry it at 40 miles an hour out of harm's way. It is the only bird with two toes, another feature which enables it to run that much faster over the grassy plains.

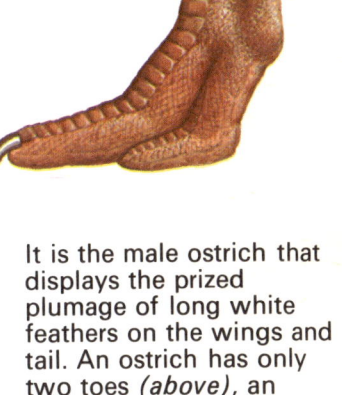

It is the male ostrich that displays the prized plumage of long white feathers on the wings and tail. An ostrich has only two toes *(above)*, an extreme adaptation for running at speed.

A Ringed Penguin *(top)* and a Gentoo Penguin *(below)* chasing fishes. Penguins use their wings as paddles and their feet as a rudder to manoeuvre themselves expertly after their prey.

Which birds 'fly' underwater?

In contrast to the powerful running birds we have already seen, there is one group of flightless birds that at best can only waddle on land. These are the penguins, but what they lack in walking ability they certainly make up for in skill at swimming. Their flipper-like wings are useless for flying but are ideal for propelling the streamlined penguin through the water at speed. Penguins waddle on land because their feet are set so far back on the body. This is just the right position for a rudder, however, and this is how the penguin steers underwater. Penguins are so agile in the sea they can be described as 'flying' underwater.

The King Penguin incubates the single egg on its feet, under an insulating flap of skin.

(Left) Adelie Penguins congregate in their noisy thousands at nesting grounds called rookeries. The nest is a pile of pebbles on which the eggs are laid.

How do penguins cope with the cold?

Some penguins breed during the Antarctic winter and often have to stand around in freezing blizzards of driving snow for hours on end. They withstand such conditions by having a very dense plumage all over the body (unlike the plumage of other birds). Underneath this thick coat of closely packed feathers there is an insulating layer of blubber. This helps maintain the body warmth, and stores food and water as well. If the temperature drops too low, penguins resort to huddling together in an attempt to conserve body heat.

(Right) The Emperor Penguin is the largest penguin at 4 feet, and is shown here next to an Adelie Penguin, as a comparison of their sizes. Both have chicks in attendance.

An Emperor Penguin parent fussing over its chick.

The Great Crested Grebes *above* and *below* are displaying to each other prior to mating. The displays are very elaborate and a number of characteristic movements can be recognized.

(Below) The toes of the Great Crested Grebe have flaps along their length. As the feet thrust through the water the flaps are spread and act like paddles to propel the bird along.

What are these grebes doing?

If you are a bird watcher you may have been lucky enough to watch the spring courtship displays of Great Crested Grebes. The birds face each other and shake their heads in opposite directions, or they may dive and surface with weed in their beaks, rear up breast to breast and sway from side to side. These displays are very exciting to watch. Both male and female grebes have strikingly coloured plumes and ear tufts which emphasize the head movements.

The Great Crested Grebe is a water bird, of course, and you can often see it on gravel pits, reservoirs and large lakes. It is in its element in the water and rarely leaves it, building a nest of floating vegetation in which to lay the eggs. The nest is abandoned as soon as the eggs hatch and the young grebes climb on to the backs of the parents for journeys around the lake. They are even carried underwater when the parent bird dives for food, although sometimes they are dislodged and can be seen to bob up to surface, none the worse for the experience.

Why are albatrosses ringed?

A small metal ring clipped to the leg of an albatross provides valuable information about the extent of the bird's travels if it can be recovered.

This man is carefully placing a metal ring or band on the leg of an albatross. Many species are ringed in this way by bird organizations in order to study bird movements. Many birds migrate – albatrosses travel enormous distances – and much is learnt about this phenomenon by analysis of the information the recovery of the rings provides. The rings are stamped with the name of the organization carrying out the research, and numbers which indicate the place of ringing, the date, and other relevant information. If you ever find a bird with a ring, send the ring to the appropriate people, for you will be helping them to carry out their valuable work.

The slender, long wings of the albatross enable it to soar effortlessly over the ocean for miles and miles. Albatrosses feed on fishes, squids and crustaceans that they can catch on the surface of the sea. They will follow a ship for miles to feed on the refuse dumped overboard.

Does the bill of a pelican 'hold more than its belly can'?

The pouch of a White Pelican from south-east Europe, Asia and Africa holds three gallons, more than twice the capacity of its stomach. This gives the impression that the pelican uses its enormous pouch to store food. Indeed it is often said that when full the food in the beak lasts the pelican for a week. However, the pouch is used not for storage but for fishing and all the fishes caught are eaten immediately. Pelicans sometimes fish together in line and drive the fishes into shoals. They all dip their beaks in together and scoop out the fishes.

The Chilean Pelican *(above left)* and the Spotted-billed Pelican *(above)*. In spite of their size and awkward shape, pelicans are graceful fliers. They fly in formation with wing beats synchronized.

(Right) The strong webbed foot of a pelican.

(Left) The Shag is a cormorant found along the shores of Europe.

How do cormorants fish for man?

In China and Japan the ancient art of cormorant fishing dates back for hundreds and hundreds of years. The cormorants are trained to fish tied to a long lead and with a leather thong around their necks. This prevents the birds from swallowing their catches which they disgorge into the boat when the owner pulls them in. At the end of the night's fishing the owner unties the thong and gives the cormorants their share of the catch to eat. Modern methods have made cormorant fishing uneconomic in Asia but it is still demonstrated as a tourist attraction.

Cormorant fishing is carried out at night. Large flares in the boats attract fishes to the fishing area.

Why is the frigate bird the 'pirate of the seas'?

The piratical behaviour of buccaneers of old has been compared to the way a frigate bird obtains food at certain times of the year. By flying alongside another bird and pecking at it until it realizes it cannot escape, the frigate bird obtains a meal for nothing. If the victim has just fed, its crop will be full of half-digested mush. In fear, or to lighten its load so that it can escape the frigate bird, the bird will disgorge the contents of its crop. This the frigate bird pounces on as it falls and scoops it into its beak before it hits the water. You will realize from this that the frigate birds are superb fliers.

The Magnificent Frigate Bird inflates its colourful throat pouch in the breeding season to attract a mate.

How do herons and bitterns deal with fish slime?

Herons and bitterns are long-legged water birds. They wade about in shallow water darting their long beaks under the surface now and again to grab fishes. Alternatively they may stand still in the water and wait for their prey to come to them. They also eat small animals – frogs, water voles, rats, other water birds and even young rabbits – but fishes are the main part of their diet. As everybody knows, freshly caught fishes are very slimy and so the heron soon gets a lot of fish slime on its feathers. The bittern has more of a problem. It is partial to eels which are covered with even more slime than fishes and which wriggle a great deal more when caught.

Herons and bitterns remove the slime by dusting themselves down with a fine powder produced from patches of special feathers. These feathers never fall out and are continually fraying at their ends to form the powder. Herons distribute the powder over their feathers using the beak. Bitterns rub their slimy heads in the powder patch. After a short time the powder absorbs the slime and the birds clean their plumage by combing it out with a specially serrated claw on the middle toe.

Herons *(left)* nest in tree-top colonies. The nests are platforms of twigs and they are used year after year.

The bittern *(below left)* is adopting the defensive motionless posture. The bittern *(below right)* is cleaning eel slime from its beak with its serrated claws.

Why does a bittern freeze when startled?

Rather than run away when disturbed, a bittern will thrust its head and neck into the air and stand motionless. This bird lives in the dense reed beds of marshes and it relies on its remarkable camouflage to escape detection. The striped plumage of its breast blends perfectly with a background of reeds. By squinting under its beak in this position, the bittern can accurately judge the range of the intruder, and decide whether or not to fly off.

Why were the egret's feathers nearly its downfall?

In the breeding season many egrets display beautiful long feathery plumes which grow from the head, breast and back. At the turn of the century, these plumes, called aigrettes, became very popular for decorating hats. The millinery trade demanded enormous numbers of aigrettes and thousands and thousands of birds were killed at a time of year when they were most vulnerable. Nests were deserted and chicks left to die to increase the disastrous effect of the slaughter. In the end, due to the efforts of conservation bodies publicizing the plight of the egrets, public opinion was turned against the use of aigrettes in hats and the demand slumped. The birds are now protected in many parts of their range.

These Little Egrets at nest from southern Europe and Asia, Africa and Australia show the fine, trailing plumes that were so prized for decorating hats.

Where do spoonbills and ibises live?

Spoonbills and ibises are wading birds of the same bird family. They live in flocks and fly with the head held straight out in front and the legs trailing behind. Both groups fly slowly, but whereas spoonbills fly with regular wingbeats, all the ibises in a group alternate flapping with gliding so that they fly in unison. The Common Spoonbill breeds in northern and southern Europe, southern Asia and Africa. The Roseate Spoonbill is found in the southern United States and through much of South America. The Scarlet Ibis lives in tropical America from Venezuela to Brazil.

The bill of an ibis is downcurved for probing along the lake shore, while that of a spoonbill is spoon-shaped for sifting small organisms from mud and water. Roseate Spoonbills *(below left)* and Scarlet Ibises *(top right)* are shown.

(Above) The strange-looking beak of the flamingo is unique in the bird world.

Why do flamingos have bent beaks?

The beak of a flamingo looks as if it has been broken in half and the halves bent downwards and rejoined. As you might expect there is a very good reason for this peculiar shape. Flamingos like to live in shallow lagoons and lakes. Despite their large size and their large beaks flamingos feed on the smallest of organisms in the water. The flamingo stalks along with its head bent right down to dip the beak in the water. In this position the upper half is underneath and the beak is now an ideal scooping organ. The flamingo sweeps its head from side to side through the water to collect tiny molluscs, crustaceans and single-celled algae. As the tongue pumps water through the beak, this food is caught on a sieve-like structure inside and passed down the throat.

(Below) Greater Flamingos looking after a group of youngsters.

Two beautiful flamingos from high altitude lakes in South America: the rare James' Flamingo *(left)* and the Andean Flamingo *(right)*.

Why is this duckling following a model mother?

It has been known for a long time that the young of ducks, geese and chickens sometimes behave very strangely after hatching. If the parent duck, for example, is absent for some reason, ducklings will form an attachment with any object or person that comes close to them. To them the new object or person becomes their 'mother' and they will trail behind if the 'mother' moves. It seems that the strong attachment is made at a particular time after hatching and if the parent bird should appear later it will be ignored by the duckling. Some very strange friendships indeed have been made by young birds. One became firmly attached to a ping-pong ball, imagining it to be its mother, and others have adopted a person as their parent, following him everywhere. When the ducklings hatch normally they form this strong attachment to their natural mother, of course. This ensures that when she leaves the nest and waddles to the comparative safety of the water, they will all waddle closely behind. They realize at this time that they are ducks and not ping-pong balls or people, and so will be able to recognize their own kind later in life.

The newly hatched duckling *(above)* will adopt an artificial 'mother' in the absence of its real mother. It will even climb obstacles to follow a model duck *(above left)*.

All these red-faced ducks are Muscovy Ducks although they have quite different colouring.

Where do ugly muscovies come from?

You may be feeding the ducks one day when a scruffy fat duck with a red knobbly face and black and white plumage swims on the scene. This is a Muscovy Duck and others will probably soon appear although all will have slightly different plumage. Muscovies originally came from the forests of Central and South America. There the wild birds are much more attractive with glossy green feathers. Centuries of domestication have resulted in the muscovies having a rather drab appearance and varied colouring.

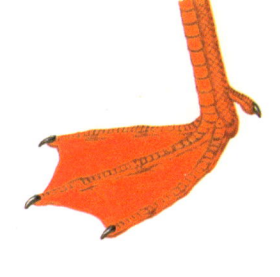

The male Mallard *(left)* loses its colourful plumage at the end of the breeding season. The Mallard's feet *(above)* are strongly webbed like all ducks'.

Which duck provides eiderdown?

As you snuggle under your soft and beautifully warm eiderdown, spare a thought for the Eider Ducks from whose nests the down is collected. Eider ducks are northern sea ducks and breed in colonies on the coast. Man soon realized the value of the down which the birds pluck from their breasts to line their nest. In Scandinavia and Iceland the birds are encouraged to breed in specially prepared and protected areas. The down is harvested from these eiderdown farms twice in each breeding season.

The down from the Eider Duck *(right)* is also used in sleeping bags.

Why shoot nets over geese?

On page 155 we learnt that much valuable information about the movements of birds can be obtained by ringing (or banding). Obviously, the more birds ringed, the better the chance there is of recovering a good proportion. An easy way of catching whole flocks of large birds, like geese, is by cannon or boom net. The net is carefully folded up on the ground next to a known feeding area of the geese. One edge is secured, but to the other, weights are attached. When the geese are feeding, explosive devices fire the weights high over the flock. The net soars into the sky and falls gently over the birds.

Cannon or boom nets are used to catch whole flocks of large birds for ringing experiments. The recovery of the rings gives important information about the migrations of the birds.

(Below left) A tame goose confronts a stranger by lowering its head and hissing and honking loudly.

Which is the best known American goose?

The goose most familiar to North Americans is the Canada Goose. It is a very handsome bird with a black head and neck and a distinctive white cheek patch. The Canada Goose lives in Alaska, Canada and the northern United States. Each winter it migrates south to escape the harsh northern weather. When the warmer weather returns it migrates north again to breed and its arrival there is said to

(Above) Geese are grazers and their bills have serrated edges for cropping grass and plants.

(Right) Three types of domesticated goose. Geese make very amiable pets and soon learn to recognize their owner.

herald the return of spring. In the seventeenth century Canada Geese were introduced to Europe to grace the ornamental ponds and lakes of country houses and parks. They settled down well and are now established as semi-wild birds.

Do geese make good pets?

Geese have been kept as pets for hundreds of years. They are reputed to be extremely good 'watchdogs' and will react very fiercely to anyone they do not recognize. You will need to make some sort of enclosure to prevent your geese wandering and, of course, a large country garden is an ideal place to keep them. Apart from this their requirements are few. They are vegetarian and do not need much feeding. In fact geese will save you mowing the lawn for some time.

Three species of wild goose from *left* to *right*: the Canada Goose, the Greylag Goose and the Brent Goose.

Trumpeter Swans have completely black beaks. These large North American swans were reduced to near extinction by overshooting only forty years ago. Fortunately, vigorous protection measures and breeding programmes have re-established the Trumpeter Swans in North America.

Is the Mute Swan really mute?

It is easy to understand how the Mute Swan came to be so called. Gliding gracefully along with head held high, it looks too gentle to be a noisy bird. It is not altogether a silent bird, however. A party of swans moving up a stream will often make small grunting noises to each other, for example. Other 'conversational' sounds made by Mute Swans include growls and short yaps, and all these sounds probably serve to keep the group together. A more sinister sound is made when the Mute Swan is angry. It arches its neck and half raises its wings before lunging at an intruder with fierce hissing sounds. (It is well known among anglers that you can usually deter a swan from coming too close by hissing loudly at it.)

The Mute Swan *(below)* occasionally gives its cygnets a ride on its back.

What is swan-upping?

The Mute Swan has been a domesticated bird in England for over 800 years. It is sometimes called the 'royal' bird and in fact by the thirteenth century all the swans in England belonged to the Crown. People were allowed to keep swans on open water as long as the birds were prevented from flying away, and they carried their owner's mark. Hundreds of swan marks were developed. Birds usually had a series of notches or a symbol on the orange part of their beak. One man, the Royal Swanherd, was responsible for registering all the marks and for actually marking the birds. Each year he would set out on swan-upping expeditions to gather all the year's cygnets for marking. This ancient practice is still carried out each year on the River Thames where all the swans belong to the Queen.

Which are the black swans?

Not all swans have pure white plumage. Two species, one from Australia and New Zealand and one from South America, have black plumage. The Black Swan must have been an amazing sight to the seventeenth century explorers of Australia who had previously seen only white birds. Black Swans soon arrived in England and America and were popular as decorative curiosities on the lakes and ponds of stately homes. The other black swan, with less black in its plumage, is the Black-necked Swan from South America. It has a black head and neck, a white eye stripe and a red bill. It occurs from southern Brazil to Patagonia and also breeds in the Falkland Islands.

The Black Swan of Australia (*left* and *top*) is not entirely black. It is not apparent from the bird at rest but the trailing edges of the wings are white. The Black-necked Swan (*above*) has a curious, red knobbly bump on its beak.

(Right) Falcons hunt their prey by rushing at it from a great height and stunning it with a tremendous blow from their talons.

(Below) These two birds illustrate the range in size of birds of prey. The smaller is a falconet, about 6 inches in length, and the larger is an Indian Vulture about 30 inches in length. Other vultures are even longer than this.

What is a bird of prey?

Birds of prey are birds which feed on other animals. They catch and eat animals that are usually smaller than themselves, on the ground, in the air, or in water. Not all bother to chase their prey. Some prefer feeding on the flesh of animals already dead. Birds of prey have strong wings and are powerful fliers: some – the vultures – have mastered

(Right) The feet are the main killing weapons of birds of prey and owls. They often suffer damage through injury from constant use. It is interesting to notice that these feet are an owl's and that they are feathered. Owls swallow their prey whole and so do not feed as messily as birds of prey.

(Above) A Kestrel hunts by hovering over open ground and then plunging down on to its prey before it can escape.

the art of soaring flight. They all have curved talons for grabbing and holding their prey, and large hooked beaks for tearing at flesh.

There are several different methods of hunting. Where there is sufficient cover, some eagles hide in a tree and wait for their prey to wander into a clearing. Where the ground is more open, Kestrels and other birds of prey hover over likely places, scouring the ground for the slightest tell-tale movement of a mouse or vole. Over undulating country a slow gliding flight at low level may be used by harriers to cover a wide area with the minimum effort. Carrion eaters soar on outstretched wings at considerable heights for hours on end, peering down for animals already dead, or one about to die. In contrast, small birds of prey like the Sparrowhawk dash at high speed through trees and along hedgerows, hoping to surprise a smaller creature. Buzzards, eagles, falcons, harriers, hawks and vultures comprise the birds of prey; owls also catch smaller animals but they are usually treated separately.

Why do birds of prey have bare feet?

Birds of prey kill with their feet. Some also use the beak but the sharp curved talons of the feet are the main killing weapon. The rear and inside talons are usually larger than the middle and outer talons, and with these the bird exerts a strong pincer grip on the prey. The neck of the creature is dislocated or it is fatally pierced or crushed, but however it dies it is soon torn to pieces by the beak. This is a messy way of feeding and if the feet of a bird of prey were feathered they would soon become matted and bloodstained. Most have bare feet since these are much easier to keep clean.

(Above) A selection of feet of birds of prey illustrating the variety in size and strength. Each type of foot suits each bird for its particular diet and method of hunting.

(Left) A number of Old World vultures clustered on the carcase of a zebra.

The colourful King Vulture *(below)* from Mexico and Argentina is the third largest of the New World vultures.

How do vultures find their prey?

Any animal that has just died in an area frequented by vultures is soon picked over by a horde of these ugly birds. How can they all arrive at one spot so quickly from the huge areas they patrol? Vultures, of course, are the soaring birds of prey mentioned earlier. They have excellent eyesight but they examine not only the ground as they glide high in the sky. They also closely watch each other and the descent of any one bird is always noticed by at least one other. All the vultures from a wide area soon swoop down to see what it was that interested the first bird.

Vultures have weak beaks and feet adapted for running rather than killing. They have bald faces for the same reason that other birds of prey have naked feet. The Sociable Vulture *(top)* is one of the first to arrive at a carcase and tears off large pieces of flesh. The Egyptian Vulture *(bottom)* arrives later and its narrower beak is more suitable for picking the bones left by the larger birds.

How big is the Andean Condor?

The grotesque-looking Andean Condor is one of the two largest flying birds found today. Almost 4 feet in length, with a wingspan of 10 feet, it weighs up to 28 pounds. The California Condor is similar in size. A bird as big as this requires a lot of food and the Andean Condor has to eat at least a pound of meat a day. Condors spend hour after hour gliding effortlessly over enormous areas in search of carrion, although if this is scarce the Andean Condor will attack and kill lambs and calves. It will also come down to feed on stranded animals on the shore, including whales if it is lucky enough to find one.

There are two unrelated groups of vultures, one from the Old World (Europe, Africa and Asia) and one from the New World (North, Central and South America). The New World group includes the condors.

(Below) Large vultures spend hours wheeling and soaring in thermals of warm air rising from the ground.

(Right) The naked head of the Andean Condor is suited to poking around a decomposing carcase.

Golden Eagles will return year after year to the same eyrie. Sites include cliff ledges and caves, trees and sometimes hollows in the ground.

Where do Golden Eagles nest?

In Asia, Golden Eagles have been trained by tribes to hunt wolves.

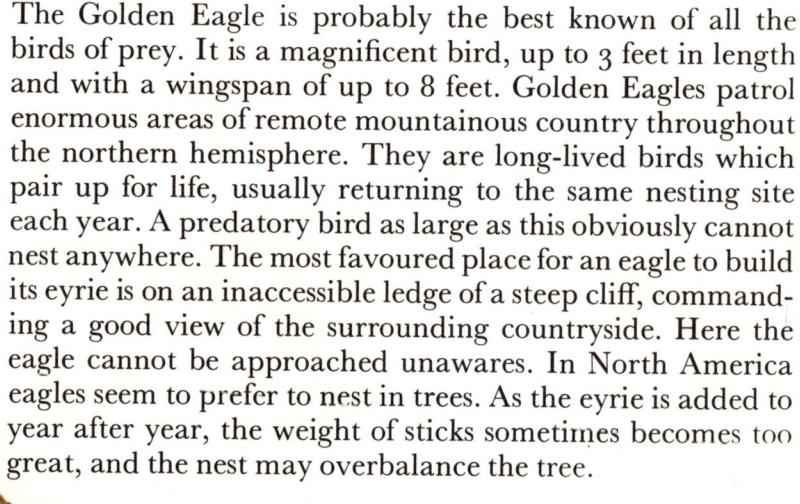

The Golden Eagle is probably the best known of all the birds of prey. It is a magnificent bird, up to 3 feet in length and with a wingspan of up to 8 feet. Golden Eagles patrol enormous areas of remote mountainous country throughout the northern hemisphere. They are long-lived birds which pair up for life, usually returning to the same nesting site each year. A predatory bird as large as this obviously cannot nest anywhere. The most favoured place for an eagle to build its eyrie is on an inaccessible ledge of a steep cliff, commanding a good view of the surrounding countryside. Here the eagle cannot be approached unawares. In North America eagles seem to prefer to nest in trees. As the eyrie is added to year after year, the weight of sticks sometimes becomes too great, and the nest may overbalance the tree.

This is the underside view of a Golden Eagle gliding directly overhead.

How many young are reared?

Two eggs are usually laid by the Golden Eagles, the second within a few days of the first. One eaglet is therefore slightly bigger than the other. If food is scarce the stronger will bully the weaker of the two to the extent that it eventually dies. The stronger bird therefore has a better chance of survival during the periods when its parents are unable to find much food. If food is plentiful, both eaglets survive.

(Right) This sequence shows the development of a Golden Eagle from the newly hatched eaglet *(top)* through the half-grown stage *(middle)*, to the immature bird *(bottom)*. Eaglets leave the eyrie after ten weeks but usually stay nearby to learn the skills of hunting from their parents.

(Above) The white-bellied Sea Eagle lives along the coasts of South-east Asia and feeds on fishes, corals and sea snakes.

How does the Osprey catch fishes?

The feet of an Osprey are adapted for holding fishes. One foot is placed in front of the other on the fish's back, so that the four toes on either side have a very secure hold. The Osprey sometimes disappears from view when it hits the water. In the United States this bird is called the Fish Hawk.

The Osprey is a bird of prey that specializes in catching fishes. You can see this by looking at its feet. Instead of the usual bird of prey arrangement of three front toes and one rear, the Osprey has two at the front and two at the rear, all of equal length. Each toe bears a razor-sharp talon curved downwards, and underneath a patch of special spine-like scales. Both these features enable the Osprey to grasp fishes securely, however slippery. The Osprey circles slowly over water looking out for fishes just below the surface. Once the prey is spotted, the Osprey hovers for a moment, and then plunges downwards. Just before hitting the water it swings its feet forwards to grab the fish. It struggles for a moment to rise again and then flaps up from the surface with its prey held firmly in a vice-like grip.

How does the Secretary bird catch snakes?

The Secretary bird prefers to walk around looking for its prey rather than to fly. As a result its feet are less adapted for killing. The Secretary bird strides around African grasslands on its long legs hoping to disturb its prey. It catches insects, small mammals and lizards, but it is best known for eating snakes. It attacks a snake by shielding itself with open wings and trampling and battering the snake with its feet. Its long scaly legs give it good protection and eventually the snake is beaten to death.

(Right) South African farmers sometimes keep pet Secretary birds to control the snakes and rats on their land.

(Above) The falconer ties a bell around the foot of his bird so that if it flies out of sight he is still able to follow it.

What is falconry?

Falconry is the ancient practice of training birds of prey to kill for man. It dates back thousands of years, the earliest falconers probably using the birds as a means of obtaining food. It soon developed into a sport for kings and queens and the well-to-do, and became very fashionable during the Middle Ages in Europe. Today it is much less widely practised, but small groups of dedicated enthusiasts still train birds for this exciting sport. It is not a sport that anyone can take up, however. For a start, in most countries birds of prey are protected species and in Britain you need a licence to take one from the wild. Immense patience and understanding are needed to train the young birds to fly after prey, kill, and then return to the falconer. It is something you cannot teach yourself and for this reason the sport is exclusive.

The falconer's arm is protected from the bird's claws by a leather gauntlet. He holds the bird by leather straps called jesses which are attached to its feet.

(Left) A made-to-measure leather hood fits snugly over the heads of the falconer's birds, to prevent them being distracted before the moment of flight.

The plumage of the Red Jungle Fowl *(far right foreground)* contrasts with that of a domesticated chicken *(background)* and a variety bred for improved laying *(right)*.

An Australian Mallee Fowl standing beside its nesting mound inside which the eggs are incubated. The mounds vary from 1 to 4 feet in height above ground level and can be 15 feet in diameter.

Which bird operates its own incubator?

Most birds use their body heat to incubate their eggs. However, one bird from Australia utilizes the warmth of a pile of rotting vegetation, a primitive method we first saw demonstrated by a reptile (see page 133). The Mallee Fowl builds an elaborate nesting mound of decaying leaf debris and lays its eggs in the middle. Instead of simply leaving them there, the male Mallee Fowl goes to enormous lengths to ensure that conditions are just right for the eggs. He digs down into the egg chamber every day and checks the temperature. If too warm he will scrape away some of the nest material to allow the eggs to cool down. If too cool he will either expose the eggs to the sun if it is shining, or cover them up well to prevent heat loss. When the eggs hatch the chicks have to struggle their way to the surface.

The male peafowl erects his 'train' when excited and displays to the female by shivering the feathers. She often takes very little notice of this remarkable sight, and is herself drably coloured in contrast. When not displaying, the peacock carries his train just above the ground.

Is the Red Jungle Fowl a chicken?

The brightly coloured Red Jungle Fowl can be found in the forests of the warmer parts of Asia. It looks very much like the chickens you may keep in your garden, and in fact it is probably the ancestor of the domesticated birds. Man first started keeping jungle fowl thousands of years ago. Innumerable improved strains have been bred over the years and some now look very different to their wild relations.

How many feathers are there in a peacock's tail?

Peafowl are birds domesticated for their looks rather than for food. Their haughty appearance and the beautiful tail fan of the male have made them popular decorative birds in the grounds of many a stately home. The male bird grows to $7\frac{1}{2}$ feet in length, two-thirds of which is the 'tail'. This is actually made up of elongated feathers from the lower back and is composed of about 150 magnificent plumes. When these are erected in a fan over the male's body, the effect is extremely impressive.

The Takahe is a primitive flightless bird, about 2 feet high, related to rails and coots. It seems to be a naturally declining species, and is easy prey to weasels and stoats and other predators. The map shows the only area of New Zealand in which it survives.

What is the rarest bird in the world?

The Takahe of South Island, New Zealand has a strong claim to this title. Before 1900 only four birds had ever been caught. Furthermore, Takahe bones were often found with those of the extinct moas (see page 149), and so the Takahe was also considered to exist no longer in the wild. Then in 1948 the ornithological world was rocked by the discovery of a tiny colony of Takahes that had survived in a remote valley on South Island, New Zealand. About two hundred pairs are alive today but although protected, the Takahe shows signs of soon becoming extinct naturally.

Why do cranes dance?

Cranes start dancing by walking stiffly round each other with half-spread wings. They begin to leap high into the air, first one and then the other, drifting slowly down with wings spread and legs trailing. Sticks and leaves may be thrown up during the dance and much bowing and stretching goes on. Dancing is not confined to the breeding season and it often involves whole flocks of birds, including juveniles. It seems that the birds dance for the fun of it and the performance may merely be a spectacular way of working off surplus energy.

The Sarus Crane (above) is one of the largest cranes, and stands 4 feet high. Even cranes as large as this make graceful dancing displays.

The African Jacana *(right)* often carries its young tucked under one wing while stepping out across the lilies. The wide spread of the long toes *(below)* makes this possible.

Which birds trot over lilies?

The jacanas, or lily-trotters, are small birds with very long legs, toes and claws. There are seven species of these interesting birds found in pools, lakes and slow-moving rivers of Central and South America, Africa, southern Asia and Australasia. Although they are wading birds, jacanas much prefer to run lightly over the leaves of floating water plants in a jerky, high-stepping movement. They can do this because the spread of their spindly toes evenly distributes the weight of the body over a wide area. Waterlily leaves can easily support these nimble little birds. They sometimes look as if they are walking on the surface. They can swim but they prefer not to and spend their time running nimbly over lilies in pursuit of insects, molluscs and small fishes.

The dance of the Crowned Crane. This crane has a particularly striking golden crest to enhance the spectacular effect of the high-leaping dance.

Are these birds really injured?

The communal distraction display of pratincoles is designed to prevent predators from finding the vulnerable nests on the ground.

Some birds become very angry if their nesting sites are disturbed. Owls and terns, for example, show little fear and will not hesitate to attack an intruder. Other birds have developed more unusual ways of preventing the discovery of their nest. Pratincoles nest on the ground in regions of Asia, Africa, Australia and southern Europe. If you happen to stumble into a nesting area the birds would probably 'freeze' on their nests in the hope that you wouldn't notice them. If you show no sign of going away the pratincoles begin their distraction display. A group of about twenty birds flutters and crawls about, trailing wings and making plaintive cries. They look as if they are mortally injured. This display is very convincing and the intruder usually follows the birds, which look such easy game, and is skilfully led away from the eggs and chicks.

Male Ruffs develop a collar or ruff of brightly coloured feathers in the breeding season. In America Greater Prairie Chickens put on similar displays to attract females.

Why does a gull have a red spot on its beak?

You may have noticed a red, or sometimes a black spot near the end of a gull's beak. When the parent bird arrives at its nest the spot catches the eye of the newly hatched chick and it instinctively pecks at it. This action stimulates the parent bird to regurgitate some food from its crop and, of course, the chick promptly eats it. This form of communication between young and parent birds has been studied intensively in the Herring Gull. A series of cardboard models of bird heads were presented to chicks to test the pecking reaction. It was discovered that the chick would peck at more or less any shape, as long as the red spot was present. It seems that the red spot is all important in this curious 'begging' behaviour in young gulls.

In tests young gulls pecked at odd cardboard shapes with red spots but not at those without the spot.

A parent Herring Gull is stimulated to disgorge food from its crop by the pecking action of its young.

What are these Ruffs doing?

These birds are also putting on a display, but for a different reason. Whereas most birds pair up in the spring to build a nest and raise a family, male and female Ruffs come together only very briefly at this time. The male birds develop an elaborate head and neck plumage and they strut around in a special area of open ground called the 'lek'. Each defends his own small patch and all this showing-off activity attracts the females to the lek. After selecting the males of their choice, they mate and then go off to build the nest and lay the eggs.

The skimmer's bill is an adaptation to a specialized way of feeding. There are three species of skimmers: one from North and South America, one from Africa and one from India.

The Great Auk *(above)* has been extinct for over a hundred years. Of the members of the auk family the Great Auk had the most obvious 'penguin look'. In fact this was the bird to be first called 'penguin', the name later becoming used for the penguins we know today.

What is the connection between auks and penguins?

The auk family of birds includes the Little Auk and Razorbill, the guillemots, puffins, murrelets and auklets. They all live in the northern hemisphere – the northern half of the world – and are unrelated to the penguins of the southern hemisphere. The interesting connection is that although auks are smaller than penguins and can fly, the two groups are similar in both appearance and habit. They are both groups of strong birds which actively swim and dive beneath the surface after their prey. It seems that the two groups evolved independently of each other in areas with similar conditions but thousand of miles apart. This is called *parallel* or *convergent evolution* (see page 206).

How does the skimmer skim?

Skimmers have a bill shape unique in the bird world. The lower half is much larger than the upper. Unless you know how the bird feeds you might think such a bill would be incapable of holding anything. The skimmer feeds by flying slowly across calm water with its bill wide open. The lower half skims along just under the surface. The instant it touches a small invertebrate or a fish, the upper half snaps shut and the skimmer lifts its head to swallow.

A close-up view of the remarkable bill of a skimmer. On hatching, the two halves of the young skimmer's bill are the same length. By the time the bird is ready to fly, the halves have developed unequally.

Which birds carry water to their young?

Sandgrouse live in desert regions of Africa, Asia and southern Europe. They rest on the ground, often many miles from the nearest waterhole. Once the chicks hatch, the parents have the problem of providing the young birds with water, without which they would soon succumb to the fierce heat of the sun. The male sandgrouse wades into the shallows of the waterhole and thoroughly soaks the specially absorbant feathers on its belly. It then flies back to the nest, laden with water, and the chicks are able to drink by sucking at the feathers.

Sandgrouse are rather plump, streamlined birds related to pigeons. They are good fliers and sometimes travel up to forty miles each day to visit a waterhole.

What is the difference between pigeons and doves?

There is no real difference between pigeons and doves. In the pigeon family there are about three hundred species. Some of these are larger and plumper than the others and have square tails – these are often called pigeons. Others are smaller, sleeker and have pointed tails – these are usually called doves.

Pigeons have been kept by man since Roman times. In those days they were fattened for food. Later on they were used for carrying messages back to their roost and today they are used for racing. Special fancy varieties are also bred for showing, like these two *right*.

Of the many sorts of pigeons there are, you are probably familiar with at least one type depending on whether you live in the town or in the country. If you live in a town you probably know the feral pigeon only too well. These pigeons are descended from domesticated birds. They gather in enormous flocks in public places where people like to feed them. They usually make a nuisance of themselves by fouling pavements and buildings. If you live in the country you probably know the Wood Pigeon best. This pigeon is also considered a pest for it loves to feed on the farmer's crops, so that he has to wage continual war on it.

Two fancy pigeons, the fantail *(top)* and the pouter *(middle)*. The Rockdove *(above)* is the original pigeon from which the fancy varieties are bred.

What do macaws feed on?

The macaws are a group of large and vividly coloured parrots from tropical America. They are popular in zoos and also make good pets. They are quite easy to keep on a T-shaped perch and will often amuse their owner by learning to talk or mimic everyday sounds. It is not known for certain exactly what the macaw's diet is in the wild. It undoubtedly eats fruits, seeds and nuts – the powerful bill cracks open the hard shells of Brazil nuts with ease – but it also probably eats insects and their larvae. In captivity it is quite happy to accept peanuts, various types of seeds, fruit and meat.

Where do budgerigars live in the wild?

The parakeets are a widespread group of small Old World parrots. Best known is the Grass Parakeet or Budgerigar which is popular as a cage bird in so many homes. Budgerigars come from Australia. Large, chattering flocks feed among the grasses of the wide, inland plains. They eat the seeds of a variety of grasses, the fresh shoots of plants and any small insects they may discover while foraging. If you keep a budgie, do not be surprised if it snaps at a fly or other insect, for it is merely supplementing its diet like its wild relatives. Wild budgerigars are predominantly grass green in colour with yellow heads and blue tails. They make a spectacular sight as they flock each morning and evening to drink at a waterhole.

The Scarlet Macaw *(above)* from Mexico and Central America is the largest of the group at 3 feet in length. Two feet of this consists of the tail.

(Right) The name Budgerigar is derived from an aboriginal word 'betcherrygah' which means 'good food'.

Why do owls have such large, flat faces?

Owls are another group of birds that catch smaller animals for food. Like the hawks and eagles (see pages 168 to 175) they also have hooked beaks and sharp talons for killing their prey, but they are not related to these groups. The major difference between owls and other birds of prey is that owls do their hunting at night. If you set out on a dark, moonless night to catch a fieldmouse you wouldn't find it easy. How does the owl manage?

The owl's senses of seeing and hearing are highly developed. Its large eyes are positioned at the front of its face so that it looks directly forward, as you do. Because the field of view of each eye overlaps, the owl can see depth and can therefore judge distance accurately. (Cover up one eye yourself and see if you can judge distance as well as with both eyes open.)

The owl's greatest aid to night-hunting, however, is its excellent hearing. Its ears are large but are of course hidden under its feathers. The large dish shape of its face detects the faintest rustle from the ground, and instantly pinpoints the position of the mouse or other animal that made it.

Another refinement of the owl is its ability to fly without making a sound. Soft down on the flight feathers of each wing muffles their beating through the air. This has two advantages. The owl's sensitive hearing is not distracted, and the mouse nestling in the undergrowth has no warning of the owl's approach.

Owls vary greatly in size as can be seen by the contrast between the Great Eagle Owl *(top)*, which is as big as an eagle, and the tiny 5½-inch Elf Owl.

The owl's characteristic dish-shaped face shows very clearly in these Barn Owls *(right)*.

The Great Grey Owl *(below)* is another large owl at 2½ feet in length, whereas the Little Owl *(left)* is an 8-inch bird.

Can an owl turn its head right round?

The owl has to turn its head to see things on either side because both eyes are at the front. It has been said that if you walk several times round the tree an owl is perched in, by trying to follow you with its eyes, it will throttle itself. This is of course complete nonsense. The owl turns its head half way round, and then quickly switches to the other side, so it only appears to turn its head right round in a full circle.

What is an owl's pellet?

As we have learnt already (see page 168), owls swallow their prey whole. The strong digestive juices in the owl's stomach soon dissolve away all the soft tissues, but the fur or feathers and the bones of the prey remain. This indigestible matter forms a ball and the owl eventually coughs it up as a pellet about 1 to 2 inches long. You may be lucky enough to find pellets beneath the tree in which an owl roosts during the day. If you soften one in a saucer of water, it is interesting to pull it apart to see what the owl has been eating.

Two examples of owls' pellets.

Oilbirds come from northern South America and from Trinidad. South American Indians obtain cooking oil from the nestlings.

How do oilbirds fly through dark caves?

Oilbirds are nocturnal birds that roost inside caves, sometimes up to half-a-mile from the entrance. Every evening they leave the caves to feed and fly down the narrow twisting passages in the pitch blackness without hitting the sides. They do this by using a system of 'echo-location', rather like that used by bats (see page 209). As they fly along they send out a series of clicks which bounce off the walls and projections inside the cave. The echo of each click returns to the oilbird and from the time interval it is able to tell the direction and distance of the projections from which it bounced.

A close relative of the oilbirds is shown *(left)*. Nightjars comprise a large family of night-flying birds that feed by catching insects on the wing. The Long-tailed Nightjar shown is from South-east Asia.

Oilbirds are also interesting because they are the only nocturnal birds to feed solely on fruit. They eat only the rich, oily fruit of certain palm trees and will fly many miles each evening to feed on fruit of the correct ripeness. The young are also fed on the rich fruit and so become very fat until they learn to fly.

Which nests are used in bird's nest soup?

The swiftlet is another bird which nests in caves (and also uses echo-location to fly in darkness). Like other swifts, the swiftlet uses saliva to build its cup-shaped nest on to the cave walls. However, the swiftlet uses a lot more saliva and less additional nesting material. Some nests are constructed purely of saliva and these are the ones that are most prized for making bird's nest soup. The nests are gathered twice a year for the Chinese soup industry by men climbing up on poles to knock them down.

Swifts *(above)* are a group of small birds that spend most of their lives in the air catching insects.

Swiftlets *(right and below)* are closely related to swifts and nest in huge colonies in caves in South-east Asia and on islands of the western Pacific.

What is the Laughing Jackass?

The Laughing Jackass or Kookaburra of Australia is a member of the kingfisher family of birds. Not all kingfishers live near streams and catch fishes. One group lives far from water and feeds on a variety of animals. The Laughing Jackass, 17 inches long, is the largest of this group and is probably best known for its raucous, cackling cry, which can sound almost human.

How do hummingbirds hover?

Hummingbirds have developed the most amazing powers of flight. They can fly straight up and down, forwards, sideways and backwards, and even hover stationary in front of a flower while probing with their bills. To be as manoeuvrable as this in the air, the hummingbird's wings have to beat at a very high speed. A definite hum is produced as these beautiful birds dart from flower to flower sipping sugary nectar, and their wings disappear into a faint blur. The secret of the hovering flight lies in the attachment of the hummingbird's wings to its shoulder. This is a swivel joint and instead of beating up and down, the wings swivel round to beat backwards and forwards in a figure of eight motion. At each stroke forwards and backwards air is forced downwards so that the hummingbird is able to 'hang' in the air. Hummingbirds use up an enormous amount of energy in this high-powered flight and are continually feeding on nectar rich in energy-giving sugars, and insects.

The Laughing Jackass *(above)* is a large kingfisher, valued in Australia for its preference for eating poisonous snakes. It either batters them to death, or flies up and drops them to the ground.

There are over three hundred types of hummingbirds found in the New World. All are small birds with beautiful, iridescent plumage. The Sword-billed Hummingbird is shown *above right*.

Which bird imprisons its mate?

Hornbills tend to nest in tree-holes, either natural or perhaps those left by woodpeckers. When the female is about to lay she is walled up in the hole by the male using a mixture of mud, regurgitated food and saliva. He leaves a small hole through which to feed his mate, who remains within the well-protected nest until the eggs have hatched.

The female hornbill may be confined for up to six weeks within the nest. Her mate is faithful to her all this time and gathers food to regurgitate through the hole for her to eat. Two hornbills from southern Asia are shown *left*.

(Left) A honeyguide leading the way through the African forest to a wild bees' nest. The bird usually enlists the help of a honey badger but has been known to lead Africans to a nest for the same purpose.

The beautifully coloured bill of the Sulphur Toucan.

Which bird leads the way to honey?

Honeyguides are a small group of African birds that feed mainly on insects. They are particularly fond of bees and wasps and some will even enter bees' nests to snap up the insects and their larvae. One or two honeyguides are actually known to eat the beeswax of which the nests are constructed. This is a very rare habit among birds. Even more interesting is the way the birds enlist the help of a honey badger to break open the nest so that they can get at the beeswax. Once a honeyguide discovers an occupied nest it flies off for a short distance and then chatters loudly from a low bush. A honey badger attracted by the urgent

The toucan's bill is very useful for fruit picking.

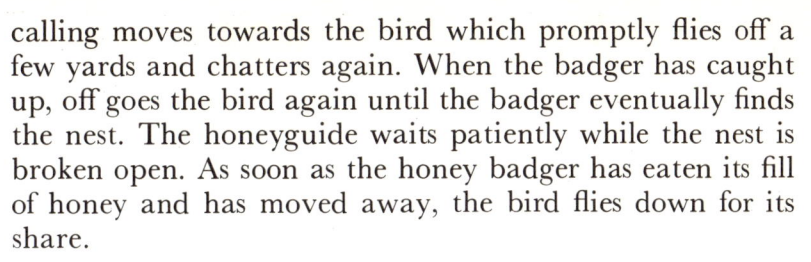

calling moves towards the bird which promptly flies off a few yards and chatters again. When the badger has caught up, off goes the bird again until the badger eventually finds the nest. The honeyguide waits patiently while the nest is broken open. As soon as the honey badger has eaten its fill of honey and has moved away, the bird flies down for its share.

Why do toucans have such large bills?

The enormous, gaily coloured bills of toucans look heavy and ungainly but in fact the birds manage very well with them. The bill is not as heavy as it looks. A network of bony fibres is covered with a hard, horny sheath making the bill remarkably strong and light. It is not known exactly why toucans have such large bills. As fruit-eaters they must find the length useful for reaching out to pluck berries from branches that would not support their weight. They pick berries with the very tip and have to toss them into the air and catch them in their throats to eat them. It is unlikely that the bill evolved as an offensive weapon, but its impressive size may have had some value in frightening off would-be attackers. Another suggestion is that the distinctive colours and prominence of the bill may help the toucans with similar body colouring to recognize each other in the forest. Alternatively, the bright colours may act as signals between the birds either in aggressive displays or in courtship behaviour.

How long is the woodpecker's tongue?

Drilling the bark of trees with a chisel-like bill, the woodpecker exposes the tunnels of wood-boring insect larvae. It flicks in its tongue (up to 6 inches long in the Green Woodpecker) and stabs the grubs with the barbed tip to withdraw them.

Special bones and elastic tissues support the woodpecker's long tongue coiled up within its head *(right)*.

Which birds sew up their nests?

Rather than occupying naturally occurring nest sites in a particular tree, one group of birds prefers to make their own. The nests of these birds fit snugly into suspended pouches or cups, each formed by the stitching together of one or more leaves on a branch. The birds are appropriately called tailor birds and it might indeed be that each pouch is 'tailor made' for its nest. The tailor bird pierces a series of closely spaced holes along the edges of the leaves with its beak, and by pulling plant fibres or silk from spiders' webs through the holes, it draws two leaves together. The ends of each individual stitch are teased out by the bird so that it is secure and the leaves are held in position. Once the pouch is ready the nest is built inside from soft plant down and fine grasses.

Two examples of tailor bird nests are shown. The main tailor bird group comes from southern Africa but there are birds with the same nest-building habit from Australia.

Which birds knit nesting 'socks'?

Have you ever watched anyone knit a sock? They start at the opening and then work downwards to join up the sock at the toe. This is exactly the method of nest construction used by a group of birds called oropendolas from North, Central and South America. The nesting material used for their 'knitting' consists of fibres stripped from palm leaves.

These are twisted around a branch to anchor the nest. A loop of fibres is hung from this foundation and more fibres are woven from it to form the walls of the nest. The loop forms the entrance, and the female oropendola always enters the nest this way to continue her building rather than from the unfinished end. As the weaving is continued downwards the nest increases in diameter until, about a month later, when it is between 3 and 6 feet long, the tube is closed to form a nesting chamber. This is lined with leaves, the eggs being laid at the bottom of the suspended 'sock'. Oropendolas live in colonies. A tree bearing up to one hundred of these long swaying nests is a remarkable sight. Hanging from the outermost branches the nests of the oropendolas are very well protected from predators.

How do honeyeaters feed?

Honeyeaters are birds that specialize in feeding not on honey but on nectar. They are another group of birds with interesting tongues (see page 193). The tongue is long enough to reach to the bottom of flowers and its tip is frayed into a brush-like structure to sweep up the nectar. The sides of the tongue curl over to form a tube through which the nectar is sucked into the mouth. The bills of honeyeaters are long and down-curved for probing into flowers. Some are so modified that they are suitable for feeding on flowers of a particular shape only.

(Above) A female oropendola checks on her nest while her mate keeps watch.

(Left) Honeyeaters are a diverse group of birds found in the Australasian region. This one is the Western Spinebill. Its bill shape is particularly suited to extracting nectar from the long flowers of the banksia plant.

(Left and below) Woodpecker Finches using cactus spines to probe the bark for insects. This is one of the very few cases of a bird using a tool.

Why is this bird holding a cactus spine?

It was Charles Darwin, a nineteenth century naturalist, who first discovered the finches that now bear his name. In 1835 he visited the Galapagos Islands and he noticed there a number of birds which were obviously related to each other but which all had very different feeding habits. He deduced that the finches were all evolved from a common ancestor that had somehow arrived on the islands from the South American mainland. In the absence of many other competing species, these original finches had multiplied and spread across the group of islands. They were able to adapt themselves to various types of habitat and sources of food.

(Below) A line of Starlings on a branch will space themselves out about 4 inches apart.

Some fed predominantly on insects and evolved thin, warbler-like bills, while others fed on cactus and soft fruit, and developed stouter bills. One finch took up the woodpecker way of life, carefully searching the crevices in the bark of trees for insects and grubs. However, this finch lacked the specially adapted tongue of the woodpecker (see page 193), and so it was unable to extract its food in the true woodpecker fashion. Instead it resorted to the use of a tool to do the same job. The Woodpecker Finch holds a cactus spine or twig in its bill and by poking this into the nooks and crannies of the bark, it hooks out the insects from their hiding places. (When the descendants of an ancestral type of animal spread into new habitats and become adapted, forming new types, the process is called *adaptive radiation*.)

Which birds tie knots?

Some of the best nest builders are members of the large weaverbird family from Africa. Using long grasses or strands of palm fibre, weaverbirds have the advantage of being able to interweave and knot one end with the bill while holding down the other end with a foot. The male Village Weaver starts off by weaving a loop from a branch. Standing inside it adds material as far as it can reach on one side and then the other to form a ball-shaped nest. A hole or funnel from underneath the structure forms the entrance.

(Above right) The stages in the construction of the nest of a Village Weaver.

Why are these Starlings evenly spaced?

Look closely at a line of birds on a telephone wire and you will probably notice that they are evenly spaced out along it. Most birds that live in flocks tend to arrange themselves like this. The distance between individuals of a species is usually always the same. Each bird has moved as close to the next bird as it dares and is just out of reach of a peck from its neighbour's bill.

How does the bowerbird attract a mate?

Most male birds advertise their presence to the females in the breeding season by bright plumage. The male bowerbird, however, displays no impressive finery and so must resort to alternative means of attracting a mate. Instead, he builds her an elaborate bower and decorates it with brightly coloured objects in order to impress her. There are seventeen species in the bowerbird group and four types of courting activity are shown. The first group does not bother with a bower at all. The second group, called 'stage-makers', clears an area of ground and lays freshly picked leaves on it. Other bowerbirds, 'maypole-builders', heap twigs around the base of a sapling until the pile is several feet high. Another heap around a neighbouring tree is joined to the first to form a tent-like bower, often with an associated 'garden'. The bird decorates the walls and floor with fresh flowers, mosses, bright berries and snails' shells. The most elaborate bowers are those of the 'avenue-builders'. The bird first lays down a floor of twigs. Then two walls of interwoven twigs are erected, arched at the top, and also decorated with objects such as pebbles, feathers and flowers. Two species even daub the walls with colouring using leaves or bark as a 'brush'.

(Above) The Golden Bowerbird builds a less elaborate maypole bower. Once the birds have mated, the female goes off alone to build a nest and lay the eggs, and the bower is abandoned.

Bowerbirds come from New Guinea and Australia. They are among the few groups of birds known to use a tool (see page 196). The bowerbird, *left*, from New Guinea has built a maypole bower and garden.

Which birds have the most attractive displays?

Of all the birds, the bird of paradise develops the most varied of spectacular plumage during the breeding season. The tails of the males are usually elaborated into beautiful fans with a pair of extra-long feathers trailing down behind. Some birds are adorned with long neck feathers which can be erected in colourful ruffs around their heads. Others hang upside-down from branches and their long plumage hangs around them, creating elegant displays.

Naturally such beautiful birds did not go unnoticed when their home, the island of New Guinea, was first explored in the sixteenth century. A tremendous trade in the birds' skins grew up to satisfy the fashion demands of the nineteenth century. Many birds became endangered. Fortunately the trade in bird of paradise feathers is now controlled and so the birds have a chance to recover their numbers.

(Right) A Magnificent Bird of Paradise displays its gorgeous crest of golden tail feathers in a specially cleared area in the forest.

(Below) The Jay is called a 'passive anter' because it allows ants to run all over it while standing still.

Why is this Jay covered in ants?

The Jay is deliberately letting the wood ants run all over its wings and body by standing near their nest with its wings spread. This is called 'anting' and many birds have been seen doing it, although others actually rub the ants into their feathers. It is thought that the formic acid from the ants (which makes the sting when the ant bites) stimulates the birds' plumage, and may perhaps act as an insecticide.

MAMMALS

What is a mammal?

The greatest disadvantage to the reptiles was their inability to control their body temperature (see page 112). The birds and mammals which evolved from them solved this problem by insulating themselves: the birds with a coat of feathers and the mammals with a covering of hair or fur. Sweat glands in the mammal's skin enabled it to regulate its body temperature – if it became too hot, water was secreted which, as it evaporated, had a cooling effect. Other improvements occurred in the mammals. Instead of hatching from an egg, the young mammal developed to an advanced state inside its mother's body. The blood systems of the developing embryo and the mother are separated by a special organ, the *placenta*. Food substances and oxygen pass from the mother's blood across the placenta to the embryo, and waste substances pass in the opposite direction. After the young mammal is born it receives further nourishment from its mother in the form of milk. This is secreted from *mammary glands* developed from the skin glands already mentioned, and the offspring is suckled until it is able to take solid food.

The mammals, then, are warm-blooded, hairy animals that suckle their young. These characteristics have made them a successful and diverse group.

(Below right) A platypus suckles its young. The milk produced by the female platypus and echidna seeps from pores rather than from proper nipples.

(Above) The platypus lays two eggs in a chamber at the end of a long riverbank tunnel.

Echidnas are sometimes known as spiny anteaters. Powerful limbs and claws are used to tear open termite nests. The egg-pouch is visible on the echidna (right).

(Right) A species of echidna with a long snout and thick black hair found in New Guinea.

Do any mammals lay eggs?

A small group of Australian mammals, the monotremes, are so primitive that they still lay eggs similar to those of the reptiles. These animals are descended from a relative of the reptile ancestor from which the mammals evolved.

The odd appearance of the Duck-billed Platypus caused quite a stir when it was first discovered. It has webbed feet, a flattened beaver-like tail and a wide shovel-like bill, all

The second claw of an echidna's hind foot is enlarged so that it can scratch between its spines.

features indicating a life in water. Indeed it is as a tunnelling, semi-aquatic mammal that the platypus has been a success. At the end of a special tunnel the female lays two leathery eggs in a breeding chamber lined with wet leaves. The young platypus is helpless when it is hatched and feeds on milk which oozes from slits in its mother's fur.

The other monotremes are the echidnas, also found in the Australasian region. They resemble large hedgehogs and lick up ants, termites and beetles with a long sticky tongue. The single egg is carried by the female in a pouch on her belly and on hatching, the young suckles her milk from a primitive mammary gland.

What is a marsupial?

We have seen how the monotremes represent an early stage in the evolution of the mammals from their reptile ancestors. Another group of animals, also found today in the Australian region, represents a later stage in this development. These are the marsupials – the pouched mammals. The young marsupial begins to develop inside its mother's body. However, the special organ (placenta) that supplies the embryo with nourishment from its mother's blood in more advanced (placental) mammals is not present in the marsupials. This means that the embryo cannot develop very far before it is born and it appears at a very immature stage with no hair, eyes, true skin or limbs. It can just about crawl, however, and it immediately seeks the safety of the pouch. It is here that the young marsupial finds the well-developed nipples of its mother's mammary glands. It attaches itself to a nipple, and is suckled for a number of weeks or even months until it has completed its development.

(*Left* and *above*) Tasmanian Devils were once found on the mainland of Australia but are now confined to scrub and rocky country of Tasmania. Persecution by early settlers and the spread of the introduced Dingo were probably responsible.

Why is the Tasmanian Devil so called?

This stockily built, fierce-looking marsupial has earned its name of 'devil' from the vicious way it attacks and kills its prey. It will eat any animal it can find and also feeds on carrion. Its powerful head with strong jaws and teeth make short work of its victims which are crushed and eaten whole. For all its ferocity, however, the Tasmanian Devil is only about the size of a small dog and seems quite harmless to humans. Some people say it makes a good pet.

Do all marsupial pouches open the same way?

When we think of a typical marsupial pouch, the one that usually springs to mind is that of a kangaroo. A kangaroo's pouch opens upwards because it spends most of its time sitting upright. If the pouch opened the other way the young kangaroo would have difficulty staying in it. Bandicoots are marsupials varying in size from rats to rabbits, which run on all fours. All bandicoot pouches open backwards between the hind legs and the young quickly scuttle to the safety of the pouch whenever danger threatens.

(Above) The Southern Short-nosed Bandicoot, a typical Australian marsupial mammal. All bandicoots have backward-opening pouches.

(Above and *right)* The loose skin between the front and hind legs of the Greater Glider Phalanger forms the gliding surface when stretched in flight.

Can any marsupials fly?

Three families of the phalanger group of marsupials have mastered the air to the extent that they can swoop down from high vantage points in long glides. As we have already seen in other animals with this ability (see pages 105 and 137) this is not true flying but is more like delayed falling, since the animal does at least have some control over the direction of the glide. The Greater Glider Phalanger is the most accomplished gliding marsupial. A skin membrane from elbow to ankle, on either side of the body, cushions the animal's fall, and it steers itself through the air with its long, fluffy tail. It can cover one hundred yards with ease in a single glide.

What is the Australian teddy bear?

Practically everyone has owned a teddy bear as a child, but not everyone realizes that the animal it is modelled on is not a bear at all. Bears are placental mammals whereas the Koala, which is often called the Australian teddy bear, is another marsupial mammal grouped with the phalanger family. It is interesting that a number of the marsupials restricted to the Australian region look and act like placental mammals found in other continents. The gliding phalanger is very much like the flying squirrel for example. Why is this?

About fifty million years ago Australia became cut off from the other continents as the mammals evolved. This allowed the marsupials to adapt themselves to live in every kind of habitat, free from competition from the more advanced placental mammals. In every other continent the placentals flourished and replaced the marsupials so that apart from Australia (and America where some opossums have somehow managed to survive), marsupials are found nowhere else in the world. So, in separate continents, representatives from two unrelated groups of mammals became adapted to live in all the available habitats. Where particular conditions were the same in either continent, the animals which evolved to suit them bear similarities in shape and behaviour. This phenomenon is called *parallel* or *convergent evolution* (see page 183).

Two more Australian marsupials from the phalanger family: the monkey-like Spotted Cuscus *(top)* and the Brush-tailed Phalanger *(above)*.

(Left) The young Koala stays with its mother for six months after leaving the pouch and often rides pick-a-back.

What does the Koala eat?

The Koala is a very specialized eater. It feeds only on the leaves of the eucalyptus tree. It will not eat any eucalyptus leaves, however, but only those that are young and tender, and even then it will eat only the very tips. Added to these preferences, some races or varieties of Koala will eat only the leaves from particular types of eucalyptus tree. The fussy feeding habits of the Koala and its inability to adapt to alternative foods make the animal particularly vulnerable. The felling of eucalyptus forests, forest fires and, in the past, the shooting of Koalas for their skins, have sadly reduced their numbers.

(Above) The tiny embryo kangaroo crawls up its mother's fur to the safety of the pouch.

(Right) Once there it quickly finds a nipple and starts to suckle.

(Below) The baby kangaroo is suckled for eight months within the pouch. After leaving its mother it still frequently returns to her for milk for another six months.

How is a baby kangaroo born?

Until about twenty years ago nobody was really sure how baby kangaroos were born. As in all marsupials, the kangaroo is born prematurely and completes its development within the pouch of its mother. What was not known, however, was how the tiny embryo managed to get into the pouch. Some people maintained the mother placed it there with her mouth, others denied this. We now know that before giving birth the mother squats down and licks her pouch and the fur down to her birth opening. The tiny inch-long embryo appears and crawls slowly up her wet fur towards the pouch. In three minutes it has climbed in and quickly closed its mouth over one of the nipples. The tip swells inside its mouth and holds it securely within the pouch while it is being suckled.

What are solenodons?

Solenodons are curious rat-sized creatures with long snouts. They were once found in North America but the only survivors of this ancient group are found on two islands of the West Indies, one species on Cuba and another on Haiti. Solenodons are members of a primitive group of mammals called insectivores. These were the first placental mammals and in general the representatives we know today are small creatures (shrew-like, mole-like or hedgehog-like) which feed on a variety of invertebrates. Solenodons are shy creatures, sleeping during the day and appearing at night to feed. They run clumsily on their toes in a zig-zag course and if chased are likely to trip over.

(Below left) Solenodons have managed to survive on two West Indian islands. Competition from man and introduced higher mammals (dogs and cats for example) has made them rare animals and they seem doomed to extinction.

Which mammals really fly?

True flapping flight, almost as proficient as that of the birds, has been achieved by only one group of mammals, the bats. Bats probably evolved from a group of early insectivores that fed by leaping from the branches of trees to catch passing insects. It is interesting that bats fly by cupping their wings in front of the body and dragging this air behind them, rather than flapping their wings up and down.

Bats can be arranged into two large groups: fruit-eaters and insect-eaters. In general the fruit-eaters are large, can see well and fly in dim light. Insect-eaters are usually smaller, have poor eyesight and have developed a good system of

In many insect-eating bats the nose is obscured by highly folded flaps of skin. Two examples are shown *above* and *below*. It is thought that this 'nose-leaf' concentrates the high-pitched squeaks emitted from the bats' nostrils, and even possibly directs them.

echo-location to enable them to fly in pitch blackness. By sending out series of ultrasonic squeaks and listening for the returning echoes with very efficient ears, the bats can navigate their way around obstacles and catch their insect prey in darkness.

Which mole has a star on its nose?

Moles, also members of the insectivore group of primitive mammals, are burrowing creatures completely adapted for an underground life. A mole on the surface can hardly move forwards at all but once burrowing it quickly disappears from sight. Short but powerful clawed limbs stick out sideways and shovel the soil behind the mole as it tunnels forwards. Moles cannot see very well, some are blind, but they have very highly developed senses of hearing and touch. To perfect its sense of touch, the North American Star-nosed Mole has a remarkable bunch of twenty-two tentacles on the end of its nose. These are highly sensitive and mobile and are brought into use when the mole is searching for food, usually under water.

(Above) The Star-nosed Mole lives near water and dives for its food which it detects with the sensitive feelers on its nose.

The hearing of insect-eating bats is well developed. The Mouse-eared Bat *(above)* is appropriately named. The fruit bats *(right)* feed on dates, figs and bananas.

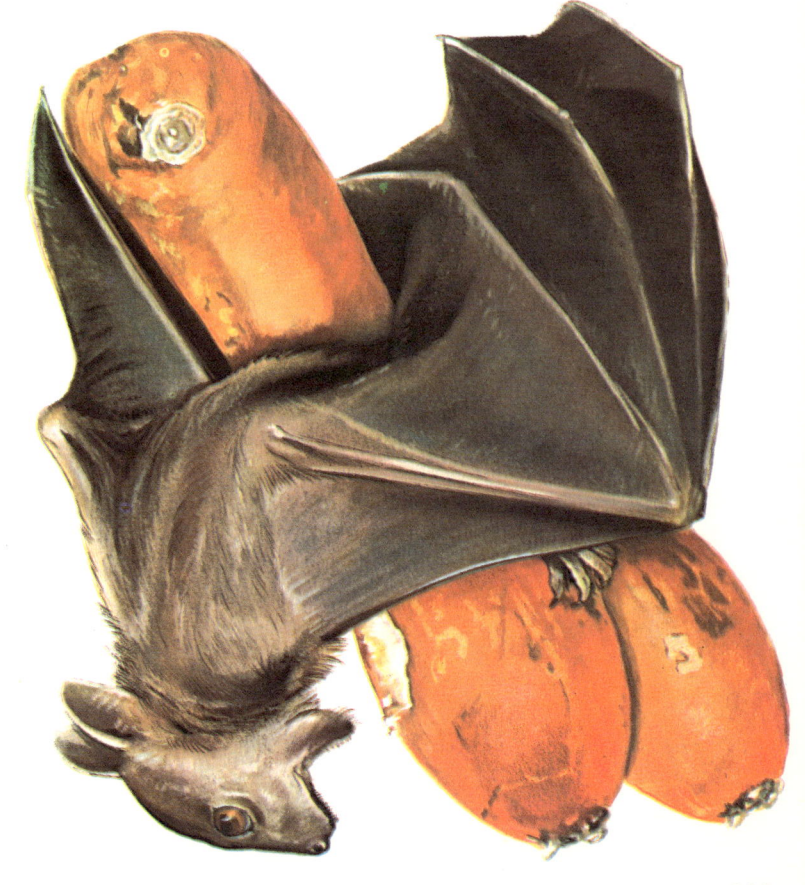

209

How advanced are the primates?

You would think that a group of mammals that included man would be the most advanced in the animal kingdom. This is not so, however. Of course, as a single species man has become the most intelligent and successful animal, but the group to which he belongs is quite primitive. The primate group branched off from the insectivores, the first placental mammals to appear. They did this by taking to the trees, becoming more active, developing grasping hands and feet and good eyesight. However, other primate features are still quite primitive when compared to further developments in other mammal groups. Primates still have five fingers and toes, for example, and simple teeth.

Indrises are found only on Madagascar. The two shown *below* are Verreaux's Sifaka *(left)* and the Indris *(right)*. Both are fond of basking in the sun among the treetops, turning over when one side is 'done'.

(Below) The Aye-Aye is another strange primate restricted to Madagascar. Its middle finger is very long and by tapping it along a branch it can detect the presence of grubs in the wood. These are quickly hooked out with the same long finger and eaten.

What are the main primate groups?

The primates are a large group of very varied animals ranging from the small, squirrel-like treeshrews to man himself. The first major division is into less advanced primates and more advanced primates. The former (prosimians) includes treeshrews, lemurs, bushbabies, indrises, the Aye-Aye, lorises and tarsiers. The more advanced primates (anthropoids) include monkeys from both the Old and New Worlds, the apes and man himself. The anthropoids have more expressive faces than the prosimians and are more intelligent. They are active during the day whereas a number of the prosimians are active only at night.

How did the Indris get its name?

Not many people have seen an Indris. It lives only in small groups on the island of Madagascar in the tree-tops of dense mountain forests. It is an odd-looking primate and at first glance could be mistaken for a long-legged man with a foxy face, crouching up a tree, wearing woolly gloves. The European to discover this primate called it an Indris because it was first pointed out to him by a native jumping up and down shouting '*indris izy*!' All the observant man was really saying in his own language was, 'There it is!' Indrises have the interesting habit of sunbathing holding their hands out to the sun to warm them.

(Below) Galagos or bushbabies are prosimian primates usually grouped with the lorises. They have long bushy tails and sleep in communal 'dormitories' during the day. The Fat-tailed Galago *(left)* is shown with a bushbaby *(right)*.

Which are the strangest-looking primates?

(Above) There are three species of tarsier from the Philippines, Sumatra and Borneo and the Celebes. The disc-like pads on the fingers increase the tarsier's grip. Treefrogs possess a similar feature (see page 105).

The tiny tarsiers have a strong claim to this title with their large ears and enormous staring eyes. The eyes are perhaps the most fascinating feature of these curious creatures. They are completely circular, set quite close together and stare straight forwards. If your eyes were in the same proportion to the size of your face as the tarsier's are, they would be at least as big as dinner plates. Tarsiers are nocturnal, as you might expect with eyes this big, and they spring from branch to branch catching insects, lizards and spiders. They are very agile, easily leaping distances of 6 feet, balanced by the long tail trailing out behind.

With long limbs and a long grasping 'extra hand' it is easy to see how spider monkeys came to be so-called. A close-up view of the sensitive bare area underneath the tip of the tail is shown *left*. There are four species of spider monkeys from the New World.

What is a prehensile tail?

Some of the best examples of prehensile tails are shown by the spider monkeys of South and Central America. Spider monkeys belong to the more advanced group of primates called anthropoid apes (see page 210). The anthropoids look more like typical monkeys than the prosimians and among them, the spider monkeys are some of the best adapted to an active tree-top life. They have slender bodies but long and powerful limbs. They travel through the trees by swinging along under the branches hand over hand. They have no thumbs and the fingers are bent so that the hands are used rather like hooks. The remarkable tail of the spider monkey is usually used as a third hand when the monkey swings from tree to tree. The tail is long, and on the underside of the tip there is a bare patch of wrinkled skin. This wraps round the branches in a grip firm enough to support the weight of the monkey. Such a grasping tail is called prehensile. Lacking thumbs, the spider monkey finds it difficult to pick up small objects. Its prehensile tail, however, is sensitive enough to pick up a peanut and put it in its mouth, so the monkey is not really handicapped.

(Right) A Proboscis Monkey family showing the range of nose development. The male is at the bottom.

How do baboons defend themselves?

Baboons are large Old World monkeys that have come down from the trees to spend most of their time on the ground. They are interesting because they are social monkeys that form well-organized family groups of about forty animals. As they move across open ground the members of the group take up particular positions within it. Young males advance first, followed by the older, more dominant males, with the females and young in the centre, and other young males bringing up the rear. The female baboons and their young are therefore protected on all sides. If danger suddenly threatens they are the first to flee to safety, while the males advance to try and ward off the attacker by presenting a united front.

(Below) An Olive Baboon showing the characteristic dog-like muzzle of the group.

Which monkey has a drooping nose?

The nose of the Proboscis Monkey is enormous. No other monkey has one quite as large. It is too long to stand out straight from the monkey's face and so it droops instead. In some males it hangs down over its mouth to below its chin. Imagine how it would feel if our noses were this long, swinging about as we walked along. Naturally it does not bother the Proboscis Monkey and although the nose must be large for some reason, we do not know what this is. As you might expect, it makes the monkey's voice sound rather odd, and when it utters its alarm cry, the nose straightens and stands out from the face. Proboscis Monkeys are large, powerfully built monkeys from Borneo.

(Left) The gibbons are the smallest of the apes but the most agile of all the mammals. Their very long arms are ideal for swinging along under the branches, and gibbons fling themselves across gaps of up to 30 feet.

What is the difference between monkeys and apes?

All the primates on these pages are apes. The apes are divided into three groups: the gibbons, the great apes, and man. Apes differ from monkeys by being tailless, having arms longer than legs and by being more intelligent.

Chimpanzees spend most of their time on the ground in the wild but climb trees to 'make their beds'.

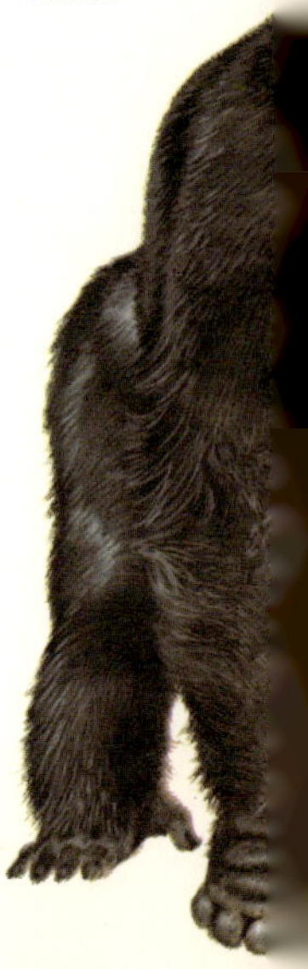

Where do chimpanzees sleep?

Every night the chimpanzee spends five minutes making its bed for the night. It bends two or three leafy branches together to make a platform quite high up in the trees. It curls up on its side with legs drawn up and soon falls asleep.

Who is the 'old man of the woods'?

The remarkable human features of the elderly Orang-utan led to it being referred to by this name. As it grows old the male Orang grows a moustache and beard, the rest of the face remaining hairless. It often develops a pot belly, its skin becomes wrinkled, and its cheeks and throat grow flabby as flaps of loose skin develop. Orangs usually live in trees, but old, fat males find they no longer have the strength to swing through the branches and so sit around on the ground instead. Like the chimpanzees, Orang-utans make a tree platform to serve as a bed for the night. The Orang's bed is improved, however, by the addition of a shelter to keep the rain off the animal while it is asleep.

There are two varieties of Orang-utan, one from Sumatra and one from Borneo. A female *(left)* and male *(right)* Borneo Orang are shown *below*. The males grow to twice the size of the females and may weigh as much as a man.

The largest of the primates, the Gorilla *(below)*, is in fact a gentle giant and prefers to avoid any contact with man.

Why do Gorillas beat their chests?

Everybody has been impressed by the size of the male Gorilla at the zoo. He can stand over $5\frac{1}{2}$ feet tall, weigh 28 stone, with an arm span of 8 feet. In the wild he gives a terrifying, angry display if he is suddenly disturbed. He rises up on his hind legs, roars loudly and runs sideways, beating his chest and throwing plants into the air. In spite of all these threats, a Gorilla has never, in fact, been known to attack a man face to face. All gorillas beat their chests and in females and youngsters it is thought that this is a way of releasing tension in the animal.

Sloths are either called two-toed *(below)* or three-toed *(left)* but this really refers to the number of fingers on the front feet. Both kinds have three toes on the hind feet.

Which animal spends its life upside-down?

In contrast to the acrobatic antics of the monkeys and apes, sloths move about the tree-tops in very slow motion. They hang underneath the branches from hooked claws of both the fingers and toes, and spend most of their lives in this upside-down position. They eat, sleep, mate and even give birth to their young upside-down. There are two interesting features of a sloth related to its upside-down way of life. The first is its ability to turn its head almost right round to compensate for its reversed position. The second is the way its hair lies in the opposite direction to that of most animals. The sloth's hair runs from its belly round to its back, and this ensures that heavy tropical showers run straight off.

Some people claim that the Giant Anteater *(left)* uses its long bushy tail to sweep ants into piles before licking them up.

Why does the anteater walk on its knuckles?

If you look closely at the feet of the Giant Anteater at the bottom of the opposite page, you will notice that they look slightly odd. The anteaters are animals with a specialized diet, feeding on termites, ants and their larvae. Specialized feeders usually have special features. The anteaters have strong claws on the front feet to break open termite nests, and a long narrow mouth with an equally long sticky tongue, to probe around and lick up the insects. It seems that the anteater walks on the knuckles of its front feet to protect the curved claws and to keep them sharp.

Most armadillos can curl up a little to protect themselves from predators. The Three-banded Armadillo rolls up completely to avoid attack.

Which animals are armoured?

The armadillos are well protected by a shell of bony plates covering the back and sides of the body. The skin of the head, tail and legs is also thickened and scaly so that the animals have an impressive, heavily armoured look. The main shell is divided across the back into a number of bands allowing some degree of movement. The number of bands varies in the different species of armadillo. Armadillos are strong burrowers and can soon disappear from sight into the ground if alarmed. One species is able to roll itself up completely into a ball.

Sloths, anteaters and armadillos comprise a group of primitive but specialized animals called the edentates. They are all found in South and Central America. These armadillos (left) are Nine-banded.

What is a pangolin?

A pangolin looks rather like an anteater with scales. In fact its habits are not unlike that of an anteater and it is thought that the resemblance between the two animals is another example of convergent evolution (see pages 183 and 206). Anteaters are restricted to the New World, of course, whereas pangolins make up a small group of animals from Africa and southern Asia. Like anteaters, pangolins feed on ants and termites and so have developed the same features for eating them: that is, a long, pointed snout and an incredibly long, sticky tongue. Pangolins are also toothless. Their most noticeable characteristic, however, is the suit of overlapping scales which covers almost all the body except the underside. The scales are actually modified hairs.

Most pangolins climb trees with the help of a prehensile tail. They have been said to resemble pine cones among the branches.

What is the difference between rabbits and hares?

Rabbits and hares belong to the same large group of mammals and are found practically all over the world. There are many species and in some cases the names rabbit and hare have become almost interchangeable. However, there are some important general differences between the two. Hares are usually bigger than rabbits, have longer legs and larger black-tipped ears. They run in zig-zagging leaps and bounds, whereas rabbits run normally. Hares tend to be solitary animals, resting during the day in a shallow depression called a form. Rabbits, on the other hand, live in colonies

The well-camouflaged Arctic Hare *(left)* of Canada burrows into the snow for shelter.

The rabbit *(left)* lives in underground warrens. It is a prolific breeder and considered a pest in many parts of the world for the damage it does to crops.

and dig complex tunnel systems, or warrens, in which they live and rear their young. These contrasting ways of life are reflected in the stage of development of the newly born young of each. Baby rabbits are born in the security of an underground burrow and are blind, deaf and practically naked at birth. They are helpless for ten days and are not fully independent of their mother for another twenty days. Baby hares are born in a depression on the surface. They are fully furred and can see at birth. On leaving the form they separate, although the mother continues to visit each in turn to suckle it. This ensures that even if one young hare is discovered by a predator, the others stand a good chance of survival.

Young hares *(left)* are born in a hollow on the ground and are well developed at birth.

All the animals on this page are rodents. Rodents make up an enormous group of gnawing mammals which are grouped into squirrel-like, mouse-like and porcupine-like animals.

How far can a jerboa jump?

The long tail of the jerboa *(below)* balances it in a long hop and props it up when the animal is resting.

Jerboas are small rodents that look rather like miniature kangaroos. Their back legs are four times as long as their front legs, and the tail is longer than the head and body put together. Like kangaroos they travel by leaps and bounds and at top speed can cover 10 feet in a single jump. The tail trails behind and helps to balance the jerboa as it shoots through the air, often faster than the eye can see. Jerboas live in desert areas of Asia and Africa and escape the fierce heat of the day by hiding in cool underground burrows.

Can a porcupine shoot out its quills?

Porcupines of the Old World are burrowers whereas those of the New World climb trees. Both have thousands of needle-sharp quills which are erected and rattled as a warning if the animal is attacked. The porcupine turns its back and either runs backwards to drive the quills into the intruder or angrily lashes its tail causing loose quills to fly out. In neither case are the quills actually fired.

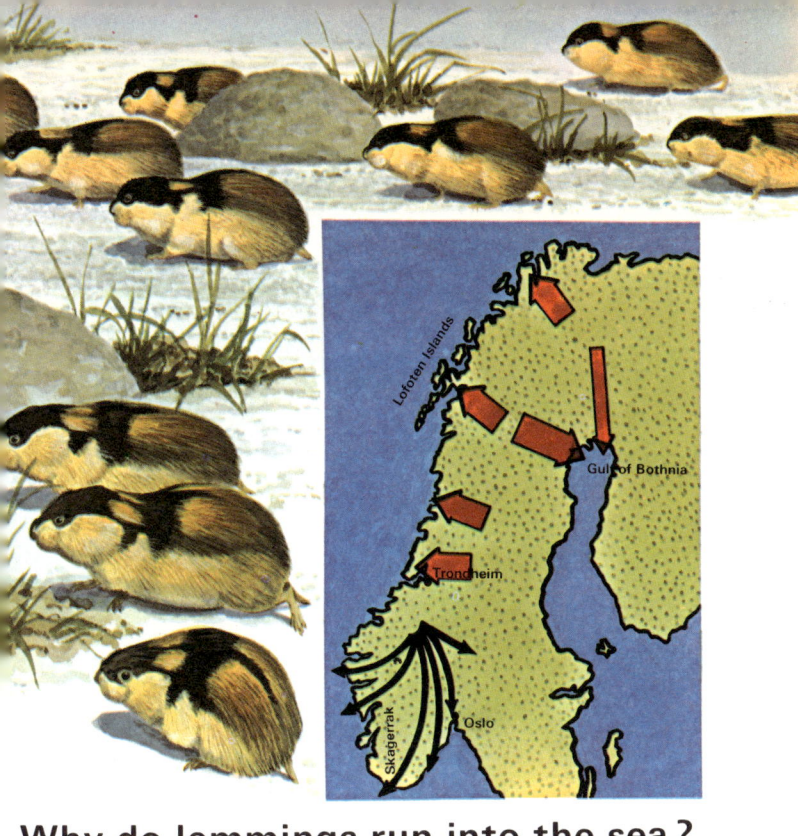

When numbers of lemmings become too great for a particular area they stream away in all directions in search of fresh food. Only some arrive at the coast and attempt to swim the ocean. The map shows the migration routes of two kinds of lemmings from Scandinavia.

Why do lemmings run into the sea?

You may have heard stories about lemmings flinging themselves from cliffs in their thousands to perish in the sea. This is only part of the whole story. The Norwegian Lemming lives high up on the mountainside and normally produces several litters of young each year. If conditions for breeding are particularly favourable over two or three years, exceptional numbers of lemmings are produced. This is called a population explosion. The available food is quickly eaten and then large numbers of lemmings migrate in all directions in search of fresh areas. They seem to panic and rush headlong down the mountains streaming through rivers, over walls and other obstacles. Usually these migrations die out inconspicuously but where a stream of lemmings reaches a cliff-top the result is spectacular.

Two species of Old World porcupine are shown *below*. They need to be treated with care for it is very difficult and painful to remove a quill which has pierced the skin.

Dolphins *(above)* differ from porpoises *(below)* by having a beak, a narrower head and a different shape of the dorsal fin.

(Above) The Sperm Whale is a toothed whale which appears to be all head. It is a valuable whale and has been ruthlessly hunted by man for centuries.

(Below) The Killer Whale is reputed to be the most ferocious animal of the sea. It hunts in packs and will feed on anything including seals, sealions, penguins and even other whales.

What makes whales mammals?

The whales are a large group of aquatic animals that vary in size from about 4 feet in length to nearly 100 feet. During the evolution of mammals tens of millions of years ago one group returned to live in water. These mammals became streamlined in shape, developed a powerful tail and front limbs for use as steering fins, and lost the use of the back limbs. Whales, descendants of this group, are mammals because they breathe air, are warm-blooded and suckle their young with milk. They have lost the mammalian coat of hair in order to help them swim, but they have replaced it with an insulating coat of thick blubber.

In America the Common Porpoise *(below)* is called the Harbor Porpoise.

How do whales feed?

We all know that the whales are huge mammals (the Blue Whale is probably the largest animal that has ever lived on the earth) but it may surprise you to learn that the biggest whales feed on the tiny organisms that make up plankton. There are two sorts of whales; the toothed whales and the baleen whales. The toothed whales have rows of large but quite ordinary teeth and catch crustaceans, squids, fishes and some smaller marine mammals. Instead of teeth, the baleen whales grow thin plates of horny outgrowths (whalebone) from the roof of the mouth, which hang down on both sides of the mouth. These plates filter out tons of plankton from the water as the whale cruises along with its mouth gaping. As the mouth closes, water is forced out through the plates, and the whale's huge tongue licks off the plankton and pushes it down its throat.

(Below left) The red arrow in this drawing shows the flow of water out through the sieve of baleen plates of a baleen whale. Some plates have been removed to make this clearer. (Rub your tongue over the roof of your mouth and you will feel the ridges similar to those from which the plates of the baleen whale have been developed.)

(Below) The dimensions of the Blue Whale are breathtaking. A 100-ton specimen and a cart-horse are shown here drawn to the same scale.

Do whales spout water?

You have no doubt seen films or photographs of whales sending up impressive plumes of what looks very much like water. The usual cry of whalers is 'Thar she blows!' for this was and occasionally still is the way the whales are spotted. However, the spout is not so much water as steam. After a dive lasting perhaps up to an hour, the used air in the whale's lungs becomes hot and laden with moisture. As it rolls on the surface the whale opens its single nostril, the blowhole, and blasts this warm humid air into air which is often freezing cold. The moisture in the whale's breath immediately condenses and it is this that pin-points its position as a spout visible from a considerable distance.

Which dog cannot bark?

The Dingo is one of the very few dogs in the world that is unable to bark. It is not a silent dog, however, as it makes up for not barking by howling and whining very loudly indeed. Dingoes are a very ancient breed of wild dog from Australia. They are probably quite closely related to the primitive dogs from which our domestic dogs of today evolved. Dingoes must have arrived in Australia with the first Aborigines to settle there from Asia. They soon went wild although the Aborigines of today still rear pups and train them for hunting. Dingoes are considered a pest in Australia because of the large number of sheep and cattle they kill every year.

The dog family belongs to a large group of mammals called the carnivores. This name means flesh-eater and apart from one or two exceptions they all have strong jaws and sharp teeth for killing and tearing the flesh from their prey.

Apart from its inability to bark, the Dingo differs from other dogs by not being able to lower its ears. A Dingo is shown living in an Aborigine camp *(left)*.

(Below) These Asiatic, or Golden, Jackals also belong to the dog family and generally live by scavenging near towns and cities.

Which dog looks like a fox on stilts?

This strange description has been used for the Maned Wolf, and if you have been lucky enough to see one in a zoo, you would understand why. The dog's fox-like body is balanced on extremely long, slender legs which give the animal a rather elegant look. As you might expect, the Maned Wolf is a good runner and ranges widely in search of prey over

The Maned Wolf is said to run faster than any other member of the dog family.

open country and small areas of forest in South America. It is rarely seen because it hunts at night and is a very wary animal.

How many wolves are there in a wolf-pack?

Each autumn the cubs born to a pair of wolves join their parents in hunting as a family group. A typical wolf-pack like this may have five members, but if the winter is particularly hard, family packs join up to form a larger pack. A large wolf-pack rarely has more than thirty wolves, however.

(Below) By hunting in packs, wolves are able to attack and kill large animals such as the moose.

Which is the biggest bear?

Imagine a bear 10 feet long, standing 4 feet tall at the shoulder and weighing nearly a ton. This is the size of the largest bear (and therefore the largest carnivore) there is, the Kodiak Bear from Alaska. You might wonder how dangerous such an enormous bear would be if you suddenly disturbed it in a clearing. Bears tend to be unpredictable creatures and often attack with no warning at all. The chances are that your encounter would be very dangerous indeed. Do not be misled by the bear's slow, lumbering movements. It is a very powerful animal and can quickly move in range to deliver deadly blows from its huge front paws. Bears do not kill by hugging but by swiping their paws, armed with sharp claws, at their prey.

Grizzly Bears and Kodiak Bears are thought to be of the same family as the Brown Bear. Brown Bears *(right)* are widely distributed and vary a lot in appearance over their range.

Which bears wear 'glasses'?

A small bear from tropical South America has rather odd face markings. The bear has a creamy yellow snout, and fur of the same colour runs from its nose in various patterns. Sometimes the lines of lighter fur encircle the eyes and cross the nose, giving the bear the comical appearance of wearing a pair of glasses. Not surprisingly the bear has come to be called the Spectacled Bear although the markings are never the same in any two bears. Some Spectacled Bears may have only the bottom half of their 'glasses', whereas in others the eye rings are so thick they completely fill the face.

All bears can climb trees but the Spectacled Bear is particularly expert at clambering among the branches to feed on leaves, fruit and nuts.

Which is the smallest bear?

The Sun Bear from southern Asia is not much bigger than a large dog, in contrast to the mighty size of the Kodiak Bear. The little Sun Bear is about 4 feet long with a 2-inch tail, and stands 2 feet tall at the shoulder. It is another bear with an odd marking, this time on the chest. Some individuals have a crescent shape in lighter fur on their front which, in the East, is said to represent the rising sun – hence the bear's name. The Sun Bear spends most of its time clambering through the tree tops in search of food. It will eat any small animals it can catch, lizards and baby birds for example, honey from wild bees' nests and some fruit.

(Above) Another excellent climber, the Sun Bear displays its characteristic chest markings from the fork of a tree.

Polar bears *(right)* are also very fast movers on ice, and can lumber along at speeds of up to 18 mph. Hair on the soles of their feet prevents them from slipping.

How well can the Polar Bear swim?

It is difficult to imagine a large, bulky animal like a bear being able to swim very far. The Polar Bear is a remarkable swimmer and has been reported swimming strongly out at sea more than 200 miles from the nearest land. The Polar Bear has a long neck and by thrusting its head out of the water and paddling with its wide front paws alone, it is able to swim steadily for long periods (actually much faster than you can walk). These bears live among the shifting pack-ice and freezing waters of the Arctic Ocean. A less inviting place for a swim would be difficult to imagine. The Polar Bear is well insulated from the cold by a thick layer of blubber and a long, thick coat of fur. Polar Bears have a varied diet but prey mainly on seals.

Although Giant Pandas are particularly partial to the tender young shoots of bamboo, they have been known to eat other food. Grasses, roots, irises and crocuses and small rodents, birds and fishes are all eaten from time to time by Giant Pandas.

What does the Giant Panda eat?

The Giant Panda has been adopted by the World Wildlife Fund to symbolize the plight of rare and endangered animals throughout the world.

Practically everyone must remember the publicity that accompanied the attempts at persuading Chi-chi and An-an to mate at the London and Moscow Zoos. However, did you know that although the Giant Panda looks very bear-like, it is in fact more closely related to the raccoons? We don't know all that much about the Giant Panda, but we do know that it is a specialized feeder. Its particular preference is for tender, young bamboo shoots, and so naturally its distribution in the wild is restricted to bamboo forests. These tend to occur in inaccessible mountainous areas of Central China, and the Giant Panda has not yet been properly studied in its natural habitat. Only a very small number of animals are kept in zoos outside China and little is known about the animal's breeding behaviour. Great excitement was shown when An-an was twice introduced to Chi-chi in the hope that he would mate with her. Alas, Chi-chi refused all his approaches.

Sea Otters even sleep floating on their backs and often wrap long strands of seaweed around their bodies to prevent themselves from drifting away. They were once abundant along the Pacific coasts but are now rare, and a protected species.

Why is this Sea Otter carrying a stone?

Otters are long, slim creatures with short paddle-like webbed feet. They are excellent swimmers. Some species live in the fresh waters of rivers and lakes while others are marine animals and live in the shallow waters of rocky coasts and islands. The Sea Otter rarely leaves the water and a lot of its time is spent floating idly on its back. It feeds on hard-shelled marine invertebrates and deals with them in a characteristic way. It dives down to collect molluscs and crabs together with a flat stone from the bottom. While floating on its back it rests the stone on its chest and smashes the shells of the animals on it, eating only their soft bodies. The Sea Otter is one of the very few mammals to use a tool.

How big are the largest otters?

The biggest otters live in the slow-moving rivers of South America. These Giant Otters are, incredibly, 6 feet long on average, some specimens reaching 7 feet. They are streamlined animals and rarely leave the water. When they do, their stumpy legs are of little use and they have to resort to sliding along on their bellies.

(Left) A Giant Otter standing, propped up by its tail. These enormous otters are rarely seen on dry land.

Palm civets from southern Asia are smaller than most civets, and spend more time in trees.
(From top to bottom): the Common Palm Civet; the Masked Palm Civet; and the large Indian Civet.

Why do civets smell?

The characteristic odour of a civet is enough to make your nose wrinkle. The smell comes from a liquid called musk secreted from glands near the civet's reproductive organs. The musk is a valuable substance and in parts of Africa civets are kept on farms and the musk collected from them several times a week. You must be wondering what possible use such a strange liquid could have. The clear, yellow liquid is collected in very small amounts and sent all over the world to the makers of the most expensive perfumes. Musk is used as a fixative in perfume making because it contains certain important oils and fats. A fixative is a substance that helps to bring out and preserve the scents of other ingredients of the perfume. Although the musk smells awful when it is secreted by the civet, once it is diluted, it begins to smell quite pleasant. The strange thing is that it is the male civets which have the more powerful smell in order to attract the females. The scent that women wear today has the opposite effect of course, by attracting men. Civets are cat-like carnivores with long bodies and tails and pointed noses.

How does a Mongoose kill a snake?

The Mongoose is best known for being able to attack and kill large poisonous snakes such as cobras. It is a slender, weasel-like animal, and the secret of its success against

(Left) The 5-foot Binturong, or Bear Cat, is the largest of all the civets. It is the only Old World Mammal to have a prehensile tail.

snakes lies in its wonderful agility. At a confrontation, the cobra rears up and faces the mongoose. The mongoose entices the snake to strike but at the same instant nimbly sidesteps the lunging fangs and crushes the snake's head in its jaws.

Are hyenas cowardly?

Hyenas seem to have gained a reputation for cowardice. They are well-adapted for killing their own prey, however, but although strong, cannot run at high speeds for any distance. Instead of being active predators themselves, their role in life seems to be clearing up after other animals. They feed on carrion and scavenge the remains of carcases left by lions, tigers and other big cats. Short, powerful jaws crunch through bones of any size and hyenas leave hardly a scrap of waste from such meat. If driven by hunger they will kill for themselves but even then will, more often than not, only attack a young or defenceless animal offering no resistance. Hyenas have been known to hunt in packs, however, harrying a zebra until it could be overcome by cooperative effort.

There are over forty species of mongooses from southern Asia, Africa and Madagascar. They all look very much alike and have similar habits. An Indian Mongoose is shown *above*.

There are two well-known species of hyena: the Striped and the Spotted *(right)*, and a third, rare, Brown Hyena, all of which come from Africa.

The cat family represents the most advanced group of carnivores (see page 225). All cats are flesh eaters. They are deadly hunters, creeping up stealthily on their prey or lying patiently in ambush.

The features that distinguish the European Wild Cat *(left)* from a domestic cat are its squarer head and flattened ears, its stouter and longer body and its shorter bushy tail with a black, rounded tip.

Is this a wild or a domestic cat?

You could easily mistake this cat at first glance for a domestic cat, but it would probably scratch you to ribbons rather than lie in your lap purring contentedly. This is a European Wild Cat and although similar in appearance to our pets it differs greatly in behaviour. It lives in the remote and inaccessible forests and mountainsides of Europe and is a rarely seen, nocturnal hunter. Wild cats have been persecuted by man over the years because of their frenzied attacks on chickens and lambs, and they are now scarce.

Large eyes and big, swivelling ears are invaluable aids to the nocturnal hunting activities of the Tiger.

(Above) All the cats walk on tip-toe so that they can run with long strides and spring at their prey. They can also withdraw their claws to protect them.

Do lions live in the jungle?

(Above) Lions live in groups (prides) and cooperate with each other when hunting. Usually the males drive the prey to where the females lie hidden, ready to make the kill.

It is easy to associate lions with jungles but in fact these magnificent beasts live in much more open country. They are found on grassy plains with few trees, in scrublands and sometimes even in deserts. Today they are restricted to two areas only – Africa and India – although they were once common all over southern Europe, southern Asia and the whole of Africa. Inevitably, lions have been unable to compete with men anxious to protect their livestock from this big predator and, more recently, from those others, anxious to secure a notable hunting trophy. Fortunately, big game hunting is now frowned upon, and lions are a protected species living in managed wildlife areas.

Another well known big cat, the Tiger, lives in jungles and forests of southern Asia and is well camouflaged for such areas. It is nocturnal, and hunts by stealth, finally rushing the last few yards to overcome its prey.

Are the tusks of the Walrus useful?

The long curving tusks of the Walrus are actually two elongated teeth growing from its upper jaw. They look rather heavy to carry around and one wonders what possible use they can have. For the Walrus they prove to be very handy teeth and they are put to a number of uses. The first is related to the Walrus diet. This consists of molluscs, starfishes and sea urchins which are dredged up from the bottom with the tusks. The Walrus's moustache of sensory whiskers help it to find this food on the bottom. Being quite large mammals (males can weigh a ton and a half), Walruses find it difficult to haul themselves out of the sea on to rocky shores or ice floes. The tusks are also useful for this job and indeed on ice the walrus can drag itself along with its tusks as fast as a man can run.

Walruses live at the edge of the polar ice of the Atlantic and Pacific Oceans. Their numbers have been severely reduced in the past by overhunting for their ivory tusks, hides and blubber.

What is the difference between sealions and seals?

Sealions, seals and the Walrus make up a group of streamlined, fin-footed mammals found along most coasts of the world. They are good swimmers using modified limbs as webbed paddles and all have a thick layer of blubber under their skin to keep them warm. Unlike the whales (see page 222) they do not spend all their time at sea, coming ashore to breed every year. The sealions (and fur seals) spend more time on land than the true seals, and can gallop clumsily along using both back and front limbs. They can turn their back limbs forward under the body to help this ungainly, humping movement. The true seals spend most of their time in water and are less active on land. They cannot use their back limbs to help, and drag themselves along on their bellies as best they can. Another difference is that sealions have small but visible ear flaps which are lacking in seals. Both groups feed on fish and have sharply pointed teeth.

Of the fin-footed mammals (sometimes all called seals) the true seals *(right)* are the most adapted to life in the water. The sealions *(above)* and fur seals spend a considerable part of each year on land.

Which seals perform in circuses?

The performing seals you may have seen balancing balls or clapping their flippers in a circus or dolphinarium are actually sealions. True seals would obviously be unsuitable for performing such antics because they are fairly inactive on land. Sealions, however, romp around with real enjoyment and are often taught a whole range of entertaining tricks.

The African Elephant *(left)* spends more time in the open and the large surface area of its ears speeds the loss of heat from its body. This is why African Elephants flap their ears to keep cool.

What is the largest living land mammal?

The largest land mammal living today is the African Elephant. A fully grown male measures 11 feet high at the shoulders and may weigh over 6 tons. It eats 700 pounds of vegetation and drinks over 50 gallons of water in a day, its trunk having a capacity of $1\frac{1}{2}$ gallons. It can walk at 4 miles an hour, which is about as fast as a man can walk, but it can run at an impressive 30 miles an hour but is unable to jump the smallest of obstacles. There is another species of elephant found today. The Indian Elephant has smaller ears, a more rounded back, a trunk with one 'finger' at the end (rather than two), a domed forehead and a smaller overall size.

The Indian Elephant *(below)* spends most of its time in dense shade.

The Indian Elephant *(right)* is found in dense forests of Sri Lanka (Ceylon), Burma, Thailand and Malaya. The African Elephant is found in most parts of Africa south of the Sahara.

Can an elephant drink through its trunk?

This is the equivalent of asking, 'Can you drink through your nose?' and of course the answer is no. The elephant's trunk is an extension of its nose and upper lip. It does not just hang limply but can be operated to carry out a vast range of tasks. The most important of these is food gathering. The sensitive finger (or fingers) at the tip of the trunk enables the elephant to pluck foliage and pass it into the mouth. The trunk is also used as a hose pipe. It can squirt water or dust over the elephant, and can also squirt over a gallon of water straight in to the mouth when the elephant is drinking. Other uses are as a snorkel or breathing tube when the elephant is swimming, as a lifting device, as a weapon for defence and lastly, for smelling, of course.

Rock Hyraxes *(below)* live on mountain slopes and among rocky outcrops. They are very active and can jump directly upwards and balance well.

Both Rock Hyraxes and Tree Hyraxes *(above)* have padded feet which act as suction cups to increase their grip. They are kept moist by sweat glands on the soles.

Why are the hyraxes a puzzle?

This small group of rabbit-sized animals from Africa has confused zoologists for a long time. Nobody has been really sure how the hyraxes are related to other larger mammals because they show an odd mixture of features. Some have teeth like rhinoceroses, others like hippopotamuses. The bone structure of their front legs and feet is like that of an elephant, as is the shape of their brain. Their back legs and feet resemble those of an ancestor of the horse and their stomach is also horse-like. Other features are intermediate between rodents and hoofed animals. It is now thought that hyraxes may have descended from a group of animals that eventually gave rise to the elephants, rhinoceroses, hippopotamuses and horses as we know them today.

What are sea-cows?

If cows lived in the sea what would they be like? They would probably be large, slow-moving mammals living in herds and feeding by grazing across beds of seaweeds. There is a group of animals that fits this description, and not surprisingly, they are called sea-cows. After the whales, sea-cows are the group of mammals most adapted to an aquatic life. Like the whales they have lost their back limbs and instead have a horizontally flattened tail. The front limbs are flippers and they have practically no hair on the skin. The two groups are unrelated, however, for the whale's ancestors were carnivores whereas those of the sea-cows were herbivorous. There are four species of sea-cows. One is the Dugong and the other three are called manatees. The Dugong has a notched tail, while that of the manatee is more rounded and paddle-shaped.

Who thought sea-cows were mermaids?

Imagine you had been a sailor on an early sailing ship passing through shallow coastal waters in the tropics. You might have been at sea for many months, and heard all sorts of seamen's yarns and tales. Suddenly a strange animal reared up out of the water to watch the ship pass. It had a fish-like tail and a face that could be vaguely human. As you look closer at this strange creature you discover that it is suckling a baby by holding it to its breast. What would you think it was? Without knowing all about sea-cows you might be excused for imagining that you had seen a mermaid, and it is thought that this is how many mermaid stories arose hundreds of years ago. Today, looking at the bald head and the wrinkled and hairy face of the Dugong, it is difficult to imagine mistaking it for a beautiful mermaid.

The Dugong *(left and above)* is found from the Indian Ocean to the northern coasts of Australia. It reaches a length of about 8 or 9 feet.

Manatees *(left)* grow up to 15 feet in length and can weigh 500 pounds.

How do sea-cows graze?

The Dugong and the manatees have slightly different methods of grazing the lush beds of vegetation that grow in the sheltered waters of tropical coasts and estuaries. The Dugong has an enormous upper lip which curls over the seaweed, pressing it against the lower lip so that it can be plucked. The manatees have a notched upper lip divided into two lobes which work against one another. These make a very good gripping organ. The manatees pluck enormous quantities of seaweed (up to 100 pounds a day), and the front flippers help by cramming the greenstuff into the mouth while it is chewed. As sea-cows are grazers, their teeth are continually wearing down. Instead of each tooth growing to replace wear, the old teeth drop out at the front of the mouth, and new ones appear at the back on a conveyor system.

The three species of manatee are the North American from the Caribbean area, the South American *(right)* and the West African.

(Left) Pitifully small numbers of Przewalski's Wild Horse live in the wild in a remote region of Mongolia. Stocks kept in zoos have been breeding successfully, however, and so the species may be saved from extinction.

Which hoofed mammals are odd-toed?

It seems strange to refer to animals as either odd-toed or even-toed but that is how the two groups of mammals that are hoofed – the ungulates – are distinguished. The herbivorous ungulates evolved on firm grassy plains – ideal places for running at high speed. The fewer fingers and toes an animal has the faster it can run. This is why you run on the very tips of your toes when you sprint for a bus, to give you more spring forwards. The fingers and toes of the ungulates became reduced, their remaining claws developed into hooves and their legs lengthened to allow fast galloping across the plains. If you draw a straight line down the middle of an ungulate's foot (this is called an axis), in some it will pass through the middle finger or toe. During the evolution of these ungulates this finger or toe has become lengthened and developed into the hoof, while the toes on either side have become lost or reduced. So the hoof is either made up of just one toe or of three in these ungulates, and they are therefore called odd-toed. Today's representatives of this group are horses, asses and zebras, and tapirs and rhinoceroses.

It is not known exactly how the domestic horse *(above)* was derived from wild horses and so it is regarded as a separate species. It is interesting to compare its appearance with the wild horse *(above left)*.

The rare Asiatic Wild Ass is now a protected species in remote areas of Asia. It is thought that the domestic donkey was derived from the African Wild Ass, now believed to be on the verge of extinction.

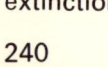

Are there any truly wild horses?

Apart from the zebras, which also belong to the horse family, the only really wild horse found today is Przewalski's Wild Horse and the Asiatic and African Wild Ass. Another wild horse, the Tarpan from the Ukraine, became extinct only recently (in 1919), and Przewalski's Horse is precariously near extinction. Wild horses of many species were once common in Europe and Asia, and from one or two of these man developed the domestic horse. Domestic breeds of horses and donkeys are now found all over the world and in many places they have gone back to the wild. These semi-wild horses readily breed with the remaining small numbers of truly wild horses, so that the pure species are gradually diminishing and will eventually disappear.

Zebras *(right* and *below)* are sometimes referred to as striped horses but their long ears, stiff manes and tufted tails make them more similar to asses.

Why are zebras striped?

This is the most obvious question to ask about zebras but unfortunately nobody really knows the answer. Looking at zebras in the zoo, the striped patterning seems very conspicuous and could hardly be thought of as protective. One theory, however, claims that this is, in fact, so. The bold stripes may serve to break up the shape of the zebra. From a distance, across the shimmering grassy plains on which the zebra lives, the blurred collection of stripes that the lion or tiger sees may not be instantly recognizable as an animal. The patterning is variable and no two zebras are exactly alike. It is interesting that African people think of zebras as black animals with white stripes whereas we think of them as white animals with black stripes.

Several odd-toed ungulates are shown on these pages. The coloration of the young Malayan Tapir bears little resemblance to that of its parent.

The head of the White Rhinoceros showing its broad square lips.

Why does the tapir have a white back?

Seen in the zoo, the coloration of a Malayan Tapir looks slightly absurd. It looks very much as if it is wearing a closely fitting white coat similar to the dog coats you sometimes see worn by the pampered pets of old ladies. To understand why such an odd-looking animal has such an odd-looking coloration we must consider the sort of places the tapir lives in and the sort of life that it leads. When we do this the tapir's appearance doesn't seem so odd after all. Tapirs are secretive, nocturnal animals living near water, in dense tropical forests. They are quite large, about as big as donkeys although with shorter legs, and being herbivorous tend to graze all night in order to find sufficient food. By moonlight their shadowy black and white outline blends well with the background so that the tapirs are perfectly camouflaged during their nocturnal wanderings. Patterning which breaks up an animal's shape like this is called *disruptive coloration*.

How many sorts of rhinoceros are there?

There are five species of rhinoceros living today, two from Africa and three from Asia. The two African rhinoceroses and one from Asia, the Sumatran, all have two horns whereas the other two Asian species have only one.

The largest of them all is the White Rhinoceros from Africa. It stands 6 feet high at the shoulder and can weigh over 3 tons. An interesting difference between this rhino and the Black Rhinoceros, also from Africa, lies in the shape of the lips. The White Rhinoceros has a wider, square

The Black Rhinoceros head-on *(above)* and from the side *(right)*.

The three Asiatic rhinoceroses: the Sumatran *(above)* the Javan *(below)* and the Great Indian *(below right)*.

mouth, very suitable for cropping grass as it grazes across the savannah. The Black Rhinoceros is more of a browser and has a pointed upper lip for grazing and plucking leaves and shoots from shrubs and bushes. The other two-horned species, the Sumatran Rhinoceros, is the smallest of them all, standing only about $4\frac{1}{2}$ feet at the shoulder.

Both the Javan and the Great Indian Rhinoceros look as if they are wearing heavy armour plating held together with rivets. This effect is given by thick skin hanging in deep folds and hard raised knobs on the front and back ends of the animals. The Great Indian Rhinoceros may weigh up to 2 tons and so is a formidable beast, but like most rhinoceroses, it is usually anxious to avoid any confrontation with man.

All the rhinoceroses are unfortunately rare animals. They have been hunted by man for their horns for years because of the belief that magical properties are imparted to the owner.

Which mammals are even-toed?

We have already discovered that, of the hoofed mammals, some have an odd number of toes and others an even number (see page 240). Although the members of both groups have long legs and hoofs developed from a reduced number of fingers and toes, they are not related, since they evolved separately from two different ancestors. The point about this other, larger group of ungulates is that their hoofs are comprised of either two or four fingers or toes. In even-toed ungulates the axis of the foot passes between the third and fourth digit (finger or toe) and so the hoof is always made up of an even number of digits.

Wild pigs are shown from Borneo *(below left)* and the Celebes *(below)* together with two Wild Boars from Europe and Asia *(below right* and *bottom)*.

Like the odd-toed ungulates, the even-toed are grazers but they seem to have been more successful animals (there are nearly 200 species). This is largely due to the rather involved way they digest their food, using a many-chambered stomach. The food is eaten quickly and enters the first chamber. Later, when the animal is resting in a safe place with no chance of being molested by predators, it brings up this half-digested food and chews it again. It swallows it for a second time and it then passes into the other stomach chambers. 'Chewing the cud' continues until all the food has been swallowed again.

Are pigs dirty animals?

Domestic pigs in their pigsty often look as if they enjoy being thoroughly filthy animals. Wild pigs, however, are not at all dirty. They are, in fact, intelligent beasts of regular, clean habits, roaming through woodlands in search of food found just under the surface of the soil. Occasionally they take a mud-wallow but this is not a dirty habit. The mud cools them, removes parasites from the skin and generally improves their health. Indeed, mud is very good for skin.

The even-toed ungulates include pigs, hippopotamuses, camels and llamas, deer, giraffes and cattle (antelopes, gazelles, goats and sheep).

(Right) The Hippopotamus rivals the Great Indian Rhinoceros for the title of the second largest land mammal. It is 5 feet at the shoulder and weighs up to 3 tons.

Can a hippopotamus run underwater?

A hippopotamus on dry land hardly looks as if it could move with any speed at all. Its enormous bulk is supported by four stumpy limbs; a less streamlined shape would be hard to imagine. Hippopotamuses spend a lot of time in the wide rivers of Africa. Once immersed, the body weight is lessened and the stumpy limbs thrash the water to propel the animal along quite quickly. They either cruise with only nostrils, ears and eyes above water level, or dive to the bottom to run along the river bed. They can stay under water for up to ten minutes. A lot of time is spent in water but hippopotamuses come out on to land at night to feed on vegetation.

(Right) The second species of hippo, the Pygmy Hippopotamus is very much smaller and spends less time in the water than the first species. It stands about 2½ feet at the shoulder and weighs about 400 pounds.

The camels shown *above* are two-humped or Bactrian Camels. The only other species is the one-humped Arabian Camel which is no longer found wild.

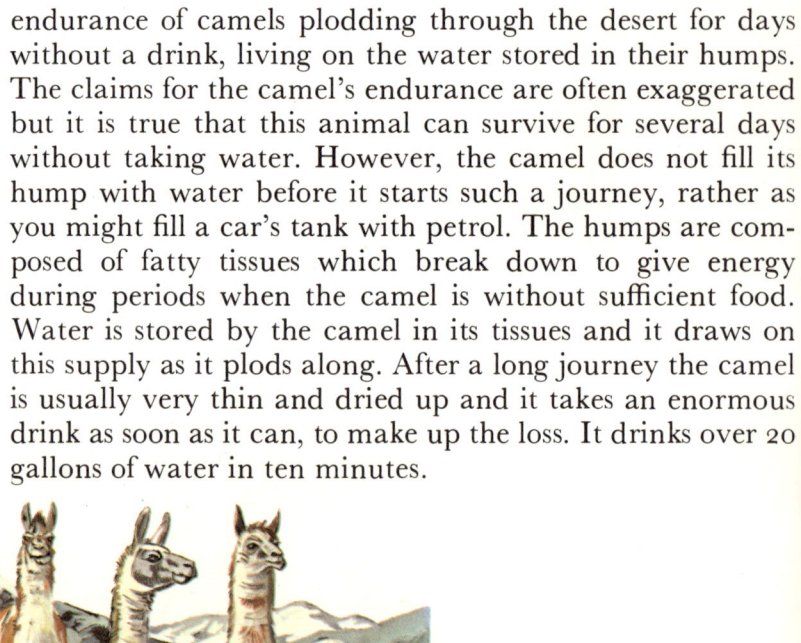

What does a camel store in its humps?

You have no doubt heard stories about the wonderful endurance of camels plodding through the desert for days without a drink, living on the water stored in their humps. The claims for the camel's endurance are often exaggerated but it is true that this animal can survive for several days without taking water. However, the camel does not fill its hump with water before it starts such a journey, rather as you might fill a car's tank with petrol. The humps are composed of fatty tissues which break down to give energy during periods when the camel is without sufficient food. Water is stored by the camel in its tissues and it draws on this supply as it plods along. After a long journey the camel is usually very thin and dried up and it takes an enormous drink as soon as it can, to make up the loss. It drinks over 20 gallons of water in ten minutes.

The South American owner of a herd of Llamas *(left)* can make rugs and clothing from their fur, sandals from their hides, candles from their fat and fuel from their droppings.

Do all camels have humps?

Apart from the two species of camel already mentioned, there are four other members of the camel family which do not possess humps. These are the Llama, Guanaco, Alpaca and Vicuna, all from South America. From the time of the Inca civilization these animals have been domesticated by man, and to this day they are invaluable to Indians living at high altitudes. They are used mainly as beasts of burden and will happily bear loads of up to 100 pounds in weight if properly handled. A Llama that is annoyed will spit in the face of the offender with great accuracy.

What use are antlers?

The male of most species of deer bears antlers. As these are grown throughout the year only to be shed soon after the breeding season they seem to be rather pointless. During the breeding season males spar by clashing antlers together but these are more trials of strength than serious fights. A recent, most interesting theory on the purpose of antlers is that they help to keep the deer cool during the summer months. As they grow, they are covered in skin richly supplied with blood vessels. In warm weather body heat would quickly be lost from such surfaces. As the time for breeding approaches, the skin (velvet) falls off. Many of the even-toed ungulates bear paired bony outgrowths from their skulls. Some are skin covered and either drop off each year (for example, in deer) or are permanent (for example, in the giraffe). Others are covered in horn (for example, in cattle).

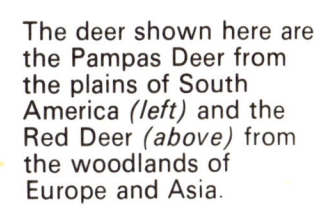

The deer shown here are the Pampas Deer from the plains of South America *(left)* and the Red Deer *(above)* from the woodlands of Europe and Asia.

Male Okapis have a pair of short, skin-covered bony horns which they keep all the year round. The females usually have a pair of bumps on the head.

What is the Okapi?

The Okapi looks as if it is a cross between a zebra, a donkey and a giraffe. It is a very recognizable animal and is quite large, as big as a horse, and yet it was first discovered only about seventy years ago. It is very shy and retiring, living in the densest tropical rain forests of the Congo. The Okapi is the only living relative of the Giraffe. It has a giraffe-like supple neck and a long tongue for plucking the leaves from trees.

Why is the Pronghorn so called?

Often misleadingly called an antelope (antelopes come from Africa and Asia), the North American Pronghorn derives its popular name from the forward-pointing branch of its horns. The Pronghorn's horns are extremely interesting. They are composed of two parts: a bony central cone

Once near extinction but now a successfully conserved species, Pronghorns inhabit dry areas of western North America and Canada.

which is permanent like those of the true antelopes, and a sheath of fused hairs supplying the horny covering. The branched horny covering splits each year and is shed revealing a new growth of horn underneath.

How long is the Giraffe's tongue?

The Giraffe is easily the tallest of the mammals at 18 feet. Apart from its legs and neck another long feature of the Giraffe is its tongue. When fully extended to pluck a distant leaf or twig, the Giraffe's tongue is 17 inches long. The Giraffe feeds on the foliage of acacia trees on the savannahs of South Africa, and because it usually browses around the trees at a constant height, they often end up with an hourglass shape. The long neck is ideal for reaching up into trees but is not as convenient for drinking. The Giraffe has to splay its front legs or bend its knees in order to reach the ground to drink.

There is only one species of Giraffe, but a number of races with slightly different colouring are recognized.

The North American Bison was slaughtered by the thousand throughout the nineteenth century during the exploration of the American West. Numbers have been built up from a few hundred to the 20,000 animals of today.

How many sorts of bison are there?

Most people know that there is a North American Bison, sometimes called the Buffalo, but there is another species which comes from eastern Europe, the European Bison or Wisent. Both are enormous shaggy animals with humped backs. The American species is an animal of the open plains whereas the European prefers thick woodland and forest. Both have come close to extinction in the past but are now protected in parks and reserves in their respective countries.

What are the true buffalos?

The best known true buffalo is the Asiatic Water Buffalo, of the cattle group of mammals. This buffalo has been domesticated for hundreds of years and is the 'work-horse' of all tropical Asia, being used for a whole range of tasks on the land. It is an immensely strong beast with impressive horns over 6 feet in length. There are two African Wild Buffalos,

The Gaur *(far left)* is the largest of the wild cattle and small herds are found in mountainous forest areas of southern Asia. Although domesticated, the Asiatic Water Buffalo *(left)* will attack anyone without provocation and can do great damage with its enormous horns.

Rocky Mountain Goats are found in the North American Rockies. Their coats and beards of long white hair are particularly striking.

the common form and a smaller and rarer forest form. The African Buffalo also carries massive curved horns and lives in herds in moist swampy areas. The Dwarf Forest Buffalo is more retiring and large herds move through thick forest without drawing much attention to themselves.

What are rock-goats?

There are four species of goat that are true rock-dwellers. The Goral, Serow, Chamois and Rocky Mountain Goat are known for their remarkable ability to bound up and down steep mountainsides and cliffs. All goats are sure-footed but rock-goats are particularly skilful climbers. They seem to defy gravity by walking along vertical cliff faces using footholds only half-an-inch wide.

Throughout history the domesticated even-toed ungulates have provided man with food, drink, clothing and transport. Pigs, camels, llamas, deer, cattle, goats and sheep all belong to this important group of mammals.

There are a number of sure-footed wild goats called Ibexes, living in mountainous areas. Their horns are particularly strong with large, evenly spaced ridges along their length.

INDEX

Figures in bold type refer to illustrations

Acorn worm **64**, 65
Adaptive radiation 197
Adder 143, **143**
Adelie penguin **152**, **153**
Aesop prawn 42, **42**
Air bladder, *see* Swim bladder
African elephant 236, **236**
    jacana **179**
    lungfish **94**, 95
    wild ass 240
    wild buffalo 250–1
Age of reptiles 114
Agouti **135**
Aigrette 159
Albatross 155, **155**
Algae 28, 31, 39, 88, 161
Alligator 188, **188**
Alpaca 247
American chameleon 122, 122–3
Amoeba **8**, 9
Amphioxus 65, **65**, 68–9
Anaconda 135, **135**
An-an 228
Andean condor 171, **171**
    flamingo **161**
Annelida 36–7
Anole lizard 122, **122–3**
Ant 50, 51, 56, 57, **57**, **198**, 199
Ant lion 51, **51**
Anteater 217, 218
Antelope 244, 248
Anthropoids 210, 212–5
Anting 199
Ape 210, 214–5
Aphaneramna **99**
Aphid 50, **50**
Arabian camel 246
Arachnids 38, 58–9
Arapaima 77, **77**, 79
Archaeopteryx **148**, 149
Archegosaurus **98**
Archerfish 86, **86**
Archeria **99**
Arctic hare **219**
Armadillo 217
Army ants 57, **57**
Arrow poison frog 103
Arthropoda 38–59
Asiatic jackal **224**
    water buffalo 250, **250**
    wild ass **240**, 241
Ass 240, 241
Auklet 182

Australian cassowary 150–1, **150**
    lungfish 95, **95**
    teddy bear, *see* Koala
Axlotl **100–1**, 101
Aye-Aye 210, **210**

Baboon 213, **213**
Bacteria 11, 39, 49
Bactrian camel **246**
Baleen whale 223, **223**
Baler shell 31, **31**
Ball python, *see* Royal python
Bandicoot 205
Banding, *see* Ringing
Barbel 80
Barn owl **186**
Barnacle 38, 40, **40**
Basking shark 71, **71**
Bat 208–9
Bath sponge 11, **11**
Beak, *see* Bill
Beak-heads 114
Bear 226–227
Bear cat, *see* Binturong
Beeswax 192
Bill, of finch 146–7
    flamingo 160, **160**
    goose **165**
    gull 181
    honeyeater 195, **195**
    ibis 160, **160**
    macaw 185
    owl 186
    skimmer **182**, 183, **183**
    spoonbill 160, **160**
    toucan 192–3, **193**
    woodpecker 193, **193**
    vulture 170, **170**
Binturong **230**
Bird of paradise 199, **199**
Bird-eating spider **59**
Bird's nest soup 189
Birds of prey 168–75
Bison 250
Bittern 158, **158**
Bivalve molluscs 24–9, 33, 60, 61
Black rhinoceros 242–3, **243**
Black swan 167, **167**
Black-necked swan 167, **167**
Bleak 80
Blue shark **70**
    whale 223, **223**
Boa 134
Boa constrictor 134, **134**

Boom net, *see* Cannon net
Bowerbird 198, **198**
Bowfin 75, **75**
Brazilian horned toad 109
Brent goose 165
Brown bear **226**
Brown hyena **231**
Brush-tailed phalanger **206**
Budgerigar 185, **185**
Buffalo 250
Bumblebee **56**
Bush cricket **44**
Bushbaby 210, **211**
Butterfly 44, **45**, 46, 52–5, **52**, **55**
Buzzard 169
Byssus thread 25, **25**, 26, **26**
By-the-wind sailor 13

Caecilian 99, 100, 101, **101**
Caiman 118, **119**
Camel 244, 246, 247
Camouflage
    bittern 158, **158**
    caterpillar 54–5
    giant frog **107**
    insect 46–7, **46**, **47**
    plaice 93, **93**
    trapdoor spider 59, **59**
    tree boa **134**
    tree frog 105
    vine snake 136
Canada goose 164–5, **164–5**
Cannon net 164, **164**
Carnivores 224–33
Carp family 80–1
Cassowary 150, **150**
Cat family 232–3
Caterpillar 44, **45**, 52–5, **53**, **54**
Catfish 79
Cattle 244, 247
Caviar **74**
Centipede 38, 43, **43**
Cephalopods 34–5, **35**
Chameleon 121, **121**, 122
Chamois 251
Chi-chi 228
Chicken 162, 177, **177**
Chilean pelican **156**
Chiton 22, **22**, 25
Chimpanzee 214, **214**
Chlamydomonas **8**, 9
Chordata 64
Chub 80
Cicada **44**
Civet 230, **230**
Clawed frog 106, **106**

252

Cleaner wrasse 88, **88**
Clownfish 87, **87**
Coat-of-mail shell, *see* Chiton
Cobra 140–1, 230–1
Cockle 25, 27, **27**
Coelacanth 94, **94**
Coelenterata 12–7
Coiling thread cell 12, **12**, 13
Colonization of land 98–100, 112
Combjelly, *see* Sea gooseberry
Common carp 80, **80**
  chameleon **121**
  European treefrog **105**
  newt **100**
  palm civet **230**
  porpoise **222**
  scorpionfish **91**
  skate **73**
  spoonbill **160**
  toad **108**
Complete metamorphosis 44, **45**, 54–**5**, 55
Concertina locomotion 128, **128**
Condor 170
Conger eel **82**
Convergent evolution, *see* Parallel evolution
Cooter, *see* Terrapin
Copepod 39, **39**, 71
Copperhead 137, **137**
Coral 12, 16, 17, **17**, 88, **88**
  reef 16, 17, **17**
  snake 141, **141**
Cormorant fishing 156, **156–7**
Cowry 32, **32**
Crab 38, 41, **41**, 73
Cradle shell, *see* Chiton
Crane 178
Crayfish 42
Crested newt **100**
Crocodile 114, 118–19
Crowned crane **179**
Ctenophora 15
Crustaceans 38–41
Cuttlebone, *see* Cuttlefish
Cuttlefish 22, 34, **35**

Dace 80
Daddy longlegs 58
Darwin, Charles 196
Darwin's frog 106, **106**
Deer 244, 247
Desert locust **44**, 45
Diatryma **148**, 149
Dimetrodon 112, **112**
Dingo 204, 224, **224**
Dinosaur 112, **112**
Disruptive coloration 242 (*see also* Zebra)
Dog family 224–5
Dogfish 71, **71**
Dolphin 86, **222**

Dolphin fish 86, **86**
Domestic cat 232
  dog 224
  donkey 240, 241
  horse **240–1**, 241
  pig 244
Dove 184
Dragonfish 91
Dragonfly 48, **48**
Driver ant, *see* Army ant
Duck 162–3
Duck-billed platypus **202**, 203, **203**
Duckling 162, **162**
Dugong 238, **238**, 239
Dwarf forest buffalo 251

Eagle 169, 172–3, 186
Earthworm 37, **37**
Eastern diamond rattlesnake **144**, 145
Echidna 202, 203, **203**
Echinodermata 60–3
Echo-location
  bat 208–9
  oilbird 188
  swiftlet 209
Edentates 216–17
Eel 82–3, **82**, 158
Egg
  butterfly 52, **52**, 53, **53**
  caecilian **101**
  Darwin's frog 106
  dinosaur **112**
  flying fish **84**
  frog 102, **102**
  locust 45
  penguin **152**
  pike **78**
  plaice **92**
  ray **73**
  reptile 112
  sea catfish 79, **79**
  shark **70**
  snake 133, **133**
  sturgeon **74**
  Surinam toad 109
Egg tooth 133, **133**
Egg-eating snake 138, **138**
Eggfish **81**
Egret 159, **159**
Egyptian vulture **170**
Eider duck 163, **163**
Eiderdown 163
Electric catfish **79**
Elegant slider **116**
Elephant 236–7
Elephant tusk shell, *see* Tusk shell
Elf owl **186**
Emperor penguin **153**
Emu 150, **150**
Euglena 9, **9**
European bison 250
European skink **124**
Eusthenopteron **98**
Even-toed ungulates 240, 244–51

Exoskeleton 38, 44
Eyed lizard 125
Eyrie 172, **172**

Falcon 168–9
Falconet **168**
Falconry 175
False coral snake **141**
Fan mussel, *see* Noble pen shell
Fantail **184**
Fanworm 36, 37
Fat-tailed galago **211**
Feather duster worm, *see* Fan worm
Fiddler crab **41**
Finch 196–7
Fire clownfish **87**
Fish hawk, *see* Osprey
Five-lined skink **124–5**
Fish finger 91
Flamingo **160**, 161, **161**
Flash colours 105
Flatfish 69, 92–3, **92**, **93**
Flatworm 18, **18**, 19
Flight
  bat 208–9
  first birds 148–9
  flying fish 84
  greater glider phalanger 205, **205**
  hatchetfish 77
  hummingbird 190
  ibis 160
  insect 48
  oilbird 188
  owl 186
  pterodactyl 113, **113**, 148
  snake **136**, 137
  spoonbill 160
  treefrog 105
Flightless birds, *see* Running birds
Flounder 92, **93**
Flower mantid 46, **46**, 47
Flying fish 84, **84**, 86, snake **136**, 137
Freshwater shark, *see* Pike
Frigate bird 157, **157**
Frilled lizard 120–1, **120**
  shark **70**
Frog 99, 100, 102–8
Frogs' spawn 102, **102**, 103
Fruit-eating bat 208–9, **209**
Fur seal 235

Galago, *see* Bushbaby
Gar 75, **75**
Gasteropods 30–3, **30**
Gaur **250**
Gavial 118, **119**
Gazelles 244
Gecko 120, **120**
Gentoo penguin **152**
Giant anteater 216, 217
  clam 28, **28**
  frog 107, **107**
  millipede **43**

253

otter 229, **229**
panda 228, **228**
tortoise 117, **117**
Gibbon 214, **214**
Giraffe 244, 247, 248, 249, **249**
Glass frog 103
Goat 244, 251
Golden
  bowerbird **198**
  eagle 172–3, **172**, **173**
  jackal, *see* Asiatic jackal
  tench 81
Goldfish 80–1 **80–1**
Goliath beetle **51**
Goose 162, 164–5, **164**, **165**
  barnacle **40**
Goral 251
Gorilla 215, **215**
Gould's monitor **126**
Grass parakeet, *see* Budgerigar
Great
  ape 214, 215
  auk **182**
  Barrier Reef **17**, 31
  crested grebe 154, **154**
  eagle owl **186**
  grey owl **187**
  Indian rhinoceros 243, **243**
  white shark 70, **70**
Greater flamingo **161**
  glider phalanger 205, **205**
  prairie chicken 180
Greek tortoise **117**
Green lizard 125, **125**
  treefrog 105
  turtle 115, **115**
  woodpecker 193
Grey monitor **126–7**
Greylag goose **165**
Grizzly bear 226
Guanaco 247
Gudgeon 80
Guillemot **182**
Gull 149, 181, **181**

Haddock 69, **69**
Hagfish 68–9, **69**
Hairy frog **103**
Halibut 93
Harbor porpoise, *see* Common porpoise
Hare 218–19, **219**
Harrier 169
Harvestman, *see* Daddy longlegs
Hatchet fish 77, **77**
Hawk 169, 186
Hermit crab 41, **41**
Heron 158, **158**
Herring gull 181, **181**
Hesperornis 149, **149**
Hibernaculum 130, **130**
Hippopotamus 237, 244, 245, **245**
Honey 56

Honey badger 192
Honeybee 56, **56**
Honeydew 50
Honeyeater 195, **195**
Honeyguide 192–3, **192**
Hoofed animals 237, 240–51
Hookworm 21, **21**
Hornbill 191, **191**
Horned
  asp **143**
  rattlesnake 145, **145** (*see also* Sidewinder)
  toad 122, **122**
Horse 237, 240–1
Horseshoe crab, *see* King crab
Hummingbird 190
Hydra 12, **12**
Hyena 231, **231**
Hylambates maculatus 105
Hyrax 237

Ibex 251, **251**
Ibis 160, **161**
Ichthyornis 149, **149**
Ichthyostega **99**
Iguana 123, **123**
Incomplete metamorphosis 45, **45**, 48
Incubation
  mallee fowl 176
  snake 133
Indian
  civet 230
  cobra **140**
  dwarf chameleon **121**
  elephant 236, **236**
  mahseer 80
  mongoose **231**
  python 139, **139**
  vulture 168
Indris 210, **210**, 211
Insect 38, 44–57
Insect-eating bat 208–9, **208**, **209**
Insectivores 208–9

Jacana 179
Jack-knife clam, *see* Razor shell
Jackson's chameleon **121**
Jacobson's organs 132
James' flamingo 161
Javan rhinoceros 243, **243**
Jay 199, **199**
Jellyfish 12, 13, 14–15, **14**
Jerboa 220, **220**

Kangaroo 205, **206**, 207, **207**
Kestrel **168**, 169
Killer whale **222**
King cobra 140, **140**
  crab 58, **58**
  penguin **152**
  snake 137, **137**
  vulture 170

Kingfisher 190
Kiwi 150, **150**
Koala 206–7, **206**
Kodiak bear 226, **226**
Komodo dragon 126, **126**
Kookaburra, *see* Laughing jackass

Labyrinth fish 90
Lamprey 68–9, **68**, **69**
Land iguana 123, **123**
Laughing jackass 190, **190**
Leaf insect 46–7, **47**
Leatherback turtle **114**
Lek **180**, 181
Lemming **220–1**, 221
Lemur 210
Leopard 139, **139**
Leptocephali 82–3, **82**
Lily-trotter, *see* Jacana
Limpet 30, **30**, 31, 33
Lion 233, **233**
Lionfish 91
Lionhead goldfish 80–1, **81**
Little auk **182**
  egret 159
  owl **187**
Living fossil
  coelacanth 94, **94**
  king crab 58, **58**
  tuatara 114, **114**
Lizard 113, 114, 122–7, 148
Llama 244, **246**, 247
Lobster 38, 42, **42**, 73
Locust 44, **44**, 45, **45**
Long-necked clam 29, **29**
Long-tailed nightjar **188**
Loris 210
Lugworm 36–7, **36**
Lungfish 95, **95**, 98

Macaw 185
Mackerel 69
Magnificent
  bird of paradise **199**
  frigate bird **157**
Malayan tapir 242, **242**
Mallard 163
Mallee fowl 176, **176**
Mammary glands 202, 204
Man 210, 214
Manatee 238, 239, **239**
Maneater, *see* Great white shark
Maned wolf 224–5, **225**
Mantid 46–7, **46**
Marine iguana 123, **123**
Marsupial 204–7
Masked palm civet 230
Matamata **115**
Medusae **12**, 14, **15**
Mermaid 238
Mermaids' purse **70**
Micropyle **52**, 53
Midwife toad **108**
Migration
  albatross 155

254

geese 164–5
lemming 221
Millipede 38, 43, **43**
Minnow 80
Mite 38, 58
Moa 149, **149**, 178
Mole 209
Molluscs 22–35
Mongoose 230–2, **231**
Monitor lizard 126, **126**, 127
Monkey 210, 212–13
Monotreme 203
Moray eel 83, **82–3**
Moth 52, 54
Mouse-eared bat **209**
Mudskipper 89, **89**
Murrelet 182
Muscovy duck **162**, 163
Musk 230
Mussel 22, **24**, 25, **25**, 60, 61
Mute swan 166, **166**, 167
Mya arenaria 29, **29**

Newt 99, 100, **100**
Nile crocodile 118, **118**
Nine-banded armadillo **217**
Noble pen shell 26, **26**
North American bison 250, **250**
Norway lobster 42
Norwegian lemming 221
Nose-leaf **208**
Notochord **64**, 65, **65**

Obelia **12**, 14
Octopus 22, 34, 35, **35**, 83
Odd-toed ungulates 240–3
Oilbird 188, **188**
Okapi 248, **248**
Olive baboon **213**
Opossum 206
Orang-utan 215, **215**
Orchid mantid, *see* Flower mantid
Oropendola 194–5, **195**
Osprey 174, **174**
Ostracod **38**
Ostrich 150, 151, **151**
Otter 229
Otter-shell clam, *see* Long-necked clam
Owl 169, 180, 186–7
Oyster 22, 25, 60, **61**, 61, 73

Paddlefish 75, **75**
Pampas deer **247**
Pangolin 218, **218**
Parakeet 185
Parallel evolution 182, 206, 218
Paramecium 9, **9**
Parasite 8, 19, 20, 39, 68
Parasol ant 57, **57**
Parrot 185
Parrotfish 88, **88**
Peafowl **176**, 177, **177**
Pelican 156, **156**

Pellets 187, **187**
Peripatus 38–9, **38**
Penguin 152–3, 182
Perentie **126**
Periwinkle 41
Phalanger 205–6
Phorohachos **148**, 149
Pig 19, 244
Pigeon 184, **184**
Pigment cells 42, 93
Pike 78, **78**
Pill millipede **43**
Piranha 78, **78**
Placenta 202, 204
Plaice 92, **92**, 93
Plankton 39, 71, 77, 223
Platyhelminthes 18–19
Poison gland 91
Polar bear 227, **227**
Polyps **12**, 13, 14, **14**
Population explosion 221
Porcupine 220, **221**
Porifera 10–11
Porpoise 222
Portuguese man-o'-war 13, **13**
Pouched mammal, *see* Marsupial
Pouter **184**
Pratincole 180, **180**
Prawn 42, **42**
Praying mantid 46–7, **46**
Prehensile tail 212, **212**
Primate 210–15
Proboscis monkey 213, **213**
Pronghorn 247, **248**
Prosimians 210–11
Protozoan 8, **8**, 9, **9**, 11, 49
Przewalski's wild horse **240**, 241
Pterodactyl 113, **113**, 148
Puffin 182
Pupa 44, **45**, **54–5**, 55
Pygmy hippopotamus **245**
Python 134

Rabbit 218–19, **218**
Raccoon 228
Radiated tortoise **117**
Radula 22, 33
Ragworm 36–7, **36**
Rattle 144, **144**
Rattlesnake 137, 142, 144–5
Ray 68, 72–3, **72**, **73**
Razor shell 27, **27**
Razorbill 182
Red
  deer **247**
  jungle fowl 177, **177**
  salamander 100
Red-tailed salamander **100**
Reef barber 88, **88**
Regal
  scorpionfish **91**
  tang **88**
Rhea **148**, 149, 150
Rhinoceros 237, 240, 242–3

Ribbon worm 20, **20**
Ringed penguin **152**
Ringhals 141, **141**
Ringing 155, 164
Roach 80, **80**
Rock hyrax **237**
  salmon, *see* Dogfish
Rockdove **184**
Rocky mountain goat 251, **251**
Rodents 220–1, 237
Roseate spoonbill 160, **160**
Roundworm 20, **21**
Royal python **134**, 135
Rubber boa **134**, 135
Rudd 80
Ruff **180**, 181
Running birds **148–9**, 149, 150, **150–1**, 152

Salamander 99, 100, **100**, 101
Salmon 68, 76, **76**
Salt-water crocodile **118**
Sand gaper, *see* Long-necked clam
Sand lizard **125**
Sandgrouse 183, **183**
Sargasso Sea 82, **83**
Sarus crane **178**
Scallop 25, 29, **29**, 61
Scampi 42
Scarab beetle 50–1, **51**
Scarlet ibis 160, **161**
  macaw **185**
Scorpion 38, 58, **58**
Scorpionfish 91, **91**
Sea anemone 12, 16, **16**, 87, **87**
  catfish 79, **79**
  cucumber 60, 63, **63**
  eagle **173**
  gooseberry 15, **15**
  hare 30, **30**
  lily 60, 62, **62**
  otter 229, **229**
  squirt 64, **64**, 65
  urchin 60, 61, 62–3, **62**
Sea-cows 238–9
Seahorse 85, **85**
Seal 235, **235**
Sealion **234–5**, 235
Seasnake 142, **142**
Secretary bird 174, **175**
Serow 251
Shag **156**
Shark 68, 70–1
Sheep 244
Shiver 80
Shrimp 38, 42
Siamese fighting fish 90, **90**
Sidewinder 128–9, (*see also* Horned rattlesnake)
Silver boa, *see* Rubber boa
Skate 68, 72–3
Skimmer **182**, 183, **183**
Skink 124, **124**, 125, 127, **127**

255

Slider, see Terrapin
Slime eel, see Hagfish
Sloth 216, **216**
Slow-worm 127, **127**
Slug 22, 30, 33, **33**
Small tortoiseshell butterfly **52**
Smith treefrog 105
Snail 22, 30, 138, **138**
Snake 114, 127, 128–45
Snake charmer 140
Sociable vulture **170**
Social insects
　ants 57, **57**
　bees 56, **56**
　termites 49, **49**
Soft-shell clam, see Long-necked clam
Soil 8, 20, 21, 37
Sole 93
Solenodon 208, **208**
South American bullfrog 107, **107**
　lungfish **94**, 95
　toad **108**
Southern short-nosed bandicoot **205**
Sparrowhawk 169
Spectacled bear 226, **226**
Sperm whale **222**
Spicule 10, **10**, 11
Spider 38, 58, 59, **59**
Spider monkey 212, **212**
Spiny anteater, see Echidna
Spiny lobster 42
Sponge 10, **10**, 11, **11**, 12
Spongin 11
Spoonbill 160, **160**
Spotted cuscus **206**
Spotted hyena 231
Spotted-billed pelican **156**
Squid 22, 34–5, **34**
Starfish 27, 29, 32, 60–1, **60**, **61**, 63
Starling **196**, 197
Star-nosed mole 209, **209**
Stick insect 46–7, **47**
Stickleback 84–5, **85**
Stinging cell 12, **12**, 13, 16, 87
Stingray 73, **73**
Striped hyena 231
Sturgeon 74, **74**
Sucker 80
Sulphur toucan **192**
Sumatran rhinoceros 242–3, **243**
Sun bear 227, **227**
Surinam toad 109, **109**
Swan 166–7

Swan-upping 167
Swift 189, **189**
Swiftlet 189, **189**
Swim bladder 74, 75, 95
Sword-billed hummingbird **190**
Symbiotic association 87

Tadpole
　frog 102–3, **102**, 106, **106**, 107
　toad **108**
Tailor bird 194, **194**
Takahe 178, **178**
Talon 169, **169**, 174, **174**, 186
Tapeworm 19, **19**
Tapir 240, 242
Tarpan 241
Tarsier 210, 211, **211**
Tasmanian devil 204, **204**
Teddy bear 206
Temperature regulation 130, 202
Tench 80, 81, **81**
Termite 49, **49**
Tern 149, 180
Terrapin 115, 116, **116**
Thirst snake 138–9, **138**
Thornback ray 73
Thread snake **139**
Three-banded armadillo 217, **217**
Three-spined stickleback **85**
Three-striped arrow poison frog **103**
Three-toed sloth 216, **216**
Tick 38, 58
Tiger **232**, 233
Toad 99, 108–9
Toads' spawn **108**
Toco toucan **192**
Toothed whale 223
Top shell 41
Tope 71, **71**
Tortoise 114–15, 116–17, **117**
Toucan **192**–3, 193
Trapdoor spider 59, **59**
Tree boa **134**
　hyrax **237**
Treefrog 105, **105**
Tree-lizard, see Anole lizard
Tree-snake 136–7, **136**
Treeshrew 210
Trout **76**
Trumpeter swan 166, **166**
Tuatara 114, **114**
Tube feet, see Water vascular system

Tumble bug, see Scarab beetle
Turbot 93
Turkeyfish 91
Turtle 114–15
Turtle soup 115
Tusk shell 23, **23**
Two-humped camel, see Bactrian camel
Two-toed sloth **216**
Tyrannosaurus **112**

Ungulates, see Hoofed animals
Univalve molluscs 30–3
Uta lizard **125**

Velella 13
Venom 140, 141, 142, 143
Vereaux's sifaka **210**
Vicugna 247
Village weaver 197, **197**
Vine snake 126–7, **136**
Viper 142–3, **142**, **143**
Volute shell 31, **31**
Volvox 9, **9**
Vultures 168–9, 170, **170**, 171, **171**

Wallace's treefrog **106**, 107
Walrus 234, **234**, 235
Wasp 56
Water flea **38**, 39
Water tortoise, see Terrapin
Water vascular system 61, 63
Water-holding frog 104, **104**
Weaver ant 57, **57**
Weaverbird 197, **197**
Wels **79**
Western
　diamond rattlesnake 145
　greater skink **124**
　spinebill 195
　toad **109**
Whale 222–43, **238**
Whale shark 70, 71
Whalebone 223
Whelk 30, 32–3, **33**, 41
White
　pelican **156**
　rhinoceros 242–3, **242**
Wild cat 232, **232**
Wisent, see European bison
Wolf 225, **225**
Wood pigeon 184
Woodpecker 193, **193**, 197
Woodpecker finch **196**, 197
World wildlife fund 228

Zebra 240, 241, **241**
Zebrafish 91